Lance Comfort

MANCHESTER
UNIVERSITY PRESS

forthcoming titles

Jack Clayton   NEIL SINYARD

Terence Fisher   PETER HUTCHINGS

Pat Jackson   CHARLES BARR

Launder and Gilliat   BRUCE BABINGTON

J. Lee Thompson   STEVE CHIBNALL

Lance Comfort

BRIAN McFARLANE

Manchester University Press

MANCHESTER AND NEW YORK

distributed exclusively in the USA by St. Martin's Press

Published by Manchester University Press
Oxford Road, Manchester M13 9NR, UK
and Room 400, 175 Fifth Avenue, New York, NY 10010, USA
http://www.man.ac.uk/mup

Distributed exclusively in the USA by
St. Martin's Press, Inc., 175 Fifth Avenue, New York,
NY 10010, USA

Distributed exclusively in Canada by
UBC Press, University of British Columbia, 6344 Memorial Road,
Vancouver, BC, Canada V6T 1Z2

British Library Cataloguing-in-Publication Data
A catalogue record for this book is available from the British Library

Library of Congress Cataloging-in-Publication Data applied for

ISBN 0 7190 5483 4 *hardback*
     0 7190 5484 2 *paperback*

First published 1999

06 05 04 03 02 01 00 99   10 9 8 7 6 5 4 3 2 1

Typeset in Scala with Meta display
by Koinonia, Manchester
Printed in Great Britain
by Bookcraft (Bath) Ltd, Midsomer Norton

For Tom Ryan, with grateful thanks

also by Brian McFarlane

The Oxford Companion to Australian Film, OUP, 1999
(with Geoff Mayer and Ina Bertrand)

An Autobiography of British Cinema, Methuen, 1997

Novel to Film: An Introduction to the Theory of Adaptation, Clarendon Press,
OUP, 1996

Sixty Voices: Celebrities Recall the Golden Age of British Cinema, British Film
Institute, 1992

New Australian Cinema: Sources and Parallels in American and British Film,
CUP, 1992
(with Geoff Mayer)

Australian Cinema 1970–1985, Secker and Warburg, 1987

Words and Images: Australian Novels into Film, William Heinemann, 1983

Martin Boyd's 'Langton' Novels, Edward Arnold, 1980

Cross-Country: An Anthology of Australian Poetry, William Heinemann, 1984
(with John Barnes)

Contents

List of plates

Every effort has been made to trace the copyright owners of these illustrations; any person claiming copyright should contact the publisher.

Series editors' foreword

The aim of this series is to present in lively, authoritative volumes a guide to those film-makers who have made British cinema a rewarding but still under-researched branch of world cinema. The intention is to provide books which are up-to-date in terms of information and critical approach, but not bound to any one theoretical methodology. Though all books in the series will have certain elements in common – comprehensive filmographies, annotated bibliographies, appropriate illustration – the actual critical tools employed will be the responsibility of the individual authors.

Nevertheless, an important recurring element will be a concern for how the oeuvre of each film-maker does or does not fit certain critical and industrial contexts, as well as for the wider social contexts, which helped to shape not just that particular film-maker but the course of British cinema at large.

Although the series is director-orientated, the editors believe that a variety of stances and contexts referred to is more likely to reconceptualise and reappraise the phenomenon of British cinema as a complex, shifting field of production. All the texts in the series will engage in detailed discussion of major works of the film-makers involved, but they all consider as well the importance of other key collaborators, of studio organisation, of audience reception, of recurring themes and structures: all those other aspects which go towards the construction of a national cinema.

The series will explore and chart a field which is more then ripe for serious excavation. The acknowledged leaders of the field will be reappraised; just as important though, will be the bringing to light of those who have not so far received any serious attention. They are all part of the very rich texture of British cinema, and it will be the work of this series to give them all their due.

Acknowledgements

My first thanks are due to Lance Comfort's son, John Comfort, for his help in answering many questions about his father's work, for giving me access to papers relating to this, and for putting me in touch with a number of his father's surviving collaborators. John acted as production manager on some of his father's later films, giving him access to his father's working habits. I thank him and his wife Maureen for their hospitality to me while I was researching this book. Among Lance Comfort's collaborators, I am grateful to the following for being generous in their recollections: editors John Trumper and Peter Pitt, continuity person Elaine Shreyeck, screenwriters Lyn Fairhurst and Peter Miller, and Roy Baird who acted as assistant director or production manager on several films. I also spoke to a number of actors who had worked with Lance Comfort and am grateful to Rona Anderson, Honor Blackman, Harry Fowler, William Franklyn, Greta Gynt, Margaret Johnston, William Lucas, Nanette Newman, Mary Parker, and Dermot Walsh for their reminiscences.

I am indebted to several members of staff and departments of the British Film Institute for their assistance: to Elaine Burrows in the Archive for considerable research help, sometimes at short notice; to Bryony Dixon, Kathleen Dickson, Steve Tollervey and George Smith in the Archive's Viewing Service for providing generous viewing facilities; to Janet Moat and Saffron Parker of the Special Materials section for allowing me extended use of their office while I examined the BFI's Lance Comfort Collection and other resources; to the BFI Library staff; and to the BFI Stills Department which provided the photographs, apart from those lent by John Comfort and Lyn Fairhurst.

My thanks are also due, in Australia, to Geoff Mayer for his helpful comments on the manuscript; to Aysen Mustafa and other staff in the

Australian Film Institute library, Melbourne; and to my daughter Sophie for typing assistance. In England, my thanks to Jeffrey Richards, Allen Eyles, and Alan Kibble; and to the Manchester University Press publishing team. And finally, for her patience and support, I must thank my wife, Geraldine, who has seen far more of Lance Comfort's work than she ever expected to.

Melbourne, January 1999   Brian McFarlane

A place in the field

'Why Lance Comfort?' This was the question one of his collaborators asked during an interview conducted for this book. The answer is in several parts, but the first must be simply that I have always liked his films since seeing *Great Day* at the age of twelve and being struck by how different it was from the Hollywood films which were what usually – and enjoyably – came my way in rural Australia. It seemed fresh, sharp and truthful, in ways I wouldn't have been able to articulate then; and it still does. This busy little film, about a village getting ready to welcome Mrs Roosevelt and putting aside but not gettting rid of personal problems and animosities, is as good an introduction to Comfort's work as any. His astute juggling of several concurrent plot strands, his prescient anticipation of postwar disaffection, the invoking of *film noir* techniques to articulate the dilemma of the tormented protagonist, and the willingness to risk his arm melodramatically: these, and other, qualities ensure that it is still a film well worth looking at fifty years later. They are the sorts of qualities one admires elsewhere in his work.

Lance Comfort had been in the film business for twenty years when, in 1946, he directed Margaret Lockwood in *Bedelia*. In that year, she was, for the first of three consecutive years, 'overwhelmingly voted Britain's best actress by the readers of the *Daily Mail*' and in the same year 'she replaced Greer Garson as Britain's favourite female star'.[1] Any director taking on a Lockwood vehicle in 1946 was clearly one who had established his credentials sufficiently to be entrusted with the No. 1 box-office star of the day. By the time of his sadly early death twenty years later, at age fifty-eight, Comfort had been making 'B' films or second features, at best co-features, for fifteen years. It will be one of the functions of this book to consider some of the possible explanations for this seemingly disappointing career decline – *and* to insist that the films them-selves have received inadequate notice, that the apparent decline is less to be located in his personal and professional capacities than in certain major changes in the contours of the British film industry.

Comfort is not the only director who enjoyed his greatest prestige in the 1940s and drifted into providing fodder for the bottom half of the double-bill in the ensuing decades, though it is at least arguable that he maintained a higher, more uniform level of achievement than such contemporaries as Arthur Crabtree, Leslie Arliss, Lawrence Huntington or Bernard Knowles. To refer briefly to Pierre Bourdieu's idea of the 'field of cultural production'[2] may suggest ways in which Comfort's predilections as individual artist, and British cinema (embracing production, exhibition, audience reception and critical discourse) as the site of his activity, helped to shape a career lasting four decades, two-and-a-half of these as a director. What follows is not remotely intended as a fully Bourdieu-based, primarily theoretical study of Comfort's films. I want simply to make use of certain of Bourdieu's key distinctions – concepts and terms – which have been hovering behind my thinking about the uneven course and achievements of Comfort's career. Before going further, I shall draw attention to, and make clear how I interpret, those which seem to me most helpful and to which this study will refer from time to time.

In particular, Bourdieu's concepts of *habitus* and *field*, and their interrelationship, work towards positing a more complex under-standing of how cultural products are made and received. Habitus, tersely summarised by Bourdieu's editor as 'a notion of the agent' (that is, the agent as cultural producer),[3] replaces the notion of *auteur*, the Romantic ideal of the artist as individual creator, with the concept of 'systems of dispositions ... realised only in relation to a determinate structure of positions'.[4] These 'systems of dispositions' act through perceptions which respond to a 'sense of social directions which orients agents.'[5] Bourdieu's interest is in

French literature and art, not at all in cinema, but the value of the concept of habitus in film study is that it releases us from the unproductive élitism of auteurist criticism. This latter has celebrated the individual film-maker as the author of his films at the expense of those other interacting elements – social, cultural, economic – which elaborate the idea of the agent as being more than an individual film-maker practising his art. In relation to cinema, the agent or habitus may not always refer to a director; it may equally be applied to a producer, or a studio, or a production company or to some combination of these, and this study will take such potential influences into account. Habitus has sometimes been described as 'a feel for the game' and summarised by Bourdieu as a system of 'durable, transposable dispositions'.[6] The complementary concept of the field implies a context for such 'dispositions' to operate in. It is conceived of as being in a state of constant change, as a site of struggles for dominant 'positions' and is not to be confused with a purely sociological explanation of the workings of cultural production. Not all the elements of Bourdieu's theory of the latter relate neatly to film, which is so immensely more expensive to create than, say, literature or painting, and which is, though criticism has sought at various times to elevate the director, so obdurately a collaborative art. However, the idea of there being, at any given time, certain *dominant positions* in the field and, therefore, a concomitant range of *dominated* ones is easily recognisable in film, and particularly in British cinema during the period in which Lance Comfort was working. Whatever 'disposition' the 'agent' may evince, it will be to little avail if, for one or other reason, no congenial 'position' can be found in the field. I shall suggest that the 'positions' Comfort found for the exercise of his talents and the network of affiliations he had established would alter dramatically from the early 1950s on.

Habitus/field, disposition/position and dominant/dominated are all distinctions worth bearing in mind in examining Comfort's career. So are others such as those between *trajectory* and *strategy*, between *symbolic* and *economic* capital, between the *heteronomous* and the *autonomous* cultural producers, and those among several 'competing principles of legitimacy'.[7] Whereas strategy 'results from unconscious disposition towards practice',[8] and has obvious connections with habitus, trajectory refers to the successive positions occupied by an agent in the field, at various times corresponding to dominant and dominated. Since it is unusual for a film-maker to remain in a fixed position in relation either to his fellows or to his audiences, this concept may be particularly useful. As to the kinds of 'capital' available to the cultural producer, in the production of such expensive 'goods' as film, 'the pursuit of economic profit, which treats the cultural goods business as a business like any other',[9] must always be an issue. Films must find large audiences to ensure profitability and thereby to ensure continuity of product from the cultural producers. For the artist, another kind of reward is also important: what Bourdieu calls the 'accumulation of symbolic capital', which may involve becoming a recognised name. In the case of film the film-maker could achieve this by being the object of critical approval or attracting the commendation of one's peers. For a short time, as we shall see, Comfort seemed well placed for acquiring both sorts of 'capital', until he lost his privileged position in the field around 1950. He then became one of those heteronomous cultural producers 'who can offer the least resistance to external demands, of whatever sort',[10] and can exercise the least control over their choice of subject or the scope of the enterprises open to them. These are distinct from the autonomous producers, who can call the shots with least regard to economic pressures or to those of popular taste, giving most nearly unfettered heed to their own proclivities, because they are the producers most welcome in the field at the time.

There is no wish on my part to impose, in grid-like fashion, a theoretical apparatus, designed specifically to account for cultural phenomena in other fields, on a field about which its author has expressed little interest. My aim is simply to make use of such concepts when they seem helpful in accounting for the sort of career trajectory mapped out near the start of this chapter. Lance Comfort clearly had the necessary 'disposition', in the sense of both a feeling for film-making, particularly for melodramatic film-making, and a background of technical know-how and of useful collaborators, acquired over the years 1925 to 1940 when he carried out a range of functions in several dozen films. When he made a success in 1941 of *Hatter's Castle*, his second feature film as a director, he ought to have found a tenable position in the field of production as it was at the time. And so, up to a point, he did: for the next few years he was very busy, making several popular wartime films, but never quite acquiring the symbolic capital that, say, David Lean or Carol Reed did during the period. Their films both carried a more personal stamp and related clearly to the social and cultural climate of their time, attracting both critical cachet (symbolic capital) and widespread popular acceptance (economic capital) as well.

Partly as a result of the work of such directors as Lean and Reed, the critically approved strands of postwar British film-making were those of the prestige literary adaptation and of social realism, the latter often drawing on the techniques of the documentary movement which had first infiltrated fiction film-making during the war. Comfort did virtually no work in these modes that dominated the discourse, if not the production statistics, of the period. Also securing a great deal of economic, if very little symbolic, capital in the mid-1940s was a series of melodramas emanating from Gainsborough studios, beginning with *The Man in Grey* (1943) and providing escapism for war-weary film audiences. Since the 1980s, these films have been critically rehabilitated, for both their cinematic flair and their encoding, in period settings, of the social realities of their time, but in the 1940s one would have searched in vain for serious critical appraisal.

The dominant positions – in terms of either economic or symbolic capital – in the field of cultural production, as it obtained in British cinema in the 1940s, just managed to elude Comfort. His first melodrama, *Hatter's Castle*, came too early to catch the Gainsborough wave, and preceded a burst of much-praised work in the realist vein, described by Dilys Powell as 'the movement towards concentration on the native subject, the movement towards documentary truth in the fiction film.'[11] Realism was often construed as offering an honest reflection of the social reality, whereas, in the words of John Hill, 'Realism, no less than any other type of art, depends on conventions, conventions which, in this case, have successfully achieved the status of being accepted as "realistic".'[12]

Comfort never did any sustained work in the conventions that were approved as social realism – not that critics at the time would have written of such films in terms of conventions, but rather saw them as breaking with these. This is not the place for a full discussion of the shifting relations between realism and the British cinema. During the war and just after, it seemed (in Alan Lovell's words) to be 'most often articulated in terms of the cinema having a serious relationship with society',[13] but later this belief 'was increasingly reduced to the exploration of topical subjects from within a conventional moral/social perspective.'[14] Almost none of Comfort's work (for better and worse) corresponds to accounts such as these. On a simple level, the location shooting he often employed always seems to be there to contextualise or heighten the drama, rather than for its social significance, and his lack of interest in the realist enterprise may help to explain his critical neglect at the time.

During the war, Comfort ventured into historical drama, regional comedy and spy thrillers, but did not again attempt full-blooded melodrama during the period of Gainsborough's commercial ascendancy. When he did embark on a series of such films with *Bedelia* in 1946, the wave had broken, and other films in the melodramatic mode by other film-makers (Charles Frank's *Uncle Silas*, 1947, Lewis Allen's *So Evil My Love* and Marc Allegret's *Blanche Fury*, both 1948), all at least as accomplished as the Gainsborough films, failed to find critical or commercial favour. Further, Comfort's melodramas, including *Temptation Harbour* (1947), *Daughter of Darkness* (1948), *Silent Dust* (1949) and *Portrait of Clare* (1950), were all perhaps too sombre for popular taste. They were not reassuring films. They lacked, too, the sort of panache, deriving partly from costume design and art direction, partly from permutations on the personae of a stable of stars, of the Gainsborough films which exploited so successfully the shifting mores of the mid-1940s, especially in regard to the changing roles of women in the wartime world. His films certainly attracted some critical attention, but they were always at the outer edge of the realist and/or literary strains preferred by the taste-makers of the period. In the mid-1940s, melodrama was a critically unrewarded corner of the field of cultural production. What is surprising is that more recent theoretical interest in melodrama (see discussion in Chapter 5), and British film melodrama in particular, has not seized on his films. A case can be made for seeing his as the most consistent body of work in the genre.

The field of cultural production is not of course governed purely by critical or audience reception, and in the case of cinema the conditions of film production, distribution and exhibition all play their influential roles. Unlike, say, Arthur Crabtree or Bernard Knowles, each responsible for several Gainsborough melodramas, or Ralph Thomas with Rank at Pinewood in the 1950s, Comfort seems never to have found for long a strongly supportive studio base or production company. Now when one thinks of the Gainsborough films, one recalls, at least as readily as the directors, the repertory of stars and character players, the costume design of Elizabeth Haffenden, the art direction of John Bryan or Andrew Mazzei, the music direction of Louis Levy, or producers such as Edward Black and R. J. Minney. With this sort of continuity involved in the making of a batch of films, the concept of habitus, the system of dispositions at work in cultural production, is plainly complex but also acquires a patina of recognisability which may be denied to the less firmly-based film-maker. In his first ten years as a features director, Comfort made fourteen films for seven different companies, including four for RKO's British operation and four for British National. It may thus have been more difficult for him to build up the network of collaborators which buttressed the work of some directors of the period. According to Peter Miller who later wrote two screenplays for him, Comfort was offered a Hollywood contract following the popular success of *Squadron Leader X*, but, feeling himself committed to RKO, as well as having family ties in Britain, he turned it down and later felt he'd made a grave career error.[15]

The offer may be seen as acknowledgment of his disposition, of his 'feel for the game'. Certainly, many of those who worked with him felt that he was not ruthless enough to capitalise on the position he had acquired. Among the many actors and other collaborators who talked to me about working with him, there was acknowledgement of his professionalism and his technical exper-tise, alongside a universally expressed sense of his being an unusually affable, gentle-mannered man in an industry in which such characteristics were not notably common and in which a streak of ruthlessness might have served him better. Biographical reasons will scarcely influence one's evaluation of the films – no one in the end cares whether a film was shot on schedule or under budget or whether the director was a nice man – they may, however, help to account for a particular film-making trajectory. As a director, whether he was making 'A' films in the 1940s or co-features in the 1950s and 1960s, he seems to have given actors plenty of room to move. He 'was absolutely unpretentious ... he was very gentle; he encouraged you to try things', recalled actor William Franklyn.[16] 'He never raised his voice', recalled Roy Baird,[17] assistant director on several of his films. Greta Gynt said that 'He talked to actors in a very gentle way'.[18] It is not, either, as if he was working with nondescript actors: there were flamboyant players like Robert Newton, Eric Portman and Robert Shaw, and exotics like Simone Simon and Siobhan McKenna, and there is a striking number who worked for him on several occasions, which may be some kind of testimony to his demeanour as a director. As well, editors such as John Trumper and Peter Pitt, who each cut several of his co-features, continuity person Elaine Schreyeck, who worked on three of Comfort's key films of the 1940s, and screenwriter Lyn Fairhurst, who wrote several of his last films, all testified to the efficiency and harmony of his working arrangements.

These admirable qualities were not, however, enough to secure the place in the industry hierarchy, the position in the cultural field of British cinema, to which his undoubted success with *Hatter's Castle* would seem to have pointed. He made other excellent 'A' films in the 1940s, which, as suggested above, may have missed the most propitious timing, and which have rarely, if ever, had the attention they deserve. When he went into 'B' films and co-features (the latter may be distinguished by, say, budget, length, or stars, as Robert S. Baker has pointed out),[19] he was not necessarily doing less effective work, but he was now working in that corner of the field of production least likely to bring him any symbolic – or even much economic – capital. As to the former, his work was unlikely to be noticed outside the trade papers or the *Monthly Film*

Bulletin, which was chronically patronising about such films, and was virtually never reviewed in the newspapers that might have kept a film-maker's name to the fore. The 'B' movie was made cheaply to provide the supporting film in the days when a double-bill was the standard exhibition pattern. Such films were made fast (about three weeks at most) in the expectation of modest profit and critical neglect. Unlike their American counterparts, they have never had a cult following, but, as I wrote in 1996, 'there are British Bs worthy of anyone's attention, both for their intrinsic merits and for what they suggest about the nature of the industry and the society that gave rise to them'.[20] Lance Comfort made several of the best of these, including such titles as *Tomorrow at Ten* (1962) and *Touch of Death* (1963).

In the mid-1950s, the field threw up another even less regarded arena in which Comfort also found himself busy. This was the television playlet, which he and his contemporaries (Huntington, Arliss, Crabtree and Knowles) churned out indefatigably. Comfort either produced or directed about seventy half-hour dramas for *Douglas Fairbanks Presents,* made for American television.These were also shown on British television, and, in a few cases, by cobbling together two or three and linking them with a commentary, screened theatrically as the supporting programme on a double-bill. When the latter happened, the resulting 'films' (for example, *The Triangle,* 1953) would be routinely noted in fan and trade journals, but nowhere else. The only sustained account of the Fairbanks enterprise at Elstree stresses the speed and budget of these half-hour dramas: 'The films ... had a five-day shooting schedule. Each Friday, in preparation for Monday's shoot, there would be a script read-through with the director and artistes ... The cost of the films was between £7,500 and £8,500 each, and the directors were paid around £175 per episode.'[21] This account goes on to say that 'Many directors were used, some of the best films being directed by Lance Comfort and Lawrence Huntington, though the latter became less popular as production costs rose.'[22] These are very rigorous film-making conditions, akin to those that prevailed in the making of 'B' films for the cinema, but with at least the freshness of comparative novelty about the procedures.

Comfort also directed or co-directed seven episodes of *Ivanhoe* for
Sydney Box Productions (ITV, 1958–59), ten episodes of *The Gay
Cavalier* for George King Productions (ITV, 1957), and was one of
the three regular directors on *Martin Kane Investigator* (ITV, 1957–
58).[23] In addition, he directed or produced episodes for *Crown
Theatre* in 1956 and for *Assignment Foreign Legion* in 1956–57. He
was finding plenty of work in a developing if not yet highly regarded
nook of the field of cultural production, and so were several of
those contemporaries already referred to. *Sight and Sound* wrote of
Comfort, in a round-up of British directors in 1958, 'Like other
directors, he has recently turned to television; and like others he
has had difficulty in sustaining the vigour of his early films
through a good deal of unrewarding material.'[24] True enough in
general, but this study will suggest that even with 'unrewarding
material', he *did* sustain a good deal of his early vigour.

Genre film-making has not usually been seen as central to the
creation of British national cinema. A recent commentator has
written that 'The 1940s are characterised by an intensification of
debates around national culture and the demand for a quality
indigenous cinema that would represent the British character and
ideals to both foreign and domestic audiences.'[25] No more so than
melodrama in particular was genre at large seen to have a role in
the construction of a 'quality indigenous cinema', unless it
acquired a consecration by virtue of its roots in a certain level of
literature (say, *Brighton Rock*) or theatre (*Brief Encounter*, for
example) or with an approved realism in its narrational mode (as
in *It Always Rains On Sunday* or, even more notably, *The Third
Man*, with its panoply of famous credentials, or some of the Ealing
comedies). Only by evincing such affiliations was the genre film
likely to fall within 'the idea of the "quality film" they [the critics]
were constituting ... Crucially, the 'quality' film was something
that they passionately hoped the wide public would come to
recognise and appreciate.'[26] In recent times, there has been more
attention given to the kinds of genre film-making which, as a
quick flick through Denis Gifford's *The British Film Catalogue 1895–
1970* or David Quinlan's *British Sound Films: The Studio Years 1928–
1959*[27] will verify, clearly outnumber the exemplars of 'quality' film-
making. Marcia Landy's ground-breaking study of British film

genres[28] offers a different way of considering and categorising British cinema. Virtually all Comfort's work falls within clearly defined genre limits, most of it melodrama of various kinds, including family/sexual inflections of the mode, many thrillers, including espionage, kidnapping, wartime and heist varieties, a few regional comedies and musicals. There is the odd film which is harder to classify, such as the strange little drama of postwar malaise and childhood fantasy, *Bang! You're Dead* (1953), but it can't be said that he ever produced a major work *sui generis*. This study is not making claims for remarkable originality – by coincidence, the general release of *Hatter's Castle* in Britain occurred in the same week (2 February 1942) as another study in megalomania, Orson Welles's *Citizen Kane*, and there is an obvious contrast between the genre director (working the genre for all it is worth) and the one-off creator staking out his own dominant position in the field in one superlatively daring stroke.

It may well be a priority for those assessing the work of the field (and, in this function, constituting *part* of the field) to recognise and applaud originality of achievement, but, in relation especially to a popular art form, it should be equally ready to value – and evaluate – what is being done within more conventional parameters. If Lance Comfort's oeuvre is examined in the context of what British cinema had to offer in the period of his productivity, as distinct from what was – more narrowly – sanctioned by contemporary taste-makers, it may be possible to arrive at a juster appraisal. It is not the function of this study to adopt the auteurist's stance of looking for nuggets in every lump of quartz. To see how he dealt with what came his way (or what he sought out); to understand why a career which seemed to show every sign of commanding a respected place in the field should have been derailed into the field's more obscure corners; and to see what there is to value in this context: this seems a potentially more useful approach. My own views on the films discussed will of course emerge, but that is not my primary aim. Instead, it seems more interesting to see how the films came to be as they were, how they were presented to and received by the public and the critics. If the book throws light on such matters, a light which might reflect on to similar career trajectories of the period, it will have fulfilled my intentions.

Notes

1 David Shipman, *The Great Movie Stars: The Golden Years* (London, Hamlyn), 1970, p. 344.
2 Pierre Bourdieu, *The Field of Cultural Production: Essays on Art and Literature*, edited and introduced by Randal Johnson (Cambridge, Polity Press), 1993.
3 Randal Johnson, 'Introduction', in Bourdieu, *Field*, p. 2.
4 Bourdieu, *Field*, p. 71.
5 *Ibid*, p. 64.
6 Pierre Bourdieu, *The Logic of Practice* (1980), translated by Richard Nice (Cambridge, Polity Press), 1990, p. 53.
7 Bourdieu, *Field*, p. 50.
8 Johnson, in Bourdieu, *Field*, p. 17.
9 Bourdieu, *Field*, p. 75.
10 *Ibid*, p. 41.
11 Dilys Powell, 'Films since 1939', in *Since 1939* (London, Readers Union), 1948, p. 78.
12 John Hill, *Sex, Class and Realism: British Cinema 1956–1963* (London, BFI Publishing), 1986, p. 57.
13 Alan Lovell, 'The British cinema: the known cinema', in Robert Murphy (ed.), *The British Cinema Book* (London, BFI Publishing), 1997, p. 236.
14 *Ibid*, p. 237.
15 Author's interview with Peter Miller, October 1998.
16 Author's interview with William Franklyn, September 1998.
17 Author's interview with Roy Baird, October 1998.
18 Author's interview with Greta Gynt, October 1998.
19 'Robert S. Baker', in Brian McFarlane, *An Autobiography of British Cinema* (London, Methuen), 1997, pp. 43–4.
20 Brian McFarlane, 'Pulp fictions: the British B film and the field of cultural production', *Film Criticism*, xxi:1 (1996), p. 52.
21 Peter Pitt, 'A reminiscence of Elstree', *Film and Television Technician*, February 1989, p. 8.
22 *Ibid*, p. 9.
23 For details relating to these series, see Dave Rogers, *The ITV Encyclopedia of Adventure* (London, Boxtree), 1988.
24 'British feature directors: an index to their work', *Sight and Sound*, 27:6 (1958) 292. (No author cited.)
25 Pam Cook, 'Neither here nor there: national identity in Gainsborough costume drama', in Andrew Higson (ed.), *Dissolving Views: New Writings on British Cinema* (London, Cassell), 1996, p. 52.
26 John Ellis, 'The quality film adventure', in Higson, *Dissolving Views*, p. 69
27 Denis Gifford, *The British Film Catalogue 1895–1970* (Newton Abbot, Devon, David & Charles), 1973, and David Quinlan, *British Sound Films: The Studio Years 1928–1959* (London, B. T. Batsford), 1984.
28 Marcia Landy, *British Genres: Cinema and Society 1930–1960* (Princeton, Princeton University Press), 1991.

A long apprenticeship

Few film directors can have had a more varied experience of their trade than Lance Comfort. Fortunately this is not a biographical study since so many of the documents that might have shed light on his earlier years have been lost. According to his son John, in moving into a smaller flat in the years just before his death, Comfort destroyed virtually all his papers, consigning a press cuttings book (the work of an agency), along with bulkier items, to a warehouse from which they were never reclaimed. The cuttings book finally found its way back to the British Film Institute, via an unknown person who had sought the advice of Dilys Powell, then film reviewer for the *Sunday Times*. This study has drawn on it a good deal for contemporary production reports and reviews of Comfort's films (it is referred to as LCC in footnotes, as it forms part of the BFI's 'Lance Comfort Collection'). Unsurprisingly, though, this valuable resource dates only from the time he started making short films for children in the late 1930s, and is therefore no help in piecing together the early years.

Comfort was born in 1908 in Harrow, where he was educated, though not at the famous public school, and he died in Worthing, Sussex, in 1966. He was between 17 and 19 years old when he first began to work in films, more or less growing up with the cinema. He did not come from an affluent background nor from one with any special interest in the cinema, but seems to have gone from school into films. John Comfort's recollection was that his father 'did a little bit of sound, a little bit in the camera department, a little bit of editing ... You had a chance to really train in the making of movies ... because you learnt across the board, not just with people in one department.'¹ First-hand recollections of Comfort's early years are now almost impossible to come by. The most comprehensive primary source about what Comfort was doing during the years between 1925 and 1940 is a three-page typed sheet, perhaps typed by Lance Comfort's wife, their son thinks, entitled 'LANCE COMFORT – PRODUCTION EXPERIENCE 1925–1940'. As well as the nearly fifty 'Feature Productions' on which he worked in a variety of capacities, there are other headings as follows: 'Speciality Productions', 'Short Films', 'Special Work' and 'Speciality Work'. While it has been possible to date the feature productions, using such sources as Denis Gifford's *The British Film Catalogue 1896–1970*,² the other work eludes precise dating. Most references suggest that Comfort came into films in the latter half of the 1920s. *The British Film Yearbook 1949–50* states in the biographical entry on Comfort: 'He entered the film industry in 1926 as animator and cameraman on a series of medical research films for Community Service Ltd',³ and later writers, further from the source, have repeated this claim, though sometimes varying the date of entry. *Sight and Sound*, for instance, in its round-up of British directors in 1959, claimed that Comfort 'became animator and cameraman on medical research films in 1928'.⁴ Among the list under the heading 'Speciality Productions' are such titles as 'British Social Hygiene' and 'Venereal Diseases', respectively 6 and 12 reels, on which Comfort is credited as 'Cameraman', these presumably being the 'medical films' referred to. He worked as cameraman on documentary and advertising films (for example, for Dunlop, United Dairies, Max Factor) and had experience as cameraman at 'Ealing, Islington, Southall and Gaumont' according to the *Yearbook*. He was termed 'Trick Cameraman' not only in 'Speciality Productions' but also on the 1928 version of *The Constant Nymph* and the 1931 version of *The Ghost Train*. For Kingsway General Films, he was both Trick Cameraman and Production Manager. He was a 'Newsreel Cameraman' for Topical Films, 'Night Scene Cameraman' on Reginald Fogwell's *Madame Guillotine* (1931) and 'Test Cameraman' on Harry Lachman's *The Outsider*

(1931). In later chapters on his feature films, this study will claim that Comfort had a visual flair, which kept his films at a remove from the look of what Karel Reisz once described as 'photographed radio plays'.[5] An aspect of Comfort's disposition as a filmmaker was his interest in and capacity for expressing himself and other people's ideas visually, and it is clear that from his earliest days in British cinema he found a position in the field for the exercise of such proclivities.

However, his range also included, notably, work as sound recordist. Dallas Bower recalls how Comfort came, in the early 1930s, to join his staff at Cricklewood where Bower, 'fed up with BIP [British International Pictures]' had gone to take charge of the sound department for Stoll Picture Productions. Comfort said to him, 'I've just been given a job. Will you teach me how to record?'[6] and, 'after a momentary suspicion that he was after my job', Bower did so, finding him efficient, quick to learn, and, as everyone else did, affable. Many of the films on which Comfort is credited as 'Chief recordist' for Stoll, under Bower's supervision as head of the sound department, were 'quota quickies', but there were also several films of more obvious prestige, such as *Dick Turpin* (1933), with Victor McLaglan, and *Song at Eventide* (1934), with Fay Compton. On most of the features on which he worked until 1936, he was billed as 'Chief recordist', and he was also responsible for 'Sound Recording & Editing'[7] on twenty films listed under the heading of 'Speciality Work', including titles such as *Emil and the Detectives* (perhaps the 1936 film directed by Milton Rosmer) and short films such as *Du Barry, Hungarian Rhapsody*, and *Tomb of the Unknown Warrior* (dates unknown). Under the list headed 'Short Films', his 'Capacity' is designated 'Chief recordist' on *City of St Alban and the Forgotten City of Verulamium* (1933), and a number of others which sound like travelogue films, such as *Lapland, Scotland* and *Paris*.

From 1936 on, he was credited as either 'Technical supervisor' or 'Assistant director', and all the films of this period, apart from a series of short children's films, were made for the director John Baxter, who would recur several times as producer on Comfort's own films as director. No one now seems very clear about what was comprehended by the term 'Technical supervisor', though several suggested that it probably implied a close working relationship with the director and that it involved a wide range of responsibilities of the kind which Comfort's varied experience would have equipped him for. He is 'Assistant director' on Baxter's *Old Mother Riley in Society* and *Old Mother Riley in Business* (both 1940), and, on the last two films he made with Baxter as director, *Love on the Dole* and *Old Mother Riley's Ghosts* (both 1941), he is billed as both 'Technical supervisor' and 'Associate director.' The roles seem to have been both important and difficult to pin down.

The point of adducing this information is to suggest that by the time Comfort came to directing he had had a great deal of varied and, no doubt, useful experience, which may help to account for the universally 'good press' he gets from the range of collaborators interviewed in relation to this study. In the views of editors, writers, actors and others with whom he worked on several occasions, he had a broadly based understanding of the technical aspects of film-making, so that he could appreciate the problems of other personnel. When he came to make 'B' films in the 1950s and 1960s, his wide-ranging expertise enabled him to deal efficiently with the constraints of tight budgets and schedules. This kind of broadly based experience was as much a part of the 'habitus' which disposed him to survive in the movies as, say, his undoubted visual flair. He even acted as producer on a number of films (some directed by himself, some not) of the 1950s and 1960s, and, though he never greatly warmed to this role, the sort of experience gained in the 1930s must have been useful to him in understanding the over-all processes of film-making.

During this long apprenticeship he worked on films from a wide generic range – love stories, crime thrillers, musicals, romantic comedy, romantic drama and broad slapstick comedy – and, later as director, his films were almost all in clear generic categories, often with a strongly melodramatic flavour. Though he was involved in documentary film-making in this period, it cannot be said that this seems greatly to have influenced his subsequent career, except perhaps in the predeliction for location filming, which remained with him till the end, even when it meant seeking out locations conveniently (that is, cheaply) near the relevant studio.

As well as the usefulness of learning his craft by working in half-a-dozen or more capacities and in a cross-section of the kinds of films then being made (that is, in matters of genres and of functions, entertainment or instructional), Comfort also made some contacts in the 1930s who would recur significantly in his career as a director. The most important was the populist director/ producer, John Baxter, who would act as producer on three of Comfort's films. It is obviously his work as Baxter's assistant from 1936 on which brought Comfort to the point of assuming the reins himself, though it is interesting to note crucial differences of feeling in their films. Unlike Baxter, Comfort is almost never explicitly a social commentator in his own films (*Bang! You're Dead* and *Eight O'Clock Walk* come nearest to mounting a case about socially important matters), and he is never sentimental, as Baxter often is. He might have taken the pleasure in the country-side Baxter shows in a fable like *Song of the Road* (1937), but in his features Comfort would very often undercut such scenes of pastoral beauty with a sharp critique, finding bitter rather than sentimental associations with it. The producer Victor Hanbury, with whom Comfort would have had dealings on *Dick Turpin* in 1933, would later produce three of his films as director. John Corfield, John Baxter's producer on several films, produced *Bedelia* in which Comfort directed Margaret Lockwood in 1946. The composer and music director Kennedy Russell, the art directors, Holmes Paul and Duncan Sutherland, and the editor Sydney Stone were others with whom Comfort was associated in the 1930s and who would make important contributions to his later career as director. And actors, of course: Eric Portman, Charles Victor, Marjorie Rhodes, Emlyn Williams, Enid Stamp-Taylor, Clifford Evans, George Carney, Ernest Butcher, Mary Clare, John Stuart, Maire O'Neill and others would all make their presences felt in Comfort's own feature films as director.

Towards the end of his apprenticeship, in 1938–39, he directed several short films for children. There was a gap of over a year between films for John Baxter, as he changed studio and producer, and it seems that Comfort filled this time by making these shorts. These, none of which is now available, were all made for Butcher's Two-Reelers, and all involve small children and animals. In 1938 he filmed *Sandy Steps Out*, and, in 1939, *Laddie's Day Out*, *Judy Buys a Horse*, *Thoroughbreds* and *Toddlers and a Pup*, in the last of which John Comfort, the director's small son, appeared. To judge from the press releases relating to them, these short films all appear to be aimed at very young children (maybe 10 and under); they all record adventures of small children with animals, except *Laddie's Day Out* in which the adventures befall the eponymous golden retriever, who investigates in turn a combine harvester, a silver fox farm, a rabbit farm, a riding party and kennels for French poodles. (The film's admiring attitudes to the production of fox and rabbit furs would not meet approval today.) There seems to have been a strongly anthropomorphic approach to animal behaviour and stress on 'the unspoilt countryside'[8] in these ingenuous-sounding entertainments for the young, and they all have the credit, 'Compered by Kent Stevenson', presumably referring to a voice-over guide to the narrative. From the press release descriptions of the action of these films, it seems as if Comfort may have been drawing on his documentary experience as he records the adventures of his young protagonists in such settings as a country fair (*Judy Buys a Horse*), a gypsy encampment and 'Mr Tom Walls' Stud Farm' (*Thoroughbreds*), nurseries and schools for children from babies to pre-tens (*Toddlers and a Pup*). Several of them are photographed by Jack Parker, a documentary cinematographer for G. B. Instructional, as well as being John Baxter's collaborator on eight films.

Though *Penn of Pennsylvania* (1941) is Comfort's first feature as director, I am referring to it here as the last stage in his apprenticeship because it seems so at odds with everything he did later – *and* it is so leaden that it could scarcely have launched a directorial career. Fortunately for Comfort, production on *Hatter's Castle* (1941) was well underway before *Penn* was released. This is not to say that it received universally bad notices – the *Guardian*, for instance, thought it 'A thoroughly well-documented English picture … an earnest and sincere picture of William Penn',[9] and the

Birmingham Post praised it as a 'wholesome, honest apologia'[10] –
but the general tone of the reviews suggested a lack of real energy.
Even the praise it attracted tended to be along the lines of 'sincere',
'discreet', 'straightforward', summed up rather well by *Picturegoer*'s
phrase (referring specifically to the latter two-thirds of the film), 'a
rather stereotyped parade of historical incidents without much
flesh and blood vitality'.[11] Not a description one would apply to
Comfort's next venture. Be that as it may, it was no doubt wel-
comed by Comfort as a chance to direct a feature film after fifteen
years of the most varied labours in the film studios, and several
press reports on the production drew attention to his new status,
including the *Daily Herald* which wrote of 'Mr. Lance Comfort, an
assistant director who now gets his big chance'.[12]

Allegedly, a broadcast by the US President Roosevelt inspired
the producer, Richard Vernon, to make the film, finding Roosevelt's 'character and ideals ... so much in keeping with those of
Penn, who, above all, stood for the principles of liberty and demo-
cracy'.[13] Seen today, what is most interesting about the film is its
blatant propagandist intention, which must have been still more
transparent when the film was released a few months before the
USA entered the war. William Penn (Clifford Evans) rebels against
the frivolous and licentious court of Charles II (Denis Arundell),
and against the drunken revelry of the tavern crowds, clashes with
his father, and throws in his lot with the Quakers. These opening
sequences are briskly enough done, with that feel for pacing
Comfort would so often reveal later. But once Penn's stance has
been taken, the film settles for a series of tableau-like sequences,
predictably ended with long fades. There are scenes representing
his clash with his snobbish father; his meeting with the society
beauty Guglielma (Deborah Kerr), won to his views with unlikely
celerity; his marketplace speech ('The day will come when the
world will be a just and friendly place'); his spell in gaol for
insisting on freedom of speech; his trial, at which both he and the
jury are found guilty, the jury because it refuses to reverse its
decision of 'Not Guilty'; his marriage and ensuing domestic bliss;
and so on. Not more than fifteen minutes are devoted to the
establishment of the colony of Pennsylvania where problems

(Native Americans and cruel colonists) are dealt with so summarily as not to make much impact. Comfort was one of those comparatively rare English directors who were prepared to let the camera do a great deal of a film's narration, but he doesn't offer much evidence of this skill here. The English episodes are too often rather stiffly staged, relying on a talky didacticism to make their points about brotherly love and the promise of America, and the persistent use of long fades gives much of the film a monotonous rhythm. However, even in these stately proceedings, Comfort still manages some visual élan: there are several montage sequences sharply edited by Sidney Cole, economically representing the oppression of the Quakers, the journey to America, and the growth of the colony under Penn's leadership (trees are felled, land cleared, streets mapped out, in the poetic treatment of an idea). Further, Holmes Paul's sets, though theatrical in orientation, are substantial and detailed, and well-rendered by Ernest Palmer's camera, of which Comfort makes astute use in a couple of close-ups, such as those revealing Penn's marriage to Guglielma, as the camera moves in on his hand holding hers, or in the moment of his death, as it closes in on the letter from her he has been reading.

For the most part, though, this is not a film of subtle effects. Its advocacy of freedom of speech and its brazen solicitation of US good opinion make it very much a film of its time, a time when Britain was in danger from a foreign power with scant respect for the freedom to differ, and when it urgently needed American intervention. It is with this background in mind that one needs to listen to such speeches as that made by Guglielma to her husband: 'America's a new world. You could start from the beginning. You could leave behind all the hatreds and foolish customs of the old world. We could take America and turn it into a vast continent where freedom of thought and liberty of conscience would be the birthright of every man.' And a few minutes later, she cries: 'You've got to go to America' and he intones in reply, 'Yes, it's the answer to all our problems, America!' Potent words undoubtedly – in 1941.

In using an historical setting for propaganda purposes, *Penn of*

Pennsylvania has obvious links with Thorold Dickinson's *The Prime Minister*, released in March 1941, and Carol Reed's *The Young Mr Pitt* (1942), and none of the three represents the best work of their respective directors. Of *The Prime Minister*, Jeffrey Richards has written, 'the principal interest of the film lies in its propaganda content ... Disraeli in the context of 1940 clearly stands for Churchill ... unlike Chamberlain, he stands up to the dictators',[14] and *The Young Mr Pitt* has been described as 'a nationalistic allegory in which England's struggle against the French during the Napoleonic Wars is implicitly compared to her lonely, heroic stand against the Nazis prior to the American entry into the war.'[15] Comfort's film may, from this point of view, be seen as urging America to fulfil its function as the most powerful nation of 'the free world', and this role must have given it a resonance lost to a viewer in the late 1990s.

What one is left with are some well-written and executed scenes. These include the court scene presided over by the choleric Lord Mayor of London (Joss Ambler), who crosses swords with the chairman (Edward Rigby) of the recalcitrant jury. The episode becomes a tribute to English justice when the jury finally wins the day. In efforts to bring it to heel, reference is made to instituting a replica of the Spanish Inquisition, in a not very oblique allusion to the Nazis' stifling of freedom of speech. There is also a nicely shaped sequence which begins with the dandified King having his portrait painted and making arch sexual innuendoes to Lady Castlemaine (Mary Hinton). This frivolity is interrupted by the arrival of Penn, come to claim the £17,000 the King still owes his father. Naturally, Penn wants this money for the expedition to set up an American state which could be 'a pattern for the world'. The King is allowed here to be more than a mere libertine; he listens to and comes to see the seriousness of Penn's proposal. There was presumably no mileage, in the interests of propaganda, in making the British head of state seem an idiot, and Denis Arundell makes a real character of His Majesty. There is a very large cast which does more or less what is required of it, though the characterisation is generally perfunctory. The publicity for the film stressed the re-teaming of Clifford Evans and Deborah Kerr 'who scored such a success in *Love on the Dole*'[16] (on which Comfort was assistant director to John Baxter), and reviews generally praised Evans' performance in terms such as 'sympathetic'[17] and 'acts sincerely',[18] though the latter comment was followed by 'a little lacking in fire'. Given the endlessly uplifting things he is given to say, Evans needs a more charismatically commanding presence. Some of Comfort's later actors (Robert Newton or Eric Portman, for instance) might have made something more exciting of the role, though the film is more interested in Penn's emblematic importance than in his human individuality. As Marcia Landy has noted: 'The figure of Penn is offered as the example of the freedom-loving Englishman, and the film is primarily a plea for tolerance and unity against the enemies of justice.'[19] For a costume drama, a Quaker hero provides a problem: committed to non-violence, he must rely on the quality of his words and the force-fulness of his delivery. The only violence permitted Penn is when he knocks down an English soldier in a conflict over treatment of the Native Americans to prevent his being shot by the Native American sympathiser, Captain Cockle. Though she has little to do, being presented as 'fused to her husband's values and beliefs',[20] Deborah Kerr, in her third film, was already skilful enough to make something touching of how Guglielma's ingenuous gaiety is subdued by love and idealism, and finally by stoically borne pain. (The true-life second Mrs Penn has no role in the film.) Viewed today the film is interesting both as a curiosity of its time, and as the film in which the thirty-three-year-old Comfort was given his chance to direct after a sixteen-year apprenticeship. His real reward, however, was his next film which gave him the opportunity to show where his talents truly lay – that is, as a perfervid melodramatist.

Notes

1 Author's interview with John Comfort, October 1997.
2 Denis Gifford, *The British Film Catalogue 1896–1970* (Newton Abbott, David and Charles), 1973.
3 Peter Noble (ed.), *The British Film Yearbook 1949–50* (London, Skelton

Robinson), 1949, p. 507.

4 'British feature directors: an index to their work', *Sight and Sound*, 27:6 (Autumn 1958), p. 292.

5 Author's interview with Karel Reisz, 1992.

6 Author's interview with Dallas Bower, 1998.

7 According to the document, 'Lance Comfort: Production Experience 1925–1940', mentioned earlier in this chapter.

8 Press release for *Laddie's Day Out*, 1939.

9 A. D., 'William Penn', *Guardian*, 20 August 1941. BFI 'Lance Comfort Collection' (LCC).

10 'Films in Birmingham', *Birmingham Post*, 18 August 1941. LCC.

11 Lionel Collier, 'Shop for Your Films', *Picturegoer*, 11:546 (24 January 1942), p. 12.

12 'British Film of William Penn', *Daily Herald*, 11 February 1941. LCC.

13 Press release, date and source obscured. LCC.

14 Jeffrey Richards, *Thorold Dickinson. The Man and His Films* (London, Croom Helm), 1986, pp. 89, 90, 91.

15 Robert Moss, *The Films of Carol Reed* (London and Basingstoke, Macmillan), 1987, p. 129.

16 *News of the World*, 24 August 1941. LCC.

17 *Reynolds News*, 24 August 1941. LCC.

18 *Kinematograph Weekly*, 1788 (24 July 1941), p. 23.

19 Marcia Landy, *British Genres. Cinema and Society 1930–1960* (Princeton, Princeton University Press), 1991, p. 78.

20 *Ibid*, p. 79.

Breakthrough: *Hatter's Castle* **3**

It was probably just as well for Lance Comfort's career that production on *Hatter's Castle* was well under way before his first feature,
Penn of Pennsylvania, was released. Filming on *Hatter's Castle*
began at Denham on 26 May 1941, had its West End release in
November 1941 to generally enthusiastic reviews, and its general
release in February 1942. The much less popular and accomplished
Penn was first released in August 1941; its reviews stressed its
worthiness and sincerity rather than its entertainment value. A
couple of months later, Comfort's reputation as a features director
seemed to be made when *Hatter's Castle*, made by Paramount's
British operation, opened at the Plaza, Piccadilly Circus, after a
well-publicised charity première attended by the Duchess of Kent
and luminaries such as Noel Coward.[1] Though some of the 'quality'
press reviewers were inclined to be reserved about its 'melodramatic'
excesses in matters of plotting and execution, the popular and
trade press responses were almost universally affirmative. The
film's reception will be discussed below; it is enough to assert here
that a significant new director seemed to have arrived, and
Comfort's career trajectory to have taken a notably upward turn.

Dr Cronin's 'sensational best-seller'[2]

The first name to appear on the screen after the Paramount logo
and the film's title – and in appropriately Gothic script – is that of

A. J. Cronin, author of the novel on which the film is based. The
novel had first been published in May 1931, exactly ten years
before production began on the film, and two other Cronin novels
had been filmed in England with great critical and popular success:
King Vidor's version of *The Citadel* (1938) and Carol Reed's
version of *The Stars Look Down* (1940). Much was made in the
publicity surrounding the filming of *Hatter's Castle* of the Cronin
connection, as if this were both a strong selling point and a matter
of some distinction. The film was trumpeted as an adaptation of
Cronin's 'greatly acclaimed and widely-read novel', a 'sensational
best-seller ... [which] has sold to date some three million copies
and has been translated into 19 languages'.[3] Even allowing for the
extravagance of publicists, the point is made about the popular
esteem in which the novel was held, and as a matter of *fact* the
book had been reprinted 22 times before production began on the
film. Given this and the success of the two preceding adaptations,
it is clear that Comfort was being entrusted with what must have
seemed a major enterprise. When the film was finally released in
the USA in 1948, the publicity could stress two further prestige
films made from his novels – *The Keys of the Kingdom* (1945) and
The Green Years (1946).[4] At this point, it was claimed that 'Cronin's
books are veritable magnets to movie-makers' and are 'Noted for
sustained narrative power, plus the fact that the author has
something to say.'[5] He is mentioned in every review of the film
and in most of the press releases during the months of the film's
production. Despite all this, I would claim that Comfort's film
improves on the novel in virtually every way.

In an earlier essay on Comfort's melodramas, I compared the
film's bravura effects to Cronin's 'relatively austere novel'.[6] Then
relying on memories of reading the novel some decades ago, I
now believe, on re-reading, that it is far from austere, that it is
impelled less by the melodramatic vitality which characterises the
film than by a relentless, all-but-sadistic determination to put the
reader through a sickening chronicle of brutalities. Its appeal
seems primarily directed to masochists. Posing as realism, it is
actually so unrelievedly bleak that it strains credulity. No such
problem attends the screenplay, usually attributed to playwright

Rodney Ackland, though the credits read: 'Screen Play Paul Merzbach and [in smaller letters] R. Bergaur' and under this 'Scenario and Dialogue Rodney Ackland'.[7] The film adheres to the main outline of the novel – an egomaniacal hatter, James Brodie, eventually destroys himself and most of his family through the pursuit of his vainglorious obsession – but alters a number of important elements of plotting, character, relationship and tone, invariably for the better. Reviewing the film, Elspeth Grant (much later to be co-author of Ackland's memoirs) wrote that producer Isadore Goldsmith and director Lance Comfort 'have ... turned Dr Cronin's ha'pence into guineas',[8] but most reviewers were more respectful of Cronin's novel than this. British critical discourse of the 1940s and later usually found film versions of novels inferior to the antecedent texts, and, in a cinema that privileged the literary, *Hatter's Castle* is the nearest Comfort came to filming a 'prestige' novel.

Lance Comfort's melodrama

The film is a passionate melodrama, polarising tyrant and victims. It intimates its unrestrained intentions from the outset with Horace Shepherd's wild scoring behind the credits, and the camera lighting first on the pub sign, 'Winton Arms', swinging in the wind. In hindsight, the name 'Winton' can be seen to introduce Brodie's mad social aspirations, as he insists on his connection with Lord Winton, the local grandee. In 1879, in a room of the pub in this Scottish town, Levensford, a men's club is in progress, discussing the appointment of a school physician. The mealymouthed ironmonger, Grierson (Henry Oscar), is holding forth when Brodie (Robert Newton), the hatter, strides in and takes command of the scene, dismissing the idea of appointing young Dr Renwick to the post. Brodie is established from the outset – through skill in framing, and through Max Greene's lighting, which highlights the manic quality Newton brings to the role – as a figure on a large scale, the other town worthies in the scene being reduced by the comparison. A good deal is accomplished in this opening segment of the film. The period is sketched, for example, in a brief reference to rumours of Mr Gladstone's raising the income tax by a penny in the pound, and in an off-screen rendition of 'My Darling Clementine' heard in the pub. Brodie's pre-eminence in the town – a matter of bullying and swagger, social and sexual – is also signified in every lineament of Newton's performance. The manic, bullying quality is there in his relationship with the comely barmaid Nancy (Enid Stamp-Taylor), herself conducting an affair with the shifty Dennis (Emlyn Williams), supposedly her half-brother for whose benefit she seduces Brodie into giving him a job. It is also evident in Brodie's references to Renwick (scornful) and to his son (patriarchal – 'As to the health of my boy, you can leave that to me'). On these bases, the rest of the film is built and they are set in place with easy narrative fluidity and a promise that the melodramatic potential will not be flinched from. Our opening view of the larger-than-life figure of Brodie is then capped by a long shot of his ridiculous 'Castle' – a suburban villa with parapets, the symbol of Brodie's ambitions. By the film's end, the Castle will be destroyed; he will have been bested by the scheming Dennis and deserted by Nancy; he will have failed to attend to 'the health of [his] boy'; and the despised Renwick will provide the hope of the future.

Brodie is not a tragic figure, nor is he simply the one-note brute of Cronin's novel. He is, like a number of Comfort's protagonists, an obsessive. He has been determined to assert his supremacy in Levensford, and, when his adored son, Angus (Anthony Bateman), tells him his house is mocked as 'Hatter's Castle', he replies 'There's not a man in Levensford would have had the gumption to build a house in his own way like your father has', we can respect the energy that has gone into the enterprise, however misguided it may seem. The realisation of this dream gives Brodie a stature denied to his fellow townsmen, including Lord Winton (Stuart Lindsell), who, in the central county ball sequence, makes clear he is offended by the idea of a bourgeois upstart claiming kinship with him. If the castle and what it stands for represents one obsession of his life, the other is his son Angus whom he alternately cossets and bullies, but for whom, in his own perverse way, he has some real affection. The film ends with these two patriarchal obsessions – the castle and the son who will carry on his name – linked in a climax in which the boy, unable to live up to his father's expectations or to bear longer with his tyranny, blows his brains out, and Brodie sets fire to the castle, which he now sees as the source of his griefs. Brilliantly effective as this penultimate sequence is in melodramatic terms, with Brodie's distorted face and maniacal laughter behind the leaping flames, the notion that it was for Hatter's Castle that 'I slaughtered all I hold dear' seems imposed rather than to have underlain the film's action. The film then fades to Brodie's funeral, leaving itself no time to question the delusion that informs Brodie's final act of madness. If most of the film's sympathies are with Brodie's victims, and though he is very nearly a study in unrelieved villainy, the urge to self-improvement, even in the most limited terms, and the sense of class snobbery at work against him, introduce a satisfying complexity, so that Brodie becomes what one reviewer described as 'a clever psychological study and a gripping one'.[9]

It is in his dealings with women that Brodie's bullying is at its most repellant. The novel deals more openly with the sexual relations involved, and the film, constrained by the censorship of the period, is forced to encode these through manipulations of the mise-en-scène. His contempt for his aging cancer-ridden wife (a very touching study in care-worn drudgery by Beatrice Varley) leads him to refuse her the medical treatment Dr Renwick (James Mason) insists she needs. Instead, he installs his mistress, Nancy, as household help, and the film makes cunning use of the off-screen space as we watch Mrs Brodie talking to someone working in the kitchen about what Brodie expects; the camera only then moves to reveal that the help is Nancy. In a shot of Mrs Brodie standing behind Nancy, the camera catches her realisation of this final insult Brodie has offered her. The image of her packing her bags dissolves to that of Brodie arriving home as his wife is about to leave. Comfort stages the triangular confrontation with a back view of Brodie flanked by the two women, the composition broken when he moves towards Nancy's beckoning. Mrs Brodie refuses 'to live with that woman under the same roof', but collapses before she reaches the door, dead from the cancer which Brodie has refused to acknowledge.

The other major victim of Brodie's patriarchal bullying is his daughter, Mary (Deborah Kerr). She falls in love with Dr Renwick, who is barred from the house by Brodie, but is seduced by the conniving Dennis. On the night of the county ball, Brodie learns that Mary has, against his orders, called in Renwick to treat her mother, and forbids her to attend the ball where Renwick has hoped to see her. Instead, Dennis, hearing that Mary is alone at the castle, leaves the ball, with a bottle of champagne and a music-box, and slips into the castle. This whole long sequence is articulated through a series of alternating segments, separated by dissolves, as the film moves between the county ball (where Brodie is snubbed and his wife faints) and the castle where Mary's virtue, fuddled by unaccustomed champagne, is compromised by Dennis. On one of these dissolves, the camera, leaving the ball, lights on her empty champagne glass on a small table, an example of the visual touches that point to Comfort's wish to tell the story with the camera, rather than just to offer pictures of people talking. Mary is of course pregnant by Dennis and when Brodie later discovers this he pushes her out into a night of unprecedented storm. In the handling of this archetypal melodramatic cliché, Comfort fulfils the film's early promise that it would not hold back from such representational excess. Lighting, framing, music and editing all make their contributions. The night of the storm is also the night of the famous Tay Bridge disaster, in which Dennis, leaving Levensford, dies but Mary miraculously survives, paving the way for the final scene. As she leaves her father's funeral, she is shunned by the townsfolk, but is joined by the faithful Renwick who takes her arm and leads her out into the sunlight. (Was David Lean recalling this image when he filmed the final scene of *Great Expectations* five years later?)

The major tonal distinction between the film and Cronin's novel is that Comfort, abetted by Greene, Shepherd and his other collaborators, and especially by Newton's all-stops-out performance, is absolutely committed to the flourish of melodrama and to its clear-cut world view, a concept more likely to be understood now than then. Very properly he eschews Cronin's spurious realism in favour of a rhetorical style which renders and heightens the elemental conflicts between tyrant and victims, and between good and evil. Ackland's scenario has also contributed to the film's greater holding power by paring down some of the novel's complications. For instance, Cronin gives Brodie three children: Mary, the eldest; Matt, a weak-minded young man who becomes Nancy's lover and involves his doting mother in grave financial troubles; and Nessie, the youngest and Brodie's favourite. Mary is still hurled from the house pregnant, but by a young man (called Dennis) whom she loves and to whom in her innocence she has given way sexually. He is killed in the Tay Bridge collapse when he has been planning to marry Mary. By making Dennis her father's shop assistant and Nancy's secret lover, with whom Brodie discovers Nancy embracing, Ackland has tautened the plotlines, while retaining their essential functions. Renwick's last-minute rescue of Mary in the novel is more convincingly built in the film as a result of his being made the confidant of Mrs Brodie, who has given him news that Mary has not died in the train wreck. Mrs Brodie is much less pitiable in the novel, where she is more shrewish in her dealings with all but the favoured Matt. She is a more willing victim for Brodie's cruelty and made the clear object of his sexual disgust; he even kicks her – literally – out of the bed he loathes sharing with her. In the film, Brodie's hideous old mother is dispensed with, along with many minor characters. The effect of this paring down and modification is to intensify the drama, and also, particularly in the gender-reversal of Brodie's idolised younger child, to insist on its source in patriarchal aspiration. In his determination that Angus should win the coveted Latta scholarship, the patriarchal ambition is made clearer: Angus will bring distinction to the Brodie name – and keep that name as a daughter might not have. In representing a man who treats women as chattels, the film has done wisely in the changes it has wrought.

The film's strength lies essentially in Comfort's grasp of its melodramatic potential and in his mobilising of the resources available to him in realising this. Allowing Newton to have his head is a major element in this realisation. He struts and swaggers, towers over those he intimidates, is wild-eyed with mad resolution, sometimes dangerously silent. In his final sequence, he reels in drunkenly singing 'O who will o'er the downs with me?', arriving at the line, 'Her father he has locked the door', just as Angus slips in, putting on the table the letter refusing him permission to sit the scholarship exam. Brodie hovers over the fire as the camera moves to a close-up of the letter, then, in a facial distortion that suggests a Jekyll-to-Hyde transition, Newton registers the contents of the letter, and bellows up the stairs for Angus as a shot rings out. The action here exists somewhere between tragedy and melodrama; it is filmed in a way which suggests a director who knows how effective a moment of visual restraint might be in counterpointing a moment of high emotional intensity. In Max Greene (formerly Mutz Greenbaum), the noted German camera-man, Comfort had a crucial collaborator who seems to have conceived of the film's visual sheen in terms of a powerful chiaro-scuro effect. This is another way of articulating that 'more clear-cut designing, usually a dichotomizing of existence, with divisions between the good and the evil, the weak and the strong, victors and victims, the human and the inhuman',[10] which is so charac-teristic of the melodramatic agenda. The final shot of Renwick and Mary walking out into the light and away from the hypocrisy of the church is a typical example of Comfort's allowing the meaning to unfold in visual terms.

Selling the film

While the film was in production, there was a steady stream of press releases stressing that *Hatter's Castle* was to be an important production. Much was made of the lavish production values, particularly in relation to art director James Carter's set designs, for such set pieces as the county ball. 'The Paramount reputation for lavish setting is evidently being upheld in its British product', ran one press release which went on to say that 'Large ornate chan-deliers carrying eighteen gas lamps, together with innumerable bracket lights, illuminated the brilliant scene below. The set decor, in shades of light green, offset by the gold cornices, brass rails, parquet flooring, and the many palms and gilt chairs made the whole scene a memorable one.'[11] The tasteful extravagance contrasts in the film with the absurd, cold pretension of Hatter's Castle. There was also a good deal of publicity about the elaborate setting and filming of the Levensford street scene, used on several important occasions in the film, and above all of the recreation of the Tay Bridge disaster. On this matter, one report read: 'A tank, 60 ft. by 70 ft., with 9 ft. sides, will represent the Tay in flood, with six wind machines producing mountainous waves'.[12] Carter, it added, 'was able to build a flawless period reconstruction of the station at "Levensford"'. As if to stress further the importance of the production, it was also noted several times that USA Paramount chief, David Rose, had been in England during the filming and would be taking a copy to the US for its release there. (As noted earlier, this release did not in fact happen for seven years.)

Hatter's Castle was, then, by the standards of its day, a prestige production, on which a good deal of attention and, presumably, money was lavished, and exhibitors were alerted to another Paramount-British success along the lines of such previous films from the same company as *French Without Tears* (1939) and *Quiet Wedding* (1940). It had been sold as an ambitious production with distinguished credentials, with particular emphasis on its spectacular scenes and on the elaborate camera work brought to bear on these. Its stars were to be more famous in a year or so, though Newton and Deborah Kerr had received very complimentary notices for *Major Barbara* (1941), in which Emlyn Williams, better known at the time than either, had also had a key role. Williams also had played a similarly shifty character in *The Stars Look Down* (1939), the preceding Cronin adaptation. In fact, one publicity piece is headed 'Strong Cast For *Hatter's Castle*' and *The Star* reported 'a distinguished cast of British stars'.[13] The film was not sold on the name of Lance (or 'Lancelot' as he is designated in the *Daily Film Renter*'s piece)[14] Comfort, and there are only very brief references to him as the director of *Penn of Pennsylvania*. The film's reception was to put him in a very strong position in British cinema, but for whatever reasons, personal or industry-based, he chose not to follow it with another film in the melodramatic vein and would not make another wholly in this mode until *Bedelia* in 1946. Thereafter, he ventured out of it on no more than a handful of occasions, bringing his feeling for melodrama to bear on a range of urban and rural-set dramas and thrillers.

The film and the critics

The film's reception offers a revealing insight into the critical preferences of the time. There is among several of the 'quality' press reviewers a discernible snootiness about melodrama, but nothing to compare with the antipathy they would direct towards the Gainsborough pieces ushered in by *The Man in Grey* in 1943. By 1941, the realist strain in fiction films such as *In Which We Serve* (1942), *Millions Like Us* (1943) and *San Demetrio London* (1944), drawing in varying measure on documentary techniques and interests, had not yet asserted itself and won itself a privileged critical position, and the famous series of literature and theatre-based films, such as *Henry V* (1944), *Brief Encounter* (1945), and *Great Expectations* (1946), was still several years down the track. The rise of these critically acclaimed strands of film-making, as more fitting representatives of a burgeoning national cinema, coincided with the commercially popular but critically excoriated Gainsborough melodramas. The sense of condescending to melodrama is there in some of the reviews of *Hatter's Castle*, but has not yet acquired the full negative connotation it would from the mid-1940s. C. A. Lejeune writes of Brodie as a 'beast ... who is riding for a fall. You know the fall will come, and you wait to see how big a fall. That is the entire primitive sport of *Hatter's Castle*.'[15] She goes on to list for the reader's sport nine hectic happenings, which comprise the film's last forty minutes. (It doesn't occur to her that one might reduce, say, *King Lear*, to a similarly risible narrative skeleton.) She nevertheless praises Newton's 'tour de force' and concludes that the film 'will be remembered far longer than many better pictures.' The other 'Sunday lady', Dilys Powell, though finding it 'an extremely competent piece of work', had this to say about it: 'Melodrama is all very well in the cinema, but melodrama properly treated; melodrama, that is, given the emphasis of strangeness and terror. Here it is given the emphasis of realism.'[16] This curious line of criticism leads her to the opinion that the film's treatment has not lifted it 'from a pasteboard puzzle into the realm of human enigma.' This is an idea which will be relevant to some of Comfort's later melodramas, where his concern for, say, a realist mise-en-scène or an unusual complexity of chara-cter put them at a remove from the Gainsborough films. Powell at least seems to be arguing some kind of tangled case, unlike the reviewer in *Tatler & Bystander* who wrote 'We laughed and laughed and laughed', suggesting that the film 'would have its moments of pleasure for anyone tired of real life'.[17] The *Punch* reviewer felt 'simply that the cumulative effect of a number of overwhelmingly melodramatic incidents is inevitably comic', but nevertheless felt that the movie was 'well done'.[18] Most other reviewers adverted to the film's melodramatic content but not necessarily in negative terms. One assessed it in this way: 'Melodramatic to a degree, there's not a foot of this film which isn't interesting', having referred already to how Deborah Kerr 'treads delicately, as Mary, through a maze of East Lynne-ish melodrama'.[19] The *Times* wrote, 'Told with swift inventiveness and a sure eye for an effective scene, it is, though unrelievedly sombre, the very stuff of film melodrama'.[20] The *Catholic Herald* rated it as 'grand melodrama, high in its own class', but concluded that 'there is not the stuff of greatness to be distilled from this collection of sensations.'[21] At this point, it seems as if the contempt for melodrama which was later so characteristic of much of the writing about British cinema was not yet so vehement or endemic.

Whatever the reviewer's attitude to melodrama, there was almost universal praise for the acting, especially Newton's in the leading role originally intended for Charles Laughton.[22] One wrote that 'it provides a part to tear a cat in, and Mr Newton tears his cat magni-ficently.[23] Dilys Powell enthused that he 'finely takes the chance he has so long awaited'.[24] The *Daily Mail* reviewer headed his column 'This is great acting!'[25] As one watches Newton in full cry, especially when directing his wrath at the time-serving Nancy, it is impossible, in hindsight, not to project on to his Brodie the terrifying bullying of another Nancy – as Bill Sykes in David Lean's *Oliver Twist* seven years later – or, in his berating of James Mason's gentle Renwick, his manic dealings with Mason in Carol Reed's *Odd Man Out* (1946). A 1984 article occasioned by the television screening of *Hatter's Castle* drew attention to how 'Mason would shortly graduate from this kind of pale love interest to the diabolic hero (and box-office heart-throb) he played in melodramas like *The Man in Grey*.'[26] In fact, there is virtually no adverse criticism of the acting from any of the cast: Deborah Kerr, Emlyn Williams and especially Beatrice Varley, who appeared in several more films for Lance Comfort, are often singled out for their contributions.

As for Comfort himself, his reputation as a feature director should have been made by the film's general success with critics and public alike. In those pre-auteurist days, the director was by no means assured of much attention in the daily or other press, but Comfort seems to have had a fair share of favourable notice. Dilys Powell (*The Observer*) thought he 'has directed ably'; J. E. Sewell (*Daily Telegraph*) considered 'Credit must go to Lance Comfort, the director, for some useful angle-work and for his recognition of the essential point of the piece'; the *Times* praised 'the consistent liveliness of his direction'; and 'Lance Comfort's *Hatter's Castle*' was singled out by Sewell in a round-up of the year's British films, claiming that 'the standard of British production has never been higher.'[27] The 1984 article which saw the film as a pointer to where British cinema had been heading in 1941 wrote that 'Director Comfort ... captures the dementia of Brodie's dream in a surprisingly fluid, atmospheric way. The style is not exactly expressionist, but in its sombre lighting and skilful camera movement the film is occasionally evocative of Orson Welles's contemporary tale of a family's downfall, *The Magnificent Ambersons*.' That is high praise, indeed, but the truth is that in this film Comfort did establish himself as a director with an authentic flair for melodrama and a capacity for selecting and orchestrating the sorts of talents – behind and before the camera – for giving this flair a vivid visual and emotional life.

Notes

1 'Famous men and women at *Hatter's Castle* première', a two-page spread of photographs in *Today's Cinema*, 18 November 1942, pp. 14–15.
2 Paramount Press Book (UK), held in the British Film Institute library. Pages not numbered.
3 *Ibid.*
4 There had also been two minor American films based on his work: *Grand Canary* (1934) and *Shining Victory* (1941), the latter derived from his play, *Jupiter Laughs*.
5 Paramount Press Book (US), 1948, p. 3.
6 Brian McFarlane, 'Lance Comfort: melodrama and an honourable career', *Journal of Popular British Cinema* 1 (1988), p. 133.
7 Ackland makes no mention of it in his memoirs: Rodney Ackland and Elspeth Grant, *Celluloid Mistress* (London, Allan Wingate), 1954.
8 Elspeth Grant, 'Films', *Daily Sketch*, 14 November 1941. LCC.
9 Lionel Collier, 'Shop for your films', *Picturegoer*, 11:546 (24 January 1942), p. 13.
10 Robert Heilman, *The Iceman, the Arsonist, and the Troubled Agent: Tragedy and Melodrama on the Modern Stage* (London, George Allen & Unwin), 1975, p. 22.
11 'Spectacle in *Hatter's Castle*', *Kinematograph Weekly*, 31 July 1941. LCC.
12 From unnamed source, probably *Kinematograph Weekly*. LCC.
13 *The Star* (date not given). LCC.
14 *Daily Film Renter* (28 May 1941). LCC.
15 'The films', *The Observer*, 16 November 1941.
16 'The new films', *The Sunday Times*, 16 November 1941.
17 'Entertainments', *Tatler & Bystander*, 10 December 1941. LCC.
18 'Tours de force', *Punch*, 26 November 1941. LCC.
19 '*Hatter's Castle*', *Sunday Express*, 16 November 1941. LCC.
20 '*Hatter's Castle*', *The Times*, 14 November 1941. LCC.
21 Iris Conlay, *Hatter's Castle*, *Catholic Herald*, 28 November 1941. LCC.
22 By coincidence, Laughton opened in London in the same week in the Deanna Durbin film, *It Started with Eve*.
23 J. E. Sewell, 'Powerful and lurid', *Daily Telegraph*, 17 November 1941. LCC.
24 *The Sunday Times*, 16 November 1941. LCC.
25 Seton Margrave, *Daily Mail*, 14 November 1941. LCC.
26 Richard Coombs, 'Quo vadis?', *The Listener*, 112:2879 (11 October 1984), p. 37.
27 Quotations here are all from the LCC.

'The busiest British film director' 4

Comfort might have established himself more firmly in the field of British cinema production if he had followed up his success with *Hatter's Castle* by several more films in a similar vein. Instead, among its successors during the remaining war years, only the 1945 film, *Great Day*, a surprisingly abrasive drama of village life, in part recalls the melodramatic mode in which Comfort had made his name, though the wartime thrillers no doubt have melodramatic elements. There were six intervening films, justifying the journalist who described him in early 1943 as the 'Busiest British film director … Within the last six months he's made five films, and now he's busy on a sixth [*Escape to Danger*]. And they haven't all been the same kind of movie as well.'[1] Indeed they were not. In order of release,[2] they were: the comedy-drama of London evacuees in rural England, *Those Kids from Town* (April 1942), the wartime thriller *Squadron Leader X* (November 1942), the knock-about comedy, *Old Mother Riley Detective* (January 1943), the regional comedy *When We Are Married* (March 1943), another wartime adventure *Escape to Danger* (November 1943), and the espionage thriller *Hotel Reserve* (June 1944). The heterogeneity of this prolific output may have served him less well than a more careful staking out of the line of territory in which he did his best work – the moody, atmospheric melodrama – but at least it revealed him to be a more than competent craftsman, able to turn his hand to a range of genres, as he would continue to do throughout the rest of his career.

Three of Comfort's wartime films – *Those Kids from Town*, *Squadron Leader X* and *Escape to Danger* – are simply unavailable for viewing in Britain, the USA or Australia, whether on film or video, as far as I have been able to establish, and have not been seen on television in recent decades. From what one reads of them, these films, the thrillers especially, seem to have been the subject of a good deal of publicity in their production periods and to have been well-received by critics and public.

Those Kids from Town

Comfort was back with British National for this comedy-drama, based on 'the theme of evacuation, that uprooting process which has torn the town child from the Metropolis, and thrust it down among the cowslips and cowhands'.[3] This trade press reviewer went on to say that the theme 'has not so far been explored with any thoroughness' and, in the main, approved the film, though it made 'no attempt to solve the problems with any profound searchings' and though its picture of an English country village and its characters is 'nearer burlesque than life'. *Kinematograph Weekly* assessed it as having 'some good moments and a certain amount of child psychology, but it hardly presents a good case for evacuation, nor do its social implications appear well timed.'[4] The *Daily Film Renter* rated it 'Commendable popular entertainment',[5] and drew attention to its contrast with the director's previous film. The film was based on the novel, *These Are Strangers*, by Adrian Alington, but, though its subject was a matter of contemporary importance, Comfort does not seem to have handled it with the touch of documentary realism which would distinguish a film such as *Millions Like Us* in the following year. The *Monthly Film Bulletin* mildly chided it for excluding those evacuees 'who take to their foster-parents naturally and lead a healthy but uneventful life',[6] while *Cinema* praised the 'sympathetic direction [which] cleverly sets wartime atmosphere and ... recreates convincing picture of reactions of parents, children and "hosts"', but felt it lost 'probability' in its latter half, with 'resort to frank slapstick'.[7]

These extracts suggest that Comfort, having chosen a theme of some timeliness, has chosen to treat it for comedy and easy pathos, rather than making any overt gesture towards a serious social document. To the village of Payling Green come six evacuees from the East End of London. They include two sisters, Liz and Maud, who are billeted with a stern spinster and rebel against the discipline she imposes, finding shelter with the local earl (Percy Marmont), who undertakes to sponsor a singing career for Liz. Her egalitarian father (Ronald Shiner) reluctantly succumbs to the benevolent aristocrat's intervention, in a touch of wartime consensuality. Two mischievous boys, Ern and Charlie, terrorise the Vicar's prissy son, engage in some petty theft, and find a champion in a warm-hearted novelist (Jeanne de Casalis).

It sounds schematic in its development, as it moves towards rapprochement all round, and it seems likely to have dated badly in its approach to the social phenomenon it addresses. It would be interesting to see, though, partly because it is a rare screen treatment of a major issue of the war years, and partly because Ern and Charlie are played by Harry Fowler and George Cole at the start of their careers. Cockneys both, they at least seem to have brought a touch of the real. (Years later, Fowler recalled Comfort as 'the epitome of what I, as a thirteen-year-old Cockney, saw as a "posh gent"',[8] a 'nice man' who would steer him through his very first film role. Cole had previously appeared in *Cottage to Let* (1941) and appeared to Fowler to have 'a professional approach to acting'.) Among the other 'kids' (whose screen tests were the subject of a press reception,[9] Angela Glynne (also in *Penn of Pennsylvania*) and Leslie Ascane made further films, but only Cole and Fowler went on to major screen careers, Fowler appearing years later in Comfort's *Tomorrow at Ten* (1962). One would have supposed the film seemed a minor exercise to Comfort after the challenges of *Hatter's Castle*, but at least the three he had done in a row – the historical biopic, *Penn of Pennsylvania* (1941), the melodrama of obsession, *Hatter's Castle*, and now a comedy-drama – had established his flexibility across a range of genres. This range was to be extended in his other wartime features to include three espionage thrillers and the adaptation of a popular regional comedy.

Spies

'One of the best spy melodramas yet made.'[10] This was the verdict of
Lionel Collier on the first of Comfort's wartime thrillers, *Squadron
Leader X*, made at Denham for RKO-Radio, from a story by Emeric
Pressburger. The latter's biographer writes of it as a 'more inter-
esting solo credit' than his previous film, *Breach of Promise*
(Harold Huth, 1941). It was originally entitled *Four Days in a Hero's
Life*, and 'Like his other early war films it shows a willingness to
differentiate between good and bad Germans. The story is another
variation on the "escape motif" [Pressburger] used in *49th Parallel*
and [*One of Our Aircraft is Missing*].'[11] Pressburger sold the story to
RKO-British for £1,500, and the screenplay was written by his
friend, Wolfgang Wilhelm, with further dialogue by Miles Malleson.
A further connection with Pressburger's earlier films is that the
leading role of the escaping German was played by Eric
Portman, who had played the fleeing Nazi in *49th Parallel*, and
who would star twice more for Comfort. He was the sort of tense,
edgy actor from whom Comfort would consistently draw interesting work, and in the week *Squadron Leader X* was released he was
voted one of the top ten British box-office stars.[12] Other regular
Comfort collaborators included cinematographer Max Greene,
art director William C. Andrews, music director William Alwyn
and producer Victor Hanbury, and such recurring actors as
Beatrice Varley, Charles Victor, Marjorie Rhodes, Henry Oscar
and Aubrey Mallalieu.

The ingenious-sounding plot concerns a Nazi flying ace
disguised as a British airman and dropped into Belgium where it
is his treacherous job to engage in anti-British propaganda, to
persuade the Belgians that the British are bombing civilians.
Circumstances conspire to have him smuggled back into England,
where he makes contact with his erstwhile fiancée and tries to
force her to help him get back to Germany. Most of the action then
takes place in Britain, as the flyer seeks out prewar contacts, and,
just as a British agent is on his track, he evades arrest, steals a
Spitfire and, on leaving England, is shot down by a Messerschmitt.

The trade press was kept apprised of the signing of Portman

and thirty-five supporting players, while suspense about who would be the leading lady was final resolved by the choice of US star, Ann Dvorak. The publicity also stressed the lavishness and authenticity of the settings: 'Played against forty different backgrounds ... [the film] has been produced on an extensive budget for world distribution' and 'The air-sequences, made with official Air Ministry co-operation, are among the most actionful and breath-taking ever screened.'[13] *Kinematograph Weekly* wrote of 'the superb sets for authentic backgrounds.'[14] The film's reviews tended to pick up on the matters referred to above. There was considerable praise for Pressburger's story and Wilhelm's screenplay ('the edge this film has over most of the others is a spanking good script,' wrote C. A. Lejeune[15] and she and Edgar Anstey[16] both invoked *49th Parallel* in their praise). The *New Statesman*, though concluding that it had 'everything one could want, except atmosphere', noted that 'The fact that it *is* exciting should be enough, perhaps, and in this case the background of London has been meticulously reproduced. The RAF and MI5 (new to thrillers) have co-operated'.[17] *Cavalcade* praised its 'excellent war photography.'[18] Virtually every reviewer praised the excellence of the acting, particularly of Eric Portman as the Nazi ('vividly realistic' claimed *The Cinema*)[19] and Martin Miller and Beatrice Varley ('two outstanding character studies in a cast which has not a weak spot,' wrote Collier;[20] 'Standing out above all else are the superbly naturalistic performances of Martin Miller as the terrorised hotel cook and Beatrice Varley as his quaking wife,'[21] enthused another). At a time when the director was lucky to be mentioned at all, Comfort came in for a good deal of praise: the film was described as 'slickly directed' and the director was awarded 'full marks'; he was said to have 'directed with an eye for naturalness and effectiveness';[22] and elsewhere to have handled the plot 'with a most competent sense of the dramatic, some convincing foreign agent atmosphere, and an appealing sense of humanity in his characters.'[23] More often, though, the success of the director's work is subsumed in such general terms of approval as 'There's never a false note about this grippingly imaginative story. It has atmosphere but not artiness',[24] or Anstey's calling it a 'very exciting and beautifully acted piece of work.'[25] There were very few discordant notes in the film's reception, but Dilys Powell, while allowing it to be 'a competent British piece, adequately played ... with plausible settings and an exciting story', felt it had 'nothing which for an instant fires the imagination.'[26] This was a distinctly minority opinion and other cavils were all minor, with two reviewers finding it overlong.

The overwhelming impression one gets from reading both the press releases during the production period and the contemporary reviews, including most US ones (except *The New York Times* which felt it missed out on being a 'real humdinger'), is that the film was a major enterprise in terms of budget, casting and schedule and that it was received with widespread acclaim. If Comfort was not quite securely occupying a dominant position in the field of cultural production as it applied to British cinema, he was certainly regarded as one who could be counted on to supply highly competent entertainment, with an edge in matters of melo-dramatic action, in providing deft human touches and in extracting fine performances from a well-chosen cast. In Bourdieu's term, habitus, he had shown 'a feel for the game', the disposition of the agent, and had found what looked like a promising position in the field, in relation to such matters as association with a major studio with its inbuilt distribution, and to the symbolic capital which accrued from favourable recognition. In the simplest terms, *Squadron Leader X* was a popular and critical success and Comfort seemed to be sitting pretty.

The second of Comfort's spy thrillers, *Escape to Danger* (originally entitled *Murder on a Convoy*), was in production at the time of the West End and general release of *Squadron Leader X* – that is, from November 1942 until January 1943 – and much was made of its reuniting key personnel from the earlier film, especially Eric Portman and Ann Dvorak in the leading roles. This time the role of the spy flying under false colours of several hues is played by Dvorak (living in England at the time while her British-born husband, Leslie Fenton, was serving in the Navy). If for no other reason, one would like to see the film to sort out the director's credit: it is variously ascribed to Lance Comfort (in most of the press release material while the film was in production), to Comfort and Mutz Greenbaum/Max Greene (his cinematographer on the previous film) in *The RKO Story*, to Comfort, Greenbaum and producer Victor Hanbury in *British Sound Films*, and in *Picturegoer*'s review the credit reads 'Produced and directed by Victor Hanbury, Lance Comfort and Mutz Greenbaum.'[27] In fact, the press releases seem to make clear that Comfort is the director and Hanbury the producer, but that still leaves unclear the nature of Greenbaum's involvement, as the accredited director of photography is Guy Green. The latter said in 1992 that the film was 'photographed' by Greenbaum, that he – Green – was camera operator and that he remembered 'Lance Comfort was very keen on directing with a wide-angle lens, a 28 or something like that'.[28] In any case, Comfort is reunited with several previous collaborators, including as well Wolfgang Wilhelm (with Jack Whittingham) as screenwriter and William C. Andrews as art director. The publicity emphasized the lavishness of the production design in sets representing Denmark, Lisbon, several ships at sea, and an invasion barge factory, the latter built on Stage 7 at Denham Studios. *Escape to Danger* is another expensive, large-scale production aimed at international distribution (exhibitors were encouraged to stress Dvorak's name in this respect).

The result of all this build-up seems to have been well-liked by reviewers, though one detects a sense that it was found to be somewhat highly-coloured, not always wholly convincing, and that the 'false climax' involving the death of the spy played by Ann Dvorak struck a contrived note. The word 'melodrama' or 'melodramatic' was invoked on several occasions with the usual (at least slightly) pejorative tone of the times, associating it with 'adventure' and such other epithets as 'highly coloured', 'improbable' and 'implausible'. The reviews were not as enthusiastic as those for *Squadron Leader X*, but in general most would agree with the *Daily Film Renter* review which described it as 'a forcefully exciting succession of high-geared and colourful adventure-thrills in a well-knit story'[29] or with *The Times* which claimed: 'The sum total of this film may not be particularly impressive, but many of the individual scenes have character and excitement.'[30] Once again, Comfort secured gratifying personal notices: the *Times* went on to praise the director for not being 'so concerned with the twists and turns of the plot as altogether to neglect the individuality of the characters'; and the *Sunday Express* considered that he had 'obviously spotted the total improbability of this story and gone to town instead with cartloads of thrills.'[31]

His association with RKO-British may have been the stablest and most supportive of Lance Comfort's career, though it was limited to only four films: the three spy thrillers and *Great Day*. There is in these films a continuity of distinguished collaborators that he would not enjoy again, though throughout his career, at whatever place along the dominant-dominated spectrum in the British field of production, it is instructive to see recurring names, even in the second features when he was no longer operating under the aegis of a large and powerful production company as he was with RKO. This British off-shoot of the Hollywood major had been filming in Britain since 1931 and would continue to do so sporadically until the late 1950s, sometimes also distributing films made for independent companies in Britain, including 'A' films such as *Night Without Stars* (1953) and Disney's *Rob Roy, the Highland Rogue* (1954) and 'B' films such as *The Way Out* and *The Brain Machine* (both 1956). Not that the RKO logo seems to have helped much with the US distribution of Comfort's films: according to *The RKO Story*, *Squadron Leader X* 'completed its propaganda mission successfully, then quickly faded into oblivion' (and hence is unavailable today?), *Hotel Reserve* had 'pitiful US box-office returns', and, as for *Great Day*, 'American audiences couldn't have cared less. They gave the film a wide berth and it ended up a $232,000 loser'.[32] It is worth noting that the latter two films were not released in the USA until 1946 when their timeliness would have passed.

The last of Comfort's three spy thrillers, *Hotel Reserve* (1944), made at Denham, again bore the credit 'Produced and directed by Lance Comfort, Max Greene [Greenbaum had by now anglicised his name] and Victor Hanbury'. On the available print, there is no credit for photography, except that of Arthur Ibbetson as camera operator, so again it is difficult to know the extent of Greene's contribution. It is certainly a handsome-looking film (William C. Andrews' elaborate sets are beautifully lit), but it was the least enthusiastically received of Comfort's three espionage thrillers.

Based on Eric Ambler's 1938 novel, *Epitaph for a Spy*, it is a curiously leisurely piece, with very little real excitement or suspense until its final chase on the rooftops of Toulon. In fact, though Ambler expressed his dissatisfaction with the film, the novel, too, is a low-key affair, enjoyable enough as it parades for the reader its cast of suspects somewhat in the manner of Agatha Christie. Ambler himself wrote in the Preface to the 1966 edition of the novel, '*Epitaph for a Spy* is basically a kind of detective story, and I have brought spies into it.'[33] The film assembles virtually the same cast and puts them through the same paces. Peter Vadassy, a young Austrian seeking French nationality, fetches up at the Hotel Reserve in the Riviera village of St Gatien in the late 1930s. He is arrested two days later for having prints of secret coastal fortifications on a reel of film (mostly depicting lizards) he has had developed. Obviously someone else at his hotel has used his camera and the police allow Vadassy to return there to discover the identity of this person, who they believe is linked to a spy ring. The rest of the film is concerned with Vadasssy's working his way through the list of hotel guests and somewhat ineffectually sounding them out about their interests in photography, until he is finally confronted by the spy. This leads to a dash to neighbouring Toulon, Vadassy and the police following the spy, Roux, and his wife, to the gang's headquarters, and to the ensuing rooftop chase in which Roux falls to his death.

In the Introduction to the 1984 edition of the novel, H. R. F. Keating writes that 'One reason for Ambler's convincing realism is that his stories are seen through the eyes ... of the ordinary person who becomes involved against his will, like poor Josef Vadassy.'[34] This works better on the page than on the screen where Vadassy (name and nationality changed) seems too recessive a hero to hold together the action going on around him. He is played by James Mason, in the last ingenuous-young-man role he would ever play, and, as one review said, '[he] has not a lot of opportunities'.[35] Vadassy is generally acted upon rather than acting. Until the very end, his efforts to take action usually prove misguided and it is only in the scene in which Mason confronts Herbert Lom as Roux, the latter holding a revolver under a hotel table, that he begins to show the intensity that might have made the film as a whole tauter. Years later Ambler, dismissing the film, wrote, 'The leading man was James Mason, yet to become a star with such films as *The Seventh Veil* and *Odd Man Out* ... he could never speak of *Hotel Reserve* without a shudder ... I shared his aversion to it.'[36] Ambler is, of course, entitled to his view of the film, but his chronology is defective here: Mason had had both *The Man in Grey* (1943) and *Fanny by Gaslight* (1944) released before *Hotel Reserve*, and they had made him a household name as Everywoman's favourite brute. His role and performance as soft-spoken, gentle, put-upon Vadassy, nearer in spirit to his previous work for Comfort as the sympathetic young doctor in *Hatter's Castle*, must have been a grave disappointment to his fans. In his autobiography, he wrote: 'Its relationship with Ambler was its only claim to distinction and the longer we worked on the film the more distant that relationship became.'[37] In terms of incident and character, the film hews closely to the book, so that Mason's point is not altogether sound.

What might have been claimed is that the film lacks a sense of the seriousness of the Nazi menace which hangs over the book. The book was written in 1938 when this ominous threat was very real, and it gives to the book an atmosphere missing from the film, which settles for more conventional action and suspense. Made in 1944, it has an opening title which reads: 'A holiday in France ... before the war ... yet even then the plane-trees and cypresses of the south cast shadows in the sun. It happened during 1938.' The film which follows this is altogether more playful in tone – and quite enjoyably so – than the novel, even though it adheres closely to the original plot. In view of the years intervening since the novel's publication, one might have expected a darker film, now that the threat of 1938 had materialised. A very early and cleverly contrived shot suggests that this may have been Comfort's purpose: at the police station, Vadassy is shot through a high, small, barred window, then from above as the bars cast their shadow over him while the police question him, and there is a genuinely alarming sense of human vulnerability about the way his situation is conveyed. This whole sequence, in which he is made to examine his reel of film, lizards giving way to fortifications, is executed with a tension which the rest of the film doesn't sustain. 'You were in possession of photographs calculated to endanger the Republic,' says the Police Chief (Julien Mitchell, often filmed slighty from below, at slightly tilted angles, which give his authority a sinister effect), who threatens Vadassy in ways that recall the Gestapo to whom he refers. The ensuing scenes at the hotel, as Vadassy tries to discover who stole his camera and took the incriminating photographs, are adequately rather than imaginatively staged, but the range of characters is entertaining enough (the young Lom stands out, already an authoritative figure). There are good scenes between Vadassy and several others (including Lucie Mannheim as the hotel proprietress, and Frederick Valk as Schimler, the liberal German whom Vadassy first suspects), though the suggestion of a love interest between him and a young American girl (played by Clare Hamilton, sister to Maureen O'Hara) is about as perfunctory as such things can be in a film.

Picturegoer summed it up as 'a well-designed melodrama without enough suspense, paucity of action and rather forced humour. It is quite entertaining but could have been a good deal better.'[38] *Daily Film Renter* described it as 'espionage drama moving at a laboured even pace ... [it] lacks the psychology of the original',[39] while *Today's Cinema* found it a 'Very likeable instance of spy thriller entertainment',[40] and the *Jewish Chronicle* rated it 'cleverly directed, well produced and ingeniously photographed' with special praise for Lennox Berkeley's 'fine music'.[41] From the reviews, one does not feel that the film raised Comfort's reputation particularly, though it seems to have been quite well liked by the trade press.

'If there was indeed a kind of renaissance of British commercial cinema during the war, a common critical assessment, it was confined to a very limited number of titles',[42] wrote Clive Coultass. Indeed, it is not likely that the entertainments directed by Lance Comfort were among these. The spy thrillers, for instance, were essentially genre films, executed with proficiency and some flair, but they were not influenced by the kinds of documentary techniques and interest in the everyday which made critical successes of such films as *San Demetrio London*, *The Way Ahead* or the actual documentary, Pat Jackson's *Western Approaches* (1944). He seems never to have evinced any interest in this kind of realism, or is it simply a matter of such opportunities not coming his way? Chance as well as disposition presumably plays a role in determining where in the field habitus will find position. Certainly, Comfort's two wartime comedies were unlikely to have been seen as central to the critically legitimated areas of British film-making during the war.

Low and bourgeois comedy

January and March 1943, respectively, saw the release of two films Comfort made for British National: *Old Mother Riley Detective* and *When We Are Married*. The former is far too broad to have interested critics, who no doubt lamented the vulgar taste that kept the escapades of the Irish washerwoman popular for fifteen years; the latter, based on J. B. Priestley's play of northern marriage and manners must have seemed distinctly to one side of the burgeoning realism and seriousness of the best-regarded wartime films. It is a wholly charming piece of regional comedy and one of Lance Comfort's most attractive entertainments.

Old Mother Riley Detective need not detain us for long. Comfort had worked, at British National, as assistant director and/or technical superviser to John Baxter on three of the series: *Old Mother Riley in Society*, *Old Mother Riley in Business* (both 1940) and *Old Mother Riley's Ghosts* (1941), which starred the husband and wife variety team of Arthur Lucan and Kitty McShane as Mother Riley and daughter Kitty. 'In a poll of exhibitors organised by the *Motion Picture Herald*, they were voted Britain's third top money-making stars for 1942 (George Formby came first, Leslie Howard second).'[43] In *Old Mother Riley Detective*, produced by Baxter, Mother Riley is a food-office cleaner who assists the police in tracking down black marketeers, triumphantly identifying the gang leader as her office boss. She joins the many other variety stars (for example, Will Hay and Arthur Askey) who, as Andy Medhurst has pointed out, 'were mobilised into the wider effort of propaganda' during the war to popular effect.[44]

Though Lucan was probably director-proof, the film opens with Comfort's customary speed in setting up of plot and for moving the narrative along, and he allows (if he had any choice) Lucan to have his/her head with often very funny results. (Perhaps it is a valuable element in a film-maker's 'disposition' to know when to let a particular collaborator have room to move.) The dialogue, some of it provided by Lucan, is fast, outrageous, wildly punning, innuendo-ridden. When the police take her to the station on a trumped-up charge, Mother Riley demands to know 'Is that journey really necessary?', alluding to the famous wartime cautionary question. Later, a police inspector says to her, 'My name's Cole.' 'You may be a merry old soul but I wish you'd tell your fiddlers to keep their hands off me'. And, ever more broadly, 'If I wasn't a lady, I'd give them a slap in the gob.' Lucan, making no attempt to look like a woman, plays her as a music hall turn, often seeming to bypass the plot to address the audience directly. Comfort propels the comic-strip action so proficiently that one accepts its idiocies as part of the film's appeal. Less happily, he also follows the tradition of letting the action stop for the excruciating Kitty to sing, though even here he contrives a very evocative moment as she is joined by a burst of community singing in a factory canteen to the tune of 'Let the wheels go round'. This moment of patriotic consensual activity – and what film-making innocence to let the action stop for it! – is at odds with the rest of the film's raucous good fun. Comfort's film is free from sentimentality, in contrast with Baxter's *Old Mother Riley in Society*, in which Kitty marries socially upwards and Mother Riley is afraid of bringing shame on her and disappears from her life, returning as her maid, and so – drearily – on. It is in line with Baxter's naive populism, but it is not very funny and it is surely absurd to try to whip up Stella Dallas-style pathos for a mother played by a man in drag. In fact, Comfort's films at large are remarkably free from sentimentality, whatever their genre.

Old Mother Riley Detective, the first in the series for over a year, was regarded by *Kinematograph Weekly* as 'one of Arthur Lucan's and the series' best efforts';[45] and by *Today's Cinema* as a 'sure-fire follow-up to previous "Mother Riley" successes',[46] praising its 'animated direction'. The *Motion Picture Herald* took a more patronising stance, relegating it to 'that brand of backstreet comedy which aims at the lowest common denominator of audience appeal', and adding that 'The film is adequately mounted and directed by Lance Comfort with a hand which betrays a familiarity with more worthy matter.'[47] Probably the most that can be said of Comfort's participation is that he has increased his range as a genre director. By coincidence, just as the film was released, critic Campbell Dixon linked him with Michael Powell and Thorold Dickinson as one of three British directors who 'have greatly increased their reputation' in 1942.[48] It is not likely to have brought him much of Bourdieu's symbolic capital, but there can have been no harm in showing himself efficient in another genre, and a popular one at that.

When We Are Married, firmly based on Priestley's play, sub-titled 'A Yorkshire Farcical Comedy', might have done more for Comfort if it had arrived a year or so later when adaptations from highly regarded playwrights and novelists (Rattigan, Coward, Dickens, Shakespeare) were claiming a good deal of critical attention for their contribution to a British cinema of quality. Comfort has respected his sturdy material and filmed it plainly on the whole. There is, however, some very telling use of close-up and a wonderfully over-stuffed and over-decorated mise-en-scène to signify the materialism and complacency of the three couples who, on the occasion of celebrating their joint silver wedding, find that they are not married after all, the officiating clergyman not having been authorised at the time. Just as the eponymous protagonist in Priestley's *An Inspector Calls* (filmed by Guy Hamilton in 1954) forces a bourgeois family to confront its hypocrisies, so, this time in comic vein, a 'very respectable neighbourhood with a lot of money behind it' must deal with a body blow to its much-vaunted respectability. There is much pompous talk about marriage, as 'the backbone of a decent respectable life' and 'Where would women be without marriage?'.

Set in the small Yorkshire town of Cleckleywyke at the turn of the century, the celebrations of the three couples are just getting under way when the new chapel organist, Gerald Forbes (Barry Morse), who has been the object of their husbands' narrow-minded views, breaks the news to the men that they aren't married. The three husbands are the stingy, prosing bully, Councillor Parker (Raymond Huntley), the pompous bore, Alderman Helli-well (Lloyd Pearson), to whose niece (Lesley Brooke) Forbes is secretly engaged, and the ineffectual Herbert Soppit (Ernest Butcher). Much of the comedy springs from how they and their wives react to the threat of scandal – or glimpse of freedom, according to viewpoint. Parker's gentle wife Annie (Marian Spencer) sees the opportunity for a chance of 'fun' ('just getting away from you, for instance,' she tells him); vinegary Clara Soppit (Ethel Coleridge) realises she has lost her power when the mild Herbert defies her, takes a whisky, returns her slap on the face and orders her to sit down; and Maria Helliwell (Olga Lindo) is forced to adjust to the idea that her Joe would have married easy-going Lottie Grady (Lydia Sherwood) if he hadn't already been married to her. (There's a suggestion of the motif of the 1949 US film, *A Letter to Three Wives*, here as Lottie teases the three women about the husband of one of them having been her 'gentleman friend'.) As the couples are adjusting to the news, the situation is comically complicated by the eavesdropping of the housekeeper, Mrs Northrop (Marjorie Rhodes), who spreads word at the local pub, by the arrival of reporter and drunken cameraman (Sydney Howard) from the local newspaper for a silver wedding photo, by the romance of the young lovers, and by a recalcitrant maid, Ruby (Patricia Hayes), who is not too young to understand what's happening 'because me brother keeps rabbits'. It is a rich cast, and it is richly cast with an outstanding ensemble of character players who all get their chance to hold the screen. Huntley, so often confined to stereotypical displays of purse-lipped disapproval, is very funny indeed as the miserly Parker, complete with Disraeli-style curl; and, for the generations to whom he is not even a name,

Sydney Howard's orotund, tipsily dignified photographer is a revelation of comic control and timing.

Many of the film's pleasures derive from the play, from the basic situation which it resolves with humane good humour, from the diversity of characters, and from dialogue which belongs utterly to its speakers, as if they had just thought of it. But Comfort's hand is to be felt in the shifts of mood, from the quite raucous comedy of the pub to the tenderness between Herbert Soppit and Annie Parker as they recall their long-ago affection for each other and as they now encourage the young lovers. These shifts are managed partly through the direction of the actors, partly through his control over timing and editing. For instance, there is a neat cut from the disabused men's patronising talk of 'them three poor women upstairs' (see Plates 5 and 6), as if the women will all be devastated at the news, to the woman trying on hats and boasting of clothes, as complacent in their way as the men, and when the confrontation between the two groups occurs it is accompanied by a swell of music, which underlines the women's silence. In terms of Holmes Paul's art direction, which caused a complete house to be erected at the National Studios, the apt sense of over-stuffed interiors denotes class pomposity and display, an effect carried through in the heavily upholstered costumes of the women particularly. *When We Are Married* is satirical at the expense of bourgeois values but it is in no sense a cruel film: it is true to the spirit of Priestley's tolerant liberalism, in that it is happy to make fun of human foibles without destroying the people in the process. The *Monthly Film Bulletin* praised Priestley for 'an exceedingly amusing, if somewhat unkind, picture of a Yorkshire chapel-going fraternity', adding that 'under the skilful direction of Lance Comfort all the cast bring the characters to life.'[49] The film is, in fact, a classic of regional comedy, which deserves to be more widely known. In look and sound, in its direction of actors and its command of timing and framing, it is one of Lance Comfort's most achieved – and neglected – works. His next film, *Great Day* (1945), ushers in Comfort's most substantial period of activity which includes six films all in more or less melodramatic mode.

Notes

1 *What's On*, 8 January 1943. LCC.
2 Release dates taken from Denis Gifford's *The British Film Catalogue 1895–1970* (Newton Abbot, David and Charles), 1973.
3 Aubrey Flanagan, *Motion Picture Herald*, 147:5 (2 May 1942), p. 63.
4 *Kinematograph Weekly*, 1824 (2 April 1942), p. 29.
5 *Daily Film Renter*, 1 April 1942 . LCC.
6 E. R., 'Those Kids from Town', *Monthly Film Bulletin*, 9:100 (April 1942) p. 42.
7 E. A. P., 'Those Kids from Town', *Cinema*, 28 March 1942. LCC.
8 'Harry Fowler', in Brian McFarlane, *An Autobiography of British Cinema* (London, Methuen), 1997, p. 195.
9 Unlabelled newspaper extract. LCC.
10 Lionel Collier, 'Shop for your films', *Picturegoer*, 12:574 (20 February 1943) p. 14.
11 Kevin MacDonald, *Emeric Pressburger: The Life and Death of a Screenwriter* (London, Faber and Faber), 1994, p. 195.
12 *Motion Picture Herald*'s annual poll, reported by Kay Quinlan, 'Eric Portman's dramatics', *Empire News*, 3 January 1942. LCC.
13 *The Cinema*, 4 November 1942. LCC.
14 *Kinematograph Weekly*, 2 July 1942. LCC.
15 'The films', *The Observer*, 3 January 1943. LCC.
16 'The cinema', *The Spectator* (undated). LCC.
17 *New Statesman*, 2 January 1943. LCC.
18 *Cavalcade*, 9 January 1943. LCC.
19 C. A. W., *The Cinema*, 11 November 1942. LCC.
20 Collier, *Picturegoer*, 1943, p. 13.
21 *Daily Film Renter*, 11 November 1942. LCC.
22 *Motion Picture Daily*, 3 February 1943. LCC.
23 Aubrey Flanagan, 'War melodrama', *Motion Picture Herald*, 9:149 (28 November 1942). LCC.
24 *Daily Film Renter*, 11 November 1942. LCC.
25 Edgar Anstey, 'The cinema', *The Spectator* (undated extract). LCC.
26 *The Sunday Times*, 3 January 1943. LCC.
27 See Richard B. Jewell and Vernon Harbin, *The RKO Story* (London, Octopus Books), 1982, p. 192; David Quinlan, *British Sound Films: The Studio Years 1929–1959* (London, B. T. Batsford), 1984, p. 206 (William Sistrom is listed here as producer); *Picturegoer*, 12:591 (16 October 1943), p. 13.
28 'Guy Green', in McFarlane, *Autobiography of British Cinema*, p. 133.
29 *Daily Film Renter*, 26 July 1943. LCC.
30 *Times*, 13 September 1943. LCC.
31 'A cartload of thrills', *Sunday Express*, 12 September 1943. LCC.
32 Jewell and Harbin, *RKO Story*, pp. 192, 209, 212.
33 Eric Ambler, 'Preface', *Epitaph for a Spy* (London, M. Dent), 1984 (rev. edn), p. 6.
34 H. R. F. Keating, 'Introduction', *Epitaph for a Spy*, p. vi.

35 Lionel Collier, 'Shop for your films', *Picturegoer*, 13:610 (8 July 1944), p. 13.

36 Eric Ambler, *Here Lies. An Autobiography* (Glasgow, Fontana Paperbacks), 1986, p. 189.

37 James Mason, *Before I Forget* (London, Hamish Hamilton), 1981, p. 135.

38 Collier, *Picturegoer*, p. 13.

39 *Daily Film Renter* (undated). LCC.

40 C. A. W., *Today's Cinema*, 62:5040 (2 June 1944), p. 14.

41 'Well-made spy film', *Jewish Chronicle*, 23 June 1944. LCC.

42 Clive Coultass, *Images for Battle: British Film and the Second World War 1939–1945* (Ontario and London, Associated University Presses), 1989, p. 130.

43 Geoff Brown, with Tony Aldgate, *The Common Touch: The Films of John Baxter* (London, British Film Institute), 1989, p. 91.

44 Andy Medhurst, 'Music hall and British cinema', in Charles Barr (ed.) *All Our Yesterdays: 90 Years of British Cinema* (London, British Film Institute), 1986, p. 177.

45 *Kinematograph Weekly*, 14 January 1943. LCC.

46 L. H. C., *Today's Cinema*, 60:4827 (15 January 1943), p. 9.

47 A. F., *Motion Picture Herald*, 150:7 (13 February 1943), p. 1158.

48 Campbell Dixon, 'Film notes: British triumphs against odds in 1942', *Daily Telegraph*, 14 January 1943. LCC.

49 E. W., *Monthly Film Bulletin*, 10:111 (March 1943), p. 26.

1 Portrait of Lance Comfort

facing **2** John Comfort (left) and friends in *Toddlers and a Pup* (1939)

3 Cinematographer Mutz Greenbaum (aka Max Greene), Lance Comfort and actor James Mason on the set of *Hatter's Castle* (1941)

4 Enid Stamp-Taylor as Nancy and Robert Newton as Brodie in *Hatter's Castle* (1941)

5 Ethel Coleridge (Clara Soppitt), Olga Lindo (Maria Helliwell) and Marian Spencer (Annie Parker) in *When We Are Married* (1943)

6 Raymond Huntley (Albert Parker), Ernest Butcher (Herbert Soppit), Lloyd Pearson (Joe Helliwell) and Barry Morse (Gerald Forbes) in *When We Are Married* (1943)

7 Eric Portman and Flora Robson as Captain and Mrs Ellis in *Great Day* (1945)

8 Beatrice Varley, Jill Esmond, Ian Hunter and Margaret Lockwood in *Bedelia* (1946)

9 Robert Newton as Mallinson and William Hartnell as Brown in *Temptation Harbour* (1947)

10 Siobhan McKenna (centre), as Emmy Baudine and Maxwell Read (right), as Dan in *Daughter of Darkness* (1948)

11 Robin Bailey (Dudley Wilbourne), Richard Todd (Robert Hart) and Margaret Johnson (Clare) in *Portrait of Claire* (1950)

12 Anthony Richmond as Cliff and Jack Warner as Perce Bonsell in *Bang! You're Dead* (1954)

13 Lisa Gastoni (Michele), Robert Hutton (Chuck Collins) and Michael Balfour (barman) in *The Man from Tangier* (1957)

14 Tony Britton as Greg Parker in *The Break* (1962)

64

15 Lance Comfort directs Joan Newell and David Hemmings as mother and son in *Live it Up* (1963) and explains a scene re-written by Lyn Fairhurst

facing **16** Lance Comfort talks to screenwriter Lyn Fairhurst while actors Tracy Reed and William Sylvester prepare to film a scene from *Devils of Darkness* (1964)

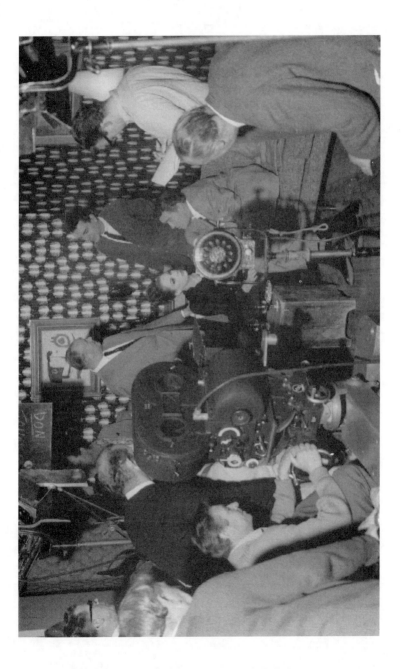

5

Dark achievement: six melodramas

The period of Lance Comfort's most sustained achievement, when he comes nearest to being (in Bourdieu's term) an autonomous cultural producer, begins with *Great Day* in 1945 and cuts off sharply with the commercial failure of *Portrait of Clare* in 1950. These two and the four intervening films – *Bedelia* (1946), *Temptation Harbour* (1947), *Daughter of Darkness* (1948), and *Silent Dust* (1959) – are all melodramas of one kind or other. To Comfort's disadvantage, they appeared when the popular vogue for melodrama was more or less over, and critics tended never to be favourably disposed to the mode. Moreover, they are generally darker in tone than the very successful Gainsborough melodramas, and in this respect have more in common with such other postwar examples of the mode as *Blanche Fury* and *So Evil My Love*, which also failed to capture public and critical acclaim. Like those two, Comfort's melodramas are at least as proficient as the Gainsborough films, and it is tempting to conclude that they simply missed the moment when they might have won at least popular support; in many ways, they also deserve more considered critical exegeses than they have had.

One of the most interesting critical reclamation projects of the 1970s through the 1990s has been that in relation to melodrama. Instead of alluding to it in purely pejorative terms, acquiescing in its consignment to the obscure corners of the field of production, and automatically denying a work or its creator Bourdieu's symbolic capital, such authors as Robert Heilman, Peter Brooks, and Thomas Elsaesser,[1] writing about theatre, novels and film, have shown melodrama to be a powerful means of ordering the world's shapelessness into potent artistic experiences, the very excess of the mode a key element of its pleasures. Critics such as Sue Harper and Robert Murphy,[2] writing specifically on British film melodrama also have seriously undermined the view that British cinema of the 1940s was actually *like* the 'quality' national cinema that critical writing at the time sought to construct through lavishing praise on privileged elements (the literary, the realist) and disregarding those which seemed at odds with this concept, specifically the melodrama, and, of course, other popular genre film-making. The mere fact that the Gainsborough melodramas were so *popular* ought to have suggested that they had a significance beyond providing mere escapism, that somehow they had tapped into aspects of the national psyche. However, in spite of this renewed interest in British film melodrama, to date there has been very little sustained attention to Lance Comfort's melodramas, or, for that matter, to those of such contemporaries as Brian Desmond Hurst and Lawrence Huntington.

The prestige of British cinema has never rested on its success in the melodramatic mode, which has been central to Hollywood film production and its dominance of world markets. For a brief period – from, say, 1943 to 1946 – the British public rewarded indigenous film melodrama with its patronage as it flocked to the Gainsborough series launched by *The Man in Grey* (1943, directed by Leslie Arliss). These films were derided by the quality critics as fit only – to invoke the class and sex bias of the critical diction – for the delectation of housemaids. It is as though they had been unduly influenced by the sententious distinctions of Anouilh's Chorus in *Antigone,* in which tragedy is found 'kingly' whereas melodrama is 'vulgar'.[3] Twenty years later, Heilman is still interested in differentiating the two modes but without implying the inevitable superiority of tragedy: 'in tragedy we put ourselves in the erring man's place; in melodrama we put the erring man in his place, or, erring or not, are put out of our own place'.[4] A little later, and with some succinctness, he summarises: 'In tragedy, dividedness is inner; in melodrama, it is outer'.[5] Though one may

not wholly accept this simplification, his summary of the nature
and rewards of the mode is useful:

> On the tragic side there are freedom, choice, acceptance of guilt,
> tensions that pull men in opposite ways ... in sum, a fundamental
> complexity and concern with the ordering of the self. On the other
> side there is a more clear-cut designing, usually a dichotomising,
> of existence, with divisions between the good and the evil, the weak
> and the strong, victors and victims, the human and the inhuman:
> sometimes a sense of innocence accompanied by littleness,
> weakness, inadequacy, deprivation, grievance; sometimes a sense
> of innocence accompanied by the spirit of blame and indignation,
> the finding of scapegoats and the punishing of the guilty; in sum, a
> concern with ordering the world.[6]

This characterisation of the melodramatic agenda seems apt in
relation to Comfort's melodramas of the latter half of the 1940s.
Indeed, it is also especially so in relation to the earlier *Hatter's
Castle*, which offers the first of his obsessive protagonists in the
tyrannical patriarch, James Brodie, in relation to whom the rest of
his family are cast as victims. In varying degree, the films from
Great Day to *Portrait of Clare* foreground characters in the grip of
obsession which brings them into powerfully articulated melodramatic conflict with those around them. The presence of the
obsessive and his/her obsession is used to highlight the kinds of
dichotomies suggested above, a species of monomania acting to
separate the character thus affected from those around him/her.
Nevertheless, closer examination of the films makes clear that
they do not opt for simple-minded oppositions: good and evil are
not so unequivocal as notions of 'Victorian melodrama' might
suggest, and, though evil is ultimately defeated, the rewards for
the innocent are sometimes very muted in kind. In fact, for the
rest of his career it is interesting to note how few times, except in
the youth-oriented musicals, Comfort settled for the conventional
happy ending, as if his sensibility reacted against easy optimism.

A transitional film: *Great Day*

Great Day is a film which belongs on the cusp of peacetime British
cinema. It anticipates a whole sub-genre of British films which
examine the problems of living with peace and finding it much
less exciting than the heightened tensions of wartime. It is a busy,
complex work, and one of Comfort's most attractive and intelligent films, showing his capacity to juggle a number of plots and to
instigate a visual patina that would register – indeed, in no small
measure, *create* – the emotional shifts and the social critique
implied in the film's various actions. In plot terms, it moves
among three major strands: the 'great day' itself refers to the
coming of Mrs Roosevelt to visit the Women's Institute of Denley
village which has been chosen as representative of what women's
war-work has achieved; the plight of Captain Ellis, a World War I
veteran, whose aimless life reaches a crisis; and the romantic
affairs of his daughter Meg, in love with a young army captain but
drawn to the security offered by a middle-aged farmer. The action
of the three strands is carefully meshed, but though the film ends
on the triumphant arrival of Mrs Roosevelt (off-screen) it cannot
be said that this closure really answers the issues that the film has
raised – or that it needs to do so.

The chief power of the film is located in the study of Captain
Ellis (Eric Portman's third lead in a Comfort film), whose distinguished World War I record is all that he has had to sustain him in
the intervening years of peace. He clings tenaciously to his
memories and will nobble anyone in the local pub who will listen
to him. 'Never lets you forget the Captain,' says the barmaid.
'Maybe that's all he's got,' answers the good-natured American
(usefully planted as an anticipation of the film's hands-across-the-
sea finale), who has tolerantly listened to Ellis's reminiscences of
the 'last war', when they knew what they were fighting for, and to
his lament that 'there's no sense of values any more'. Peacetime
life, and certainly village life, has had nothing to offer Ellis. At
every turn, his rootless, déclassé existence is vividly contrasted
with the lives around him. His wife, Elizabeth (Flora Robson) is
Vice-President of the WI and frantically involved in preparations

for the visit; when Ellis puts in an appearance at the village hall, to cadge money from her, he is merely in the way, with busy women purposefully occupied all round him. Meg (Sheila Sim), in the Land Army, works long hard hours on the farm owned by Bob Tyndale (Walter Fitzgerald) to whom she is engaged. In a striking moment of awareness, Ellis stands with Meg as a troop convoy rolls through the village at night, its sense of purpose emphasising what his life lacks. His obsession with the past, with *his* past in particular, is shown to cause nothing but heartache for his wife, his daughter and himself; in this way, he recalls James Brodie in *Hatter's Castle* and anticipates such later obsessives as Robert Rawley in *Silent Dust*.

Much of the strength of this aspect of the film is concentrated in Eric Portman's finely wrought performance. Though it might be argued that it is Mrs Ellis, important to all three of the film's plotlines, who gives the film coherence, it is from Captain Ellis's situation that it derives its power. This is not only a matter of Portman's acting in a role which recalls the Justice of the Peace (also obsessed with the past) he played in Michael Powell and Emeric Pressburger's *A Canterbury Tale* and looks forward to haunted roles in such films as Lawrence Huntington's *Wanted for Murder* (1946), Terence Young's *Corridor of Mirrors* (1948) and Compton Bennett's *Daybreak* (1948). He is certainly one of those 'volatile, brittle, intense performers'[7] from whom Comfort, according to one writer, drew 'emotional performances.' It has to do also with the structuring of the film and with its visual power. The film begins sunnily with Mrs Mumford (Marjorie Rhodes) riding round the village with news of a special meeting to be held at the village hall. When the women are assembled there, the president, Lady Mott (Isabel Jeans), introduces a visitor from the London Office, Miss Allen (Joan Maude), who tells them of the 'secret' honour bestowed on them. This scene of activity dissolves to the Ellis cottage, with the dog barking and Captain Ellis idly waiting for lunch. Embittered at having nothing to do, with 'a pack of women running everything', he quarrels with his wife, who briefly flares up with, 'The old days are dead and done with' and dismisses his nostalgia as 'nothing but a few books and a few ridiculous old photos' of his regiment'. Ellis heads out for the countryside along the river where he responds to the pastoral beauty of the scene and where he is joined by his daughter. The flight of a hawk leads to a discussion of freedom: 'No cages for him', says Ellis, who warns Meg not to get trapped, as he of course is, in his memories – and in the pretty little village which can offer him nothing. In his own way, he is as thoroughly trapped as Brodie is by his ambition, Emmy Baudine in *Daughter of Darkness* by her sexuality and Robert Rawley by his blind love of his son in *Silent Dust*. This sequence, in which the pastoral is equated with freedom, though this freedom is qualified by its lack of both purpose and responsibility, is paralleled in the third-to-last sequence of the film, thereby conferring on it a kind of symmetry and structural privilege. The later episode, again following a confrontation between Ellis, who has been arrested for stealing ten shillings in the pub, and his wife, exhausted after the day's preparations, takes place at night. Again, Mrs Ellis urges him to face the facts: 'John, you're talking to me, we're alone' as he tries to bluff his way out of the crisis of shame and humiliation to which his pathetic swaggering has brought them. She lets him go off alone, at least suspecting his suicidal intentions, and as he walks by the river this time he is again joined by his daughter, who has come to find him. He tells her he is a failure, and that he has bluffed his way out of things since the last war. Persuading him that 'It's sometimes braver to live than to die', she takes him home through the silent streets of the village. The sequence is followed by two further ones the following day: one in the Ellis home when Mrs Ellis persuades him to come to watch the arrival of the VIP and then, finally, back to the village hall for the big event.

The placement of these two crucial scenes, with their pastoral overtones, draws attention to their parallelism and to the significance of Captain Ellis in the mosaic of the bustling little village. Visually, Ellis is the subject of some of the film's most striking lighting and composition, the combined work of Comfort and cinematographer Erwin Hillier. The sunny beauty of the earlier riverside episode with its talk of freedom is recalled in the moody night lighting of the later one: what had appeared beautiful by day has now acquired an ominous quality, accentuated by a highly charged, jarring score, as the camera alternates between the silhouettes of Ellis and the alarmed Meg in search of him. In the representation of Ellis's neurosis and anguish, Comfort has drawn effectively on elements of *film noir* to render a protagonist out of kilter with his environment. This is most strikingly felt in the lead-up to his disgrace in the pub. During this sequence, which alternates with Mrs Ellis' good-heartedly making a dress for the little girl who is to present a bouquet to the visitor, Ellis has been acting the gentleman in the pub with a group of soldiers. He insists on standing another round and is refused credit by the barmaid. In a series of close-ups, at an increasingly tilted angle as the camera moves in closer on his dishevelled face, the eyes wild with the impotence of his situation, Ellis's dilemma of pain and shame is forcefully enacted. There is a distorted shot of his face seen through a glass case which catches the strength of his temptation as he steals the money from the woman's bag, and his agony is rendered in a final close-up when he has been caught by the mean-spirited man (Ivor Barnard) who has been watching him. Comfort shows here a real feeling for telling his story with the camera, as he does in the scene shortly after when Ellis is trying to explain to his wife: 'I was never frightened during the war. But I was frightened in peace – of a wife being dependent on me.' Here, his face is half-hidden from the light, while she, with nothing to hide, is softly lit full-face. Then, as he bursts out, 'I led men in the war', he is exposed to a harsh full light from a low angle: the position and quality of the lighting assume the status of meaning here – of interrogators. In a final example of how Comfort's visual style has underlined Portman's centrality in the film, there is further evidence of *noir* influences in the near-suicide scene, as the camera alternates between Ellis's face, revealingly lit from below, and his reflection in the water (a moment of near-fatal self-examination signified here). Characteristically, and intelligently, Comfort does not avoid the melodramatic potential of a scene like this, and he, Hillier and William Alwyn's emotionally charged musical score join forces to realise this to the full. In Lesley Storm's play, running in the West End at the time of the film's release, these scenes, so crucial to the film's structure have no place, as the play's whole action is confined to the village hall.

Ellis's drama is only one of the threads of the plot, but it is the dominant one. Meg's quandary is on fairly conventional triangular lines, as she is forced to decide whether to follow head or heart. Having observed her parents' marriage, ruined for her mother by 'Dad's swaggering and drinking and clinging to the last war', and having listened to her mother who tells her that 'Security may sound dull but it does give you your freedom', she accepts the proposal of Bob Tyndale to whose prosperous farm she has been assigned. In doing so, she has flown in the face of her feeling for young Captain Geoffrey Winthrop (Philip Friend). As we never see her with Bob, and as she and Geoffrey are so obviously the youngest and most attractive people in the film, it is not surprising that she finally succumbs to his argument, 'You're mixing up your future with their [your parents'] past', and after an embrace she watches as his convoy rolls off into the night. Meg's conflict is real enough, but its resolution is unsurprising. It is given some character by her mother's anxiety, by Mrs Mumford's relish for the idea of young lovers, and by the spinsterish opposition and spite of Tyndale's vinegary sister (Margaret Withers).

The third thread, that to do with the preparations for the great day, gains interest from its underlying critique of village life. Under the banner of consensus which unites the women in the common effort to be ready for the visitor, it is clear that there are undercurrents and animosities which surface at key moments. We don't have to accept Ellis's bitter remark about 'this stinking village' as the only evidence for the film's take on the confinements of life in this little community where everyone knows everybody else's business. Though Miss Allen's opening address to the women presents Mrs Roosevelt as a 'woman like yourselves', thus suppressing difference and imposing consensus, not just between women of different nations and status, but also among the village women themselves, the reality is less homogeneous. In reply to Miss Tyndale's querying why Denley should have been chosen, Mrs Mumford quells her with a very robust paean of praise about what the women have achieved, but clearly Miss Tyndale dislikes being rebuked. Miss Tyndale's scarcely suppressed, perhaps incestuously inspired jealousy of Meg, and her malice in general, manifest themselves comically in her outrage at Mrs Tracy (Maire O'Neill) who has, on this special occasion, improved her patriotically eggless cake by the addition of an egg. It is less comic when she lashes out about Mrs Ellis and Meg as 'the loving mother and the milksop daughter' whom she sees as contriving to snare her brother. At this moment, Comfort offers an overhead shot of work suspended in the hall with the women standing stock still at this outburst. This is a characteristic moment in a film which does not set out to celebrate village life but to subject it to scrutiny, not to idealise it but to dramatise a network of feelings, some positive, others not. When the news of Major Ellis's fall from grace reaches them, one of them wonders if 'poor Elizabeth' has heard about it, to which Mrs Tracy replies, 'She'll hear about it soon enough if I know this village.' It is hard to think of another film of the period – or later – which so persistently queries the picturebook pleasantness of the (usually southern) English village. Only, perhaps, Alberto Cavalcanti's *Went the Day Well?* (1942) takes a grimmer view of what is so often represented as idyllic.

Comfort's film improves in a number of ways on Lesley Storm's play, which is set entirely in the hall and is really no more than an extended conversation piece. By the inclusion of the sequences in the Ellis home and along the river, he has moulded from its somewhat meandering comedy-drama of laughter and sentiment, in which Ellis's actual suicide strikes a discordant note, a potent family melodrama set in the context of a community that offers support but also acts as a trap for animosities and passions. He has focused much more firmly on the Ellises, moving Mrs Ellis (eloquently played by Flora Robson) to the centre of the action in terms both of narrative structure and of the way the camera works to distinguish her. The other women, played by a cast of notable character actresses, have their moments but their essential function is to provide a context for the central action. The *Daily Worker*'s comment that they are 'all familiar types, over-acted, over-emphasised, and viewed with an upper-class condescension'[8] seems unduly jaundiced as the film moves to find meanness and generosity across the class range. The moment of community celebration on which the film ends – 'Jerusalem' on the soundtrack as the assembled crowd watches the arrival of the VIP car – produces its own kind of affect, without dispelling the darker insights which have made themselves felt in the preceding eighty minutes. There is no suggestion that this display of community solidarity wipes out the earlier moments of torment which have been given their full melodramatic due by Comfort. One reviewer in fact complained that 'The film's main fault is that the visit of Mrs Roosevelt neither precipitates the characters' emotional crises nor resolves them.'[9] This is true, except in the sense that the visit provides a catalyst for making the private dramas public. It is also irrelevant, in the sense that the film makes clear that a consensual community effort does not necessarily do away with individual problems.

Great Day was not very well received by reviewers, and a remark like the following from the *Spectator* suggests how wary they were about melodrama. The reviewer writing of the 'tragedy of the local retired Army Captain' goes on to say, 'Here is an adult theme conscientiously handled by director Lance Comfort, over-anxious though he is that no point shall be lost by subtlety.'[10] What a viewer sympathetic to melodrama, the 'mode of excess', might find powerful, the critic for whom 'subtlety' is the superior virtue will find over-done. There was much praise for the 'beautiful photography of rural England',[11] though no one seems to have been concerned with how this aspect of the film is integrated into its over-all pattern. The publicity for the film had stressed the location filming 'set against the lovely Cotswold country beyond the Buckinghamshire town of High Wycombe'[12] – quite a bit 'beyond', in fact. C. A. Lejeune found the film 'restful, pretty, humane, patriotic, and beautifully photographed, where the subject is trees and clouds and meadows', but also 'persistently silly' and refuses to concede any possibility of real pain at work in the Ellis character who 'Ever since the last war ... has been inexplicably peevish about something.'[13] 'Inexplicably'? 'Peevish'? One of the leading critical taste-makers of the day, Lejeune, read now, seems to have had no feeling for cinema at all, only a kind of debilitating middle-class 'good taste' that wanted people to behave well and for films to be a credit to the nation, as courage in the Blitz had been. Certainly, a skilled melodramatist such as Comfort (or Crabtree or any number of others) could expect from her no more than her relentlessly 'witty' approach. In the month after her review of *Great Day*, she summed up the achievements of British cinema during the recently ended war in Europe: 'Through necessitous circumstance, the British producer has had to work to find out what is indigenous to native art, and learn to cultivate it.'[14] The films she lists as exemplifying the 'indigenous' are almost invariably either in the literary tradition (*Major Barbara*, *Henry V*) or the realist (*The First of the Few*, *San Demetrio London*). Melodrama, as a mode, is simply outside her serious consideration, and it is in a critical climate such as this that Comfort began his string of six melodramas. His chances of acquiring the symbolic capital that comes from recognition were slight, and even those for economic capital may have been dwindling as the popularity of melodrama declined.

Murderous melodrama: Wicked ladies – *Bedelia* and *Daughter of Darkness*

If *Great Day* is only melodrama in part of its action, two further pieces centred on the activities of 'wicked women', *Bedelia* and *Daughter of Darkness*, epitomise the mode in full cry, their protagonists further exemplifying Comfort's interest in the melodrama of obsession. Both, like *Hatter's Castle* and *Great Day* before them and, later, *Silent Dust* and *Portrait of Clare*, hold up considerably better than the novel and play, respectively, on which they were based.

Of these two films, *Bedelia* is, superficially at least, the more conventional. It is based on Vera Caspary's novel, a fact to which the film's publicity drew attention, suggesting all manner of 'tie-ups' to those promoting the film. Most reviewers at the time subscribed the opinion that it was markedly inferior to *Laura* (1944), the previous film made from a Caspary thriller, a point of view it is hard to quarrel with. Otto Preminger's film, starring Gene Tierney, has rightly acquired the status of a classic *film noir*, a triumph of ambiguity and wit. What seems less clear-cut to one who has read Caspary's *Bedelia* is that the film (based on a screen-play by Caspary herself, Herbert Victor and I. Goldsmith, with additional dialogue by Roy Ridley and Moie Charles) is inferior to its source novel, as contemporary reviews suggested. To read the novel in 1998 was, to me at least, to find it crude in its plotting, characterisation and prose style. The novel is set in 1913 Connec-ticut; the film's transplantation to snowbound 1940s Yorkshire for the greater part of its action seems no more or less apt. It is also hard to see what the novel gained from being set in the earlier period. What does strike one is how much more coarsely the novel deals with its characters, especially the women: as early as page 51, 'terror possessed' Bedelia, who earlier on was too obviously described as being 'For all her vivacity ... more gentle and refined than any of her guests';[15] her husband's business partner, Ellen, is made snappish in a stereotypically spinsterish way; and Nurse Gordon (Harris in the film) is made excessively unattractive ('She used her ugliness ... to give her authority.'). In fact, Caspary seems to dislike most of her characters, and Bedelia's husband Charlie is variously described as 'pallid, angular, and restrained' (p. 1) and 'thirty-three, bland, undistinguished, going bald' (p. 27). The film gives him a little more dignity in Ian Hunter's performance, though Hunter's often stolid persona must have made him seem apt casting. This is a novel devoid of subtlety in construction and its pure functionality in verbal terms is no match for the film's visual style, with Comfort in this respect admirably served by cinematographer Freddie Young. It is, however, characteristic of reviewing at the time to find films inferior to the literary works on which they were based, without considering the distinctive ways in which film might go about achieving the emotional and other effects of novels.

Bedelia (Margaret Lockwood) has just embarked on her fourth marriage, to Charlie Carrington, and is honeymooning with him in Monte Carlo where an artist, Ben Chaney (Barry K. Barnes), wants to paint her portrait. In fact, Chaney is an insurance detective on the track of Bedelia whose previous three husbands he believes her to have murdered for their life insurance pay-outs. When the Carringtons return to Charlie's Yorkshire home, Chaney gets himself invited to paint in the Dales and eventually, when his own life has been put in jeopardy by the rapacious Bedelia, persuades Charlie to accept the truth about the wife who is currently trying to poison him. Charlie leaves Bedelia the means to bring about her own suicide. (In the US version, so as not to transgress transatlantic sensibilities and censorship codes, she confesses to the police.)

This tale of the murderous woman – 'The wickedest woman who ever loved',[16] boasted the publicity material – is one of a number of such films popular at the time. In the USA, Barbara Stanwyck seduces an insurance salesman into murdering her husband in *Double Indemnity* (1944), Lana Turner persuades her lover to murder her husband in *The Postman Always Rings Twice* (1946), Gene Tierney destroys all in her path in *Leave Her to Heaven* (1945), and Merle Oberon and Joan Fontaine poisoned their way through husbands and lovers in, respectively, *Temptation* (1946) and *Ivy* (1947). In Britain, the type and the genre were less prominent, but Googie Withers in *Pink String and Sealing Wax* (1945) and Greta Gynt in *Dear Murderer* (1947) were notable exemplars of the dangerous woman. So, of course, was Margaret Lockwood herself in two hugely popular Gainsborough melodramas, *The Man in Grey* (1943) and *The Wicked Lady* (1945); films which had propelled her to the position of box-office favourite. If she lacked, say, Stanwyck's edge or Tierney's opaque sexiness, or Withers' brazen sensuality or Gynt's slinky corruptibility, she was, in 1946 in Britain, more popular than any of them, whatever the *Daily Herald* ('I adore Miss Lockwood, but still cannot accept her as a Wicked Lady')[17] or the *Daily Express* ('But above all, can you believe in the wicked lady?')[18] thought about her capacity for rendering evil. She is the film's major publicity asset: there are numerous suggestions for soliciting female attention to her wardrobe (the work of Elizabeth Haffenden is canvassed in detail), her shoes (these receive a separate credit), and her rapport with the Siamese cat, inadvertently poisoned by Bedelia.[19] There is no mistaking the fact that this is to be sold as a 'Lockwood film' and one in a line of descent from her previous roles as treacherous women.

This kind of melodrama was in some ways a change of pace for Comfort. His previous obsessives had been men (Brodie, Ellis), but the notion of the individual propelled by an overriding and destructive motive was not new to him. The film offers Lockwood a contemporary counterpart for her Gainsborough wicked ladies, and in some ways Bedelia is drawn with more interesting depths than either Hester in *The Man in Grey* or Barbara in *The Wicked Lady*. It is obsessive greed that drives her to marry, kill and inherit, and to do so she has to overcome an inherent distaste for men which has been felt obliquely in her dealings with Ben Chaney and with Charlie, and which she spits out in a climactic moment near the end: 'I hate men. They're rotten beasts. I didn't choose them.' This line is a direct echo of the novel where she says, 'Men are rotten! ... They're rotten! Beasts.' (p. 97). The behaviour of the men in the film, while not necessarily 'rotten', is scarcely impressive. Charlie is stolidly jocular, insensitive in his parading of his partner Ellen's (Anne Crawford) virtues, and has been nannied into a state of pickled adolescence by his family's faithful retainer Mary (Beatrice Varley). Ben's whole role is based on a professionally-instigated deceit. Even the local professionals who appear for the Carringtons' first Christmas party, along with their upholstered wives, one of whom (Barbara Blair) is 'not divorcing because Alan (John Salew) is making too much money', are an unimpressive bunch.

The film does not pretend to offer a detailed case study of Bedelia, but suggestive possibilities keep escaping. Is she seeking some sort of revenge for the treatment she has received from men? Is there some kind of justified frustration at the presence of the very efficient Ellen, whose tailored suits contrast with Bedelia's own lavish wardrobe, the latter perhaps conceived as a weapon against Ellen's ideal image? Or at the presence of the kitchen staff, which assumes such proprietorial influence over Charlie, let alone the bogus Nurse Harris (played with crisp authority by Jill Esmond), who countermands Bedelia's domestic arrangements? As Marcia Landy has written in her perceptive account of the film:

On the one hand, the film can be read as a parable of housewifery gone amok. On the other, it can be read as the inevitable outgrowth of a female's resistance to domestication. In other ways, Bedelia's character seems to be a reaction to conventional treatments of women.[20]

The voice-over at the film's end simplifies the sort of response indicated in Landy's account. The film has set up more resonant possibilities than this – possibly in the interests of censorship – can accommodate. What, for instance, about Bedelia's neurotic fear of being photographed (angrily she resists Charlie's honeymoon attempt to snap her with the camera which the thoughtful Ellen has sent him), or painted by the enigmatic Ben, who strikes up a friendship with the honeymooners in Monte Carlo? 'She's not an easy subject but she is a very interesting one for a painter', he says, reinforcing the film's interest in the idea of deceiving appearances. The narrative adequately accounts for Bedelia's fear in the sense that she doesn't want to leave traces of herself to be detected, but there is a more insistent undertone that suggests she fears what such representations might reveal of those aspects of self she wants to keep hidden. The film opens on the portrait of Bedelia as light gradually crosses it, and the voice-over describes it as being 'like a poisonous flower'; it ends with the voice-over's words which tend to elide some of the more ambiguous undertones:

> There was no mystery about her motives. She killed for money but there was still an enigma, the enigma of the soul of a human being who could commit murder. Bedelia could caress and, with those same soft hands, poison in cold blood. In the delicate balance between good and evil lies this deepest of human mysteries, the problem that no detective, physician or psychologist has ever solved.

This sententious, summarising diagnosis misses some of the complexities which have made Bedelia a more teasing protagonist: it misses the obsessive urge to acquire more and more wealth, the sexual distaste, and the sympathy that her domestic confinement in Charlie's world evokes in us on her behalf.

As stated earlier, to direct Lockwood in the sort of role that had elevated her to top stardom in recent years, was to indicate Comfort's position in the industry at the time. At the very least, it points to recognition of his skill in making commercially viable entertainments. The film had only lukewarm reviews, which, again, suggest critical recoil from melodrama, a common reaction to the Gainsborough output, and there is also a suggestion that this is Hollywood territory which would be better left to Hollywood. The film is repeatedly and unfavourably compared to films such as *Laura* (especially, because of the Caspary connection) and *Double Indemnity*, without there being any sense of how differently a British version of such a tale might work. If the film points to a more domestic version of the transgressions of a wicked woman, that may simply (or complexly) point to a major national difference – and preference. This may help to account for what the *News Chronicle* saw as its inadequacies: 'This British film ... has resisted all temptations to be sordid or realistic in delineating a young and beautiful husband-poisoner, foiled in her fifth [*sic*] murder. Projected by Margaret Lockwood, she's a nice suburban girl, without passions or perversions.'[21] Part of the film's interest is in watching the machinations of just such a woman, and in watching her response to a range of pressures.

Made at Ealing, where Comfort had worked briefly as a camera operator in the early 1930s, for producer John Corfield, the film was given a lavish production. Entirely set in the studio as the publicity handouts boast (this was borne out by the film's continuity person, Elaine Shreyeck,[22] an Ealing employee at the time), it manages equally handsome Riviera settings, including a large hotel ballroom, and the recreation of Charlie's luxurious Yorkshire home. There is a no-expense-spared look about both sets and costumes which all the press releases stressed. *Bedelia* has all the appurtenances of 'A' film-making, and it represents possibly Comfort's nearest approach to what Bourdieu would call the dominant end of the field of production; not necessarily his best film, but the one that most readily bears the hallmarks of popular success.

Comfort's other 'wicked lady', and another of his obsessives, is Emmy Baudine, the protagonist of *Daughter of Darkness*, an ambitiously conceived production involving, as an item in its £200,000 budget, three weeks' location shooting in Cornwall, using Whitsands Bay as a base. 'For six weeks in all, Cornwall will be invaded by an army of executives and technicians one hundred strong getting down to the task of filming life in Ireland and Yorkshire.'[23] Actress Honor Blackman, who had her first sizeable role in it, said: 'I think I did most, if not all, of it in Cornwall'[24] and recalled the excitement of location work. The press releases relating to the film stressed this aspect of the production, and a reporter for *Picture Show* wrote: 'Sequences for an Irish village were also shot at Veryan and a sixteenth-century farmhouse in Liskeard will also be in the picture.'[25] Director Lance Comfort was clearly being entrusted with what was, for the time, an expensive production, entailing not only the kind of location work more usually associated then with extravaganzas such as *Caesar and Cleopatra* (1945) but some carefully detailed studio sets as well, including the Irish presbytery and church interior erected at Riverside Studios, home to Alliance-Paramount, the film's production company. John Comfort, Lance's production manager son, believes it was the difficulties which this film ran into, including endless wet weather in Cornwall, a fact also recalled by Elaine Schreyeck, which most importantly set back his father's career.[26] Fifty years later, it is notoriously hard to come by box-office figures to gauge how commercially successful a film was, but *Daughter of Darkness* is, on the face of it, a challenge from several points of view.

For one thing, as noted earlier the time for that kind of full-blooded melodrama had gone. Others of varying quality also released in the first quarter of 1948 included Brian Desmond Hurst's *The Mark of Cain* (January), John Clements and Ladislas Vadja's *Call of the Blood*, Marc Allegret's *Blanche Fury*, and Leslie Arliss's *Idol of Paris* (February), Lewis Allen's *So Evil My Love*, Daniel Birt's *The Three Weird Sisters*, and John Harlow's *This Was a Woman* (March), none of which enjoyed critical or popular success. The time for the escapism and other rewards offered by the popular Gainsborough films had passed, and, lurid though it may be, *Daughter of Darkness* (a January release) is about the serious and alarming matter of women's sexuality – and not even comfortably distanced into a period setting. By 1948, the sexual adventurousness of Britain's wartime women was no longer a matter even for the oblique encoding of the Gainsborough films: realism, which implied women reclaimed to those roles they had gallantly surrendered during the war, was not interested in such potentially unsettling matters. Further, whereas *Bedelia* not only subsumed its interest in a woman's sexual distaste in a familiar thriller format, here it was the centre of the film's interest, the mainspring of its action. Finally, whereas Margaret Lockwood's name was then a powerful lure at the box-office, hard as publicists worked no one had ever heard of Irish stage actress Siobhan McKenna, who had played only one small role (alongside Lockwood in Brian Desmond Hurst's *Hungry Hill*, 1947) before being given the role of Emmy Beaudine.

Sexual obsession is at the heart of *Daughter of Darkness*. Emmy is an Irish servant girl whose fascination for and with men makes her a social outcast in her village and leads the priest to send her to work on the Yorkshire farm of some English friends of his. Even at this early stage of the film our sympathies are with Emmy. Crudely, she stands for passion confronted with puritanic hypocrisy, and even the priest (Liam Redmond) seems unnerved by her. To get rid of her is perhaps as much a relief to him as to the village harpies who snarl about her in the church doorway: 'I warn you Father. We won't have any peculiar girls in our community', to which the priest can only reply weakly, 'Let me think.' 'Something terrible rises up in me and I can't breathe', Emmy tells him in what may be the frankest acknowledgment of a woman's sexual nature to be found in a British film of the period. Before leaving Ireland, Emmy's sexuality is clearly signified as a dangerous force. Dan (Maxwell Reed), a boxer with a travelling fair, is drawn to Emmy, and, in response to her sexual provocation, he bashes his opponent in the ring with untoward viciousness. Their later lovemaking ends with a scream from Dan, Emmy having torn at his face with her nails. Emmy's obsession, though apparently rooted in nymphomanic urges, is, like Bedelia's, also a matter of vengeance on the men whose passions she rouses. At the Yorkshire farm to which she is sent, she causes further havoc among the men on the place: 'When I come near you, I never seem able to hold myself back', says one of the men who falls victim to her strange beauty. Emmy is aware of the power of the sexual impulse whereas the other women on the farm, Bess (Anne Crawford) and Julie (Honor Blackman), suppress it under the clipped accents, middle-class manners and status, which they use to keep Emmy in her place. They, in consequence, sound smug and inhibited by comparison, and it is not being perverse to suggest that our sympathies remain with the transgressive Emmy.

The character of Emmy has some affiliations with the 'wicked woman' film popular in the 1940s, but Comfort brings to it a flavour of other genres which flesh out its melodramatic structure with potent resonances. The treatment of Emmy's sexuality – her luring and destroying of men – is what the film is centrally about and would have been unthinkable before the cinema embraced Freud in the early 1940s. The incessant conflict of ego caught between the claims of id and superego, the drama of suppression/ repression at work in subduing the openness of expression. The understanding of such concepts and their place in narrative paradigms is essentially a phenomenon of the decade. As well though, there are powerful elements of the Gothic, to which Comfort frequently seems drawn and, unlike most English directors of the 'quality' British cinema, he is not afraid to give vent to it. From the outset, while the credits are rolling, a note of real strangeness is struck in the images of tower, twisted trees and gnarled hands, the visual promise of Gothic excess reinforced by stirring melodramatic music, which, in turn, gives way to choral singing as the stylised church behind the credits is replaced by the interior of a 'real' church. A little later, her wild organ-playing, introduced in a close-up of her hands as the source of the powerful music on the soundtrack, and followed by the camera's tilting to reveal her obsessed face, ushers in a recurring motif in the film, a release for the sexual feeling which the men she so easily draws fail to satisfy. When I add that, at the end, she is sent out – by the forces of respectability – into the dark where Dan's dog, previously glimpsed in silhouette against the night sky, waits to savage her, it will be clear that Comfort has travelled some distance from the respectability of 1940s realism. Once again, too, Comfort uses the storm as a means of bringing emotional matters to a head, as he does in *Hatter's Castle* (the night of the Tay Bridge collapse) and *Bedelia* (the night of blizzard when Bedelia tries to escape), and as he will again in *Portrait of Clare*; he is not a director to flinch fastidiously from such vivid signification of a nature or a world in torment. Neither, of course, have such works of high culture as *Macbeth* or *King Lear* or *Uncle Vanya*, but in such texts it is regarded as symbolic and/or catalytic, whereas in melodrama it is more likely to be judged a cliché. In *Daughter of Darkness*, the storm is preceded by a church scene in which, during the singing of 'The King of love my shepherd is', a note is passed along the choir bearing the words STAND BY TONIGHT, recalling those warning notes of Dickensian melodrama, such as DON'T GO HOME in *Great Expectations*. The men are planning to pin down the midnight organist whom Bess now associates with the deaths of several young men. The village idiot's face at the window frightens Julie just before someone shouts 'Here comes the storm.' It is in this context that Bess confronts Emmy with 'What's behind this filthy thing?' by which she means sex. At this point, Emmy on the stairs above Bess has a moment of real ascendancy, but before the storm is over Bess will have followed her to the church. 'I wanted to kill you with my own hands', she claims, to which Emmy replies, 'Am I going to die?' 'I think so', says Bess, who frightens Emmy with the idea of the three dead men 'waiting' for her on the moors, and sends her out. There is the sound of Dan's dog, a scream, and a tracking shot to the stained-glass window of the church – and the viewer (this one, at least) is left with the strange feeling that the film has moved towards this resolution almost against its inclinations.

Perhaps another Gothic touch is the use, as in *Temptation Harbour*, of the carnival as a signifier of and a catalyst for disruptive forces. As Mikhail Bakhtin has noted, the carnivalesque is not merely a matter for gaiety and celebration: 'It ties into one grotesque knot the slaughter, the dismemberment and disembowelling, bodily life, abundance, fat, the banquet, merry improprieties, and finally childbirth.'[27] Or as Bakhtin's commentator, Michael

Holquist, says: 'Since the dominant ideology seeks to author the social order as a unified text, fixed, complete, and forever, carnival is a threat.'[28] In this film, on at least two occasions carnival unleashes feelings characteristically repressed in quotidian life. In Emmy's case, it seems to validate her powerful responses even when they lead to violent ends. On the second occasion, whereas the other young people on the farm see the carnival as a harmless relief from work, Emmy doesn't want to go, as if fearful of what it may involve her in. The image in silhouette of the carousel, recalling the earlier carnival scene in Ireland, suggests the inevitability of Dan's return for revenge. In a well-managed close-up, his face reveals the scars of Emmy's attack. His pursuit of Emmy, through flickering light and shadow, until she reaches an old barn, is filmed with real visual energy, and his murder, like all the moments of violence in the film, occurs suggestively off-screen: there is a scream followed by a dissolve to the carousel.

As well as its Gothic elements, the film also shares with Comfort's own *Great Day*, *Silent Dust*, *Portrait of Clare* and his sombre 1950s drama, *Bang! You're Dead* (1954), the echoes of English pastoral with sourly abrasive undertones. Cameraman Stanley Pavey's lush images of the English countryside are not allowed to lull us for long into the expectation of Emmy's coming to terms with herself in the setting of a rural idyll. In Comfort's films, pastoral usually works to establish an ominous serenity, a precarious calm, a deceptive sense of order. When the travelling fair reaches the little rural Irish village, Dan says, 'Good old Ireland ... Give me the Elephant and Castle any day'; he is in no doubt about the dubious beauties of the retired life. One recalls how the lovely daytime glow of the riverside scene in *Great Day* is replaced by the *film noir* version of the same scene by night, as if offering a commentary on the deceptive beauty of the earlier scene. The establishing shot of 'The Tallent Farm, England', accompanied by Clifton Parker's gently descriptive music, evokes a placid, pretty English pastoral life, complete with sheep and church tower, a sturdy, respectable house presided over by English-rose types, at odds with Emmy's dark Celtic beauty. The film lingers a few minutes on the pastoral activity of shearing, recalling the previous year's *The Loves of Joanna Godden*, in which the pastoral is equated with the sturdiest moral values. Not so for Lance Comfort's films, where it is seen as either delusive or inadequate or, in *Daughter of Darkness*, as the scene of destruction.

All these elements in the film's design work towards defining a potent set of narrative dichotomies: the pastoral and the world of human aspiration; the everyday and the carnivalesque; the passionate and the hypocritical; the instinctive and the restrained; the complacent middle-class and the victimised lower orders, the latter exercising a disruptive effect which must be subdued. By comparison with Max Catto's play, *They Walk Alone*, first performed in 1938, with Beatrix Lehmann as Emmy, the film is far more tightly structured and fluently executed, less marred by tediously jocular humour, and psychologically more convincingly based. Also, the film's necessary realism in matters of setting, as compared with the play's air of contrivance in locating all the action in the sitting-room of the farm, allows the development of a more potent sense of Emmy's otherness. Ireland, the fair, the church and the landscape, in their different ways, provide a diversity of ambience in which her strangeness is either called forth or suppressed. The pervasive effect is that the film provides a much more sympathetic version of Emmy, even if this may seem to be at odds with the narrative's ostensible purposes.

While many of the reviewers praised Siobhan McKenna's performance, most could not resist chiding the film for what they judged its failures in terms of realism: Dilys Powell wrote of its 'wild improbabilities', claiming that her 'own fancy is for thrillers whose whole plot makes sense',[29] revealing at once the privileging of the realist which so often relegated the melodramatic to the critical margins of British film-making. To be fair, one should record that the reviewer in the popular magazine, *Picturegoer*, proclaimed it 'an out-of-the-ordinary drama which, to me at least, was completely holding.'[30] Not many were so open to its unusualness: as a study of nymphomania, it was unique then and would remain so for at least another decade. Emmy is made to stand for a triply threatening 'Other': she is not merely a dangerous *woman*, but her class ('I'm only a servant ... I believe you're jealous') and her Celtic origins (changed from Cornish in the play, perhaps to increase the sense of her otherness) intensify our sense of the threat she poses. There was universal praise for McKenna ('one of the most interesting new faces we have seen lately';[31] 'This film introduces a brilliant newcomer, Siobhan McKenna';[32] 'a young Irish actress of quite unusual quality');[33] considerably less so for the actors playing the Tallent family ('fabulously genteel';[34] 'a farm where agriculture is conducted with unbelievable gentility by people who appear to be near relatives of the William family').[35] These actors – Crawford, Blackman, George Thorpe, Barry Morse and so on – may seem to belong to another school of British film acting, but their clipped-vowel stereotypes can also be seen as working to highlight the central strangeness of Emmy, even as they work perversely towards increasing our sympathy for her.

Comfort's handling of this highly charged piece appears not to have added to his reputation at the time. Fifty years later, however, it has an undeniable power that distinguishes it from much contemporary film-making. Prestige successes of the year included such literary adaptations and/or realist works as David Lean's *Oliver Twist*, Laurence Olivier's *Hamlet*, Anthony Asquith's *The Winslow Boy*, Launder and Gilliat's *London Belongs to Me*, Charles Frend's *Scott of the Antarctic*, the Maugham compendium *Quartet*, the Boulting brothers' *The Guinea Pig*, Carol Reed's *The Fallen Idol* and Powell and Pressburger's *The Red Shoes*. Now, that is an impressive line-up of films and one cannot readily imagine a welcoming place being found in it for a perfervid melodrama, however well-executed. *Daughter of Darkness* has little in common with that list of critically-approved titles, except perhaps with *Oliver Twist*, in which melodrama is sanitised by its association with canonical literature or with *The Red Shoes*, in which it is subsumed into the high-culture world of the ballet. On reflection, one may perhaps find that it has more in common – in its passion and visual power – with some of Powell and Pressburger's work than with any of the rest. In the USA in the 1940s and 1950s, the melodramas of Douglas Sirk were given scant attention, whereas today Sirk is admitted to the pantheon. Maybe it is not too late for such treatment to befall Comfort.

Tormented melodrama: Men and obsession – *The Silent Dust* and *Temptation Harbour*

Though *Temptation Harbour* comes earlier, in 1947 and before *Daughter of Darkness*, it is useful to consider *The Silent Dust* (1949) first because its protagonist is another of Comfort's total obsessives, belonging with Brodie, Bedelia and Emmy in this respect. In several key ways, *Temptation Harbour* stands to one side of these films, though obsession certainly overtakes its protagonist. Like *Daughter of Darkness* (and *Great Day*), *The Silent Dust* is based on a play on which it considerably improves: *The Paragon*, by Roland and Michael Pertwee, first produced in London in 1948. The screenplay is by Michael Pertwee, who has taken considerable advantage of the screen's greater ease in the representation of time and space.

Robert Rawley (Stephen Murray) is a blinded, self-made industrialist, who, like Ellis in *Great Day*, is living in the past. This time, however, it is not his own past glories he is basking in but the memory of his son, Simon, who was killed in the war and to whose memory he has had a cricket pavilion erected in the local village. In a recognisably Comfort-style touch, the film opens with a pounding melodramatic score undermining the pastoral calm of the deserted cricket field in long shot, the aural offering an ominous comment on the visual. (Over the field are superimposed the lines from Thomas Grey's 'Elegy in a Country Churchyard' from which the film takes its title, adverting to the folly of earthly monuments.) This acts as a precursor to the story of a man whose visual sense is gone but who knows the truth through the increased acuity of his other senses, notably the aural, though the tactile will also play its part. Like Mrs Ellis, Joan Rawley (Beatrice Campbell), his second wife, cautions him against letting the past dominate his life, fearing that this memorial to the dead, and the obsession that feeds it, is causing them to drift apart. The son will shortly prove not to be dead, but a coward, deserter, and murderer who turns up at Rawley's grandiose mansion to make trouble for his wife Angela (Sally Gray). She, believing him dead and unknown to Robert, has recently married Maxwell Oliver (Derek

Farr), nephew of the neighbouring aristocrat Lord Clandon (Seymour Hicks), whose own son was also killed in the war and who has tried to persuade Rawley, a comparative newcomer to the village, to dedicate the pavilion to all the local men who gave their lives. Robert is the last to know of the secret marriage, others fearing he will see it as disloyalty to Simon's memory, and he is also the last to know of Simon's return. His blindness is a metaphor for his refusal to face the truth about his son. When he is finally confronted with the facts about his son, Robert knocks him down and strikes him with his cane; as they struggle together, the father, in an Oedipal reversal, causes his son to fall to his death.

Though the film sometimes betrays its theatrical origins in its compositions, especially in some of the long dialogue exchanges, as in the other Comfort films under discussion, his melodramatic flair, operating on both visual and aural levels, rescues the film from being merely a static conversation piece. For instance, he makes use of a lying flashback to let us see the truth of Simon's wartime experiences. In what is introduced as a memory sequence, he tells his stepmother, 'You mustn't be frightened if you're an officer.' The montage of his desertion and escape to Brussels is very well shot (by Wilkie Cooper) with a touch of *film noir* in its suggestion of the deracinated ex-serviceman. Just as the flashback is creating some sympathy for Simon, his lies are made clear by the disjunction of image and voice-over: while he talks of longing for home, the images evoke a deserter making a good thing out of luxury goods. What on the stage was only a matter of dialogue is here made fluently cinematic and far more evocative than it was in the play, and it is hard to see what Lionel Collier meant when he wrote, 'it was a pity that the development was held up by a quite unnecessary flashback.'[36] The nine-minute sequence is crucial in not merely filling in Simon's history but in shaping our response to him, and it has been handled in a way that only the cinema could do. Equally cinematic is a later sequence when Robert has become aware that 'Something has turned up ... No, some*one* has turned up.' To render the blind man's sixth sense, Comfort has dissolved to a view of the room which corresponds to a photographic negative. This is an innovative way of signifying the *inner* vision of the blind man. While a good many British films of this period resembled, in Karel Reisz's previously quoted phrase, 'photographed radio plays', Comfort persistently avoided such visual dullness. Even in the dialogue groupings referred to above, he will make a point visually as when Max and Angela quarrel and the portrait of Simon looms over and between them, or when Angela, returning home after three years, sits at her dressing table flanked (imprisoned?) in the triptych mirror by a photograph of Simon. It is Robert who is the obsessive, but the other characters are represented as having difficulty in escaping the influence of his obsession.

The *Silent Dust* is not merely a proficient visualisation of a stage play in the melodramatic mode, though the latter is signalled from the beginning with an ominous score which grows more sombre as the credits near their end. Like several of Comfort's melo-dramas, it offers a muted discourse on issues of class and gender. Robert Rawley is represented as an *arriviste* in the country neigh-bourhood. He speaks scornfully of the 'tin gods' of the established families for whom 'It goes against the grain when a mongrel like me comes in.' He was born in a tenement in Leeds and the memorial pavilion may be a way not merely of perpetuating the memory of an adored son but of announcing his own arrival in the upper classes. The film is careful to represent Lord Clandon not as a bastion of reaction but as the democratic signpost to the future: he rides about the countryside on a large tricycle, with instructions from his wife to see if, in this time of postwar shortages, there is any fish in the village. There is a neat cut from the impoverished grandee teetering around on his tricycle in quest of fish to Robert and his second wife arriving at their stately home in a smart roadster. Comfort makes, visually, quite complex points about class, resisting easy class-based attitudes here: the self-made man is no philistine, the aristocrat not just an engaging eccentric; and the rapprochement of the two at the end, when Robert changes his mind about the dedication of the pavilion and Clandon takes over the messy details of Simon's death seems to be positing a less class-divided future. From this point of view, Comfort's films from *Hatter's Castle* in 1941 to *The Silent Dust* eight years later can be seen as acknowledging some shift in class attitudes, which, in varying degree, make themselves felt in his other films of the 1940s. In 1945 in *Great Day*, he promotes Lesley Storm's Mrs Mott to Lady Mott, and thus accounts for her effortless assumption of the role of President of the Women's Institute, even as she concedes that Mrs Ellis does all the work. In the hierarchy of the wartime village, 'Lady' Mott would inevitably take the highest position (and actor Isabel Jeans is wholly at home in rendering this aura of good-natured social superiority). Four years later, *Sir* Robert Rawley in the play has lost his title and is now plain 'Mr' – perhaps a gesture towards more egalitarian times. On the debit side, the cook and parlourmaid (Irene Handl and Yvonne Owen) simply go through their class-appointed paces, as laid down by innumerable West End plays: they are essentially there to provide touches of below-stairs comedy, as in the running joke about the health of the maid's mother. The old divisions, that is to say, had not wholly disappeared by 1949.

In the matter of gender representation, women are no longer seen as meekly submissive victims: the subservience of Mrs Brodie has given way, via Mrs Ellis's impatient outburst in *Great Day* and the forthrightness of Bess in *Daughter of Darkness*, to the firm-mindedness of the two women in *The Silent Dust*. Angela, believing herself widowed, has made a career for herself in postwar Germany, and Joan, once Rawley's secretary, has now assumed with aplomb the role of lady of the house. Comfort's films have their value, not merely as entertainments, but as chronicles of their age. A sense of postwar malaise also hangs over the film, in the image of the scruffy deserter on the run (thus allying it with such films as Alberto Cavalcanti's *They Made Me a Fugitive*, 1948, and Lawrence Huntington's *Man on the Run*, 1949), in the notion voiced by Simon, 'If I'd had the guts, I'd have been a conchie', and in Lord Clandon's remark, 'The peace hasn't turned out as we'd hoped'. There is a whole sub-genre of films which address the idea of ex-servicemen (very few women) coming to terms with the demands of peace.[37] This note is lightly struck in *The Silent Dust*, but it is there and it helps to give the film a richer texture, anchoring it firmly in its period.

The film attracted generally favourable notices, with emphasis on the performance of Stephen Murray as Robert Rawley: 'a powerful and moving performance';[38] 'Stephen Murray compels belief in the father's blindness';[39] and 'Mr Stephen Murray works hard, and not unsuccessfully, to give him stature and authority',[40] are typical responses. Nigel Patrick as the wastrel Simon and Seymour Hicks as Lord Clandon, shrewder than he seems, were also singled out from what one reviewer described as 'a better than average British cast'.[41] Though there was some suggestion that the film had not shaken off its theatrical antecedent, with comments on 'occasional stilted passages' in *Tatler* and dialogue that is 'a bit stiff for the screen'.[42] There was also praise for the 'impressionist glimpses of a blind man's inner vision'.[43] This was a matter which had been highlighted in the publicity material: 'what does the world he lives in look like to a blind man? ... a new technique of photography which has been planned by lighting cameraman Wilkie Cooper, is to be tried out ... the effect they hoped to achieve was similar to a negative picture with outlines felt by the blind man being brought up positive recognition.'[44] Indeed, this and the sequence of the lying flashback, as well as a general attention to framing and cutting to emphasise certain relationships and contrasts, give the lie to the *New York Times* review which claims that 'it follows a rigid stage technique, using the camera as a mere recording instrument rather than as a component part of the drama'.[45] In, for instance, comparative, juxtaposed shots of Lord Clandon's shabby but undeniably grandiose pile and Rawley's less time-honoured but more luxurious mansion, points are made about class and priorities. Cooper's camera is encouraged to swirl around the house with a fluidity at odds with the idea of 'stage-bound', picking out here the terrified eyes of the hunted man as he huddles in the dark, later echoing *film noir* stylistics again as, unshaven and in the semi-dark, he tells his lying story to his now bigamous wife. The play is, today, hard to read and the chronic awkwardness of all the action's being set in 'the study of Sir Robert Rawley's house in the Vale of Avalon'[46] helps to confine it to a bygone era of stage writing.

After what may have been the financially draining experience of filming *Daughter of Darkness*, which was meant to have been followed by *Dead Ground* at 'the new Paignton Studios in Oldway',[47] Devon, but which never eventuated, Comfort seems to have found in *The Silent Dust* a manageable project. Produced at Teddington by N. A. Bronsten for Associated British, the press releases all carried the story of a project completed under schedule, in spite of some elaborate set-pieces. These included 'a gay scene in the Café de Bruxelles, a piece of typical architecture and fruit of the art director's flying visit to the Continent'; 'A gravel quarry across the river from Teddington Studios [which] was found ideal to represent a desolate strip of war-torn terrain when suitably treated by the art department'; and 'the magnificent entrance hall and stairway of the house [which matched the style of] ... an old manor house in Bucks, which will be employed for location shots.'[48] All this care in physical production paid off in a film which might easily have looked merely stage-bound. As in those other films Comfort adapted from conventional plays, *Great Day* and *Daughter of Darkness*, he shows skill in effortlessly opening out the action beyond the theatrical convention of the missing fourth wall, without, however, the self-consciousness that sometimes marks films derived from such plays. According to his surviving collaborators, he probably never again went on locations that were not within easy reach of the relevant studios. We shall consider how he managed this constraint particularly in relation to the modest-budget productions of his last fifteen years, when as a heteronomous rather than autonomous creative artist he could offer less resistance to external pressures, economic and otherwise.

The other of the two tormented male protagonists referred to above is Bert Mallinson, a harbour port signalman who succumbs to temptations and falls into theft and murder. Based on Georges Simenon's novel, *Newhaven-Dieppe*, with the setting now an English harbour town, the symbolically titled *Temptation Harbour* is possibly Lance Comfort's finest work, its strength a curious and engrossing blend of melodrama and *noir*ish realism. Released in March 1947, it netted some excellent reviews, many of them singling out the director for special mention: 'As for the direction, this is the best thing Lance Comfort has achieved',[49] said one;

while another concluded his review with 'Lance Comfort's direction strengthens the impression that he may be one of the British screen's white hopes.'⁵⁰

Like Ellis in *Great Day*, and unlike Brodie or Bedelia, Mallinson (Robert Newton, in more subdued mode) is a man caught by circumstances rather than a figure of evil. As in *Great Day*, the obsessional element is, though important, not the whole of the film. Mallinson is a basically decent man whose life is thrown out of kilter when he dives into the harbour to rescue a man he has seen pushed, fails to save the man but does find a case containing £5,000. Structurally, the film parts company with melodrama in that what ensues is less a matter of Mallinson's being pursued by others for the contents of the case than of the conflict in his own mind. The common – and misleading – idea that melodrama has no truck with the divided consciousness breaks down as we consider protagonists like Ellis and Mallinson. As Robert Murphy has written, 'Mallinson has a strong sense of right and wrong and his falls from grace stem, ironically, from acts of kindness and generosity.'⁵¹ That he knows right from wrong has been made clear when we see him admonish his daughter Betty (Margaret Barton) for bringing home unpaid-for kidneys from the butcher's shop she works at. It is the desire to provide a better life for this hard-working daughter which first tempts him to keep the money. What clinches this decision for him is his meeting with a French carnival performer, Camelia (Simone Simon), 'the disappearing mermaid', whom he rescues from the bullying of her boss and with whom he becomes infatuated. Camelia has the resonances of a *film noir* woman: she comes with intimations of past sexual adventure and looks out of place in the domesticity of Mallinson's life with his daughter. At one point, Betty warns her father that 'the mermaid is in the parlour', a phrase which suggests Camelia's disruptiveness in their lives: the worlds she has inhabited, whether wartime France or the fairground, are outside Mallinson's customary range. His sexual obsession provides further motive for him not to return the money, even when, in a moment recalling Fritz Lang's *Scarlet Street* (1946), she mocks him for his suggestion that they might marry. The inner and the outer conflict come to a head when Brown (William Hartnell), the murderer of the drowned man, comes looking for the money and Mallinson kills him in a fight. Now Mallinson's true decency leads him to give himself up to the police, in spite of Camelia's attempts to persuade him not to and following her final taunt: 'I hate you with your big clumsy hands.' The murderer has been gradually closing in on Mallinson, but the film's real drama has been within his own mind. There was criticism of Comfort's rendering of some key moments of this inner conflict in a spoken voice-over. The *Punch* reviewer wrote: 'One point I wasn't very happy about is the film convention of "spoken thoughts"';[52] the *Spectator* complained of 'the now threadbare technique of the spoken thought';[53] and C. A. Lejeune had 'only one complaint to make against the film, and that is about its trick of expressing a man's thoughts on the sound-track, while his image, on the picture-track, gets on with the business ... This is a bad habit in the cinema, and it has got to stop.'[54] It is worth noting that, a year later, Lejeune finds no fault in Olivier's use of this 'trick' to express Hamlet's agonies of mind during the great soliloquies.[55] It seems that different criteria are applied to works judged to derive from dominant positions in the field of cultural production. On the matter of Mallinson's troubled conscience, there is, in a tobacconist's shop, a very well-composed shot of Newton, his face half-shadowed, as he holds the Meerscham he covets. As he looks up in the decorative mirror before him, he sees Brown, the murderer, and the holder of the key to his conscience, come in behind him (see Plate 9). Here, the composition does what the voice-over does elsewhere. It seems captious to object to the voice-over *per se* – to ignore its possibilities is not necessarily to be cinematic; it might just be a matter of failing to exploit one of the cinema's strategies.

As in all these films, Comfort exploits the framework of melo-drama for his underlying plot, but *Temptation Harbour* also reveals affiliations with other styles and modes. So do the films discussed earlier: *Great Day* has elements of village comedy-drama and *film noir* preoccupations in mood and style, as has *Silent Dust*; *Bedelia* belongs partly to the detective story genre; *Daughter of Darkness* is enriched by its flair for the Gothic. The *film noir* element is there in *Temptation Harbour*, not only in the woman who provides the basis for sexual fixation, but also in the character of Mallinson: the essentially good man tempted to improve the quality of the sorely constrained life he lives when a chance seems to present itself. It was not surprising that British cinema should be influenced by this dominant Hollywood style, and Britain's postwar films frequently reflect its iconography, tone and structures. The realism which won so much praise from 1940s reviewers of British films also makes itself felt in this film's unpatronising detail of working-class life, though there is also a whiff of the moody atmospherics of those French films of the 1930s and 1940s (*Quai des Brumes* and *La bête humaine*, for example, both released 1938) in which emotional and moral conflicts are enacted in dreary railway yards or on foggy wharves. The main street scene, too, with overhanging second storeys, also has a cross-channel suggestion to it, as if to imply its proximity to the source of Brown's criminal activity, and the destination of the ferries that leave Mallinson's harbour. The presence of French actor Simone Simon, star of Renoir's classic *La bête humaine*, reinforces this intertextual reference. *Temptation Harbour*, in fact, has a sombre grey look not common in British cinema of the day, for which cinematographer Otto Heller, who in the same year shot Cavalcanti's unsettling thriller *They Made Me a Fugitive*, must take the credit. He avoids the luscious black-and-white contrasts which are so rapturous an element of British cinema of the time in favour of a spectrum that stresses the in-between shades and is therefore in keeping with the troubled conscience at the heart of the film's narrative.

The film's realist aspirations – and clearly these mattered more to Comfort in relation to this film than, say, to those on either side of it, *Bedelia* and *Daughter of Darkness* – call for a little more attention. Partly they are the result of carefully undertaken location work. The publicity hand-outs record that 'for a number of weeks the complete production unit made Folkestone their headquarters, filming thrilling scenes at the cross-Channel embarkation jetty, St Margaret's Bay and special scenes were taken at night in mid-channel on board the Belgian cross-Channel steamer, *Princess Josephine Charlotte*'.[56] A *Picturegoer* columnist reported that, at Welwyn studios, '"matching shots" in the production [were used] to reproduce scenes already made on location at Folkestone and Rye (the story is not set in any specific port).'[57] Continuity person Elaine Shreyeck recalls shooting in the streets of Rye with specially erected lamp-posts.[58] The film's realist agenda is also realised in part through the work of art director Cedric Dawe, who has taken a good deal of rewarding trouble over sets. Mallinson's dingy home, which has the warmth of personal attachments but which signifies also the limitations of the life he and his daughter can afford to live; the modest hotel in which the French police inspector Dupré (Marcel Dalio) awaits Brown; the carnival with its ferris wheel and tatty 'Disappearing Mermaid' act; the steamy pub in which Camelia's pernod strikes such an exotic note; and the signal box itself from which Mallinson sees the conflict that will usher in his own: all these are observed with an eye for revealing detail. In the first of the episodes set in the fairground, Camelia tells the 'story' of her escape from war-torn France to England where she was found to have in her ear-lobe enough 'atomic energy to flatten London'; she is plainly bored while men are called up from the audience to inspect her chains before she is lowered into a glass case filled with water. While the shoddy MC, Gowshall (Charles Victor) compères the show, his pianist wife Ethel (Irene Handl) desultorily picks her teeth, in an anti-romantic gesture that anticipates the bored women's orchestra in Max Ophüls' *Letter from an Unknown Woman* (1948). Later, in their caravan, Gowshall is pouring water over Ethel's newly shampooed hair, in another moment that undercuts any possible glamour in the side-show life, complaining that he is 'sick of these French programmes. There, we've missed ITMA now', offering a sharp, unglamorous view of life behind the scenes of the fair. This is done without patronage or the suggestion of stock comedy relief, as Comfort makes idiosyncratic use of Handl and Victor, two actors often associated with stereotyped lower-orders casting in British films, both of whom worked for Comfort on several occasions. Similarly, Gladys Henson, another actor often seen in caricatures of working-class life, has a brief moment of verisimilitude as the receptionist at the hotel to which Dupré tracks Brown.

Above all, it is in the acting of the principals that the film makes its strongest claim to realism. Newton, who had given a fine, all-stops-out performance for Comfort as the monomaniacal Brodie in *Hatter's Castle*, the first big success for either star or director, here subdues his penchant for eye-rolling flamboyance. Instead, he offers something more in line with his success as suburban Frank Gibbons in David Lean's *This Happy Breed* (1944), and his first scene with his daughter establishes his every-day decency. He is an upright man struggling to achieve small aims, such as owning a fishing boat, but, as Robert Murphy has noted, 'it is a strength of the film that he is no cardboard innocent ... [he] discovers that he has interests, abilities, passions, not normally associated with railway signalmen'.[59] The images of Mallinson glimpsed in relation to chains (as he climbs up the steps of the quay after failing to rescue the drowned man) and nets (as he watches Brown hurl the man in to the water and, later, the fishing nets as he takes food to Brown in the beach hut) reinforce, visually, the sense of his imminent entrapment. Newton distinguishes finely among the acts of unpremeditated goodness (diving into the harbour to try to save an unknown man; rescuing Camelia from the bullying entrepreneur who exploits her), the moments of conscious hesitation as he fails to act on his best instincts (when he decides not to tell his hectoring supervisor about the money; when at the last minute he accepts a lift home on a friend's dray just as he is about to return the money to the police station), and the instincts he has forgotten he has and which surface in the moment when Camelia asks him, in sexual invitation, to help her take off her dress. His final decision, to give himself up, having killed Brown in a struggle in a beach hut, is made very moving in a close-up as he confronts Camelia with the determination born of his essential goodness, followed by the quietly made symbolic gestures of shutting the case of money, turning off the lights and closing the doors as he takes his leave of the domesticity that had once seemed both reassuring and confining.

There was a great deal of praise for the performance of Margaret Barton, the twenty-one-year-old actress who so convincingly plays Mallinson's sixteen-year-old daughter, Betty, poignantly registering the girl's growing fear for her father. The detail of her yearning for gaiety, but not at the cost of her father's peace of mind, places the performance at some remove from the railway buffet caricature of her preceding work in *Brief Encounter*. She is, as one reviewer noted, 'exactly what an overworked child would be',[60] and the *New Statesman* said of her, 'there is a delightfully genuine child, Margaret Barton, whose presence clinches the terror of certain moments.'[61] In one of Comfort's strongest casts, Simone Simon's slightly sing-song English stresses her otherness in this scene, as she moves between a *film noir* woman's contempt for an older man and the unforced naturalness of her scenes with Betty, whose real innocence highlights Camelia's affectation of this. William Hartnell's Brown is a character of some pathos, rather than a cardboard crook, and all the way down the cast one finds small moments of truthful portraiture that make *Temptation Harbour* a melodrama of unusual substance. This is a film which, in the collaborations which account for its look and sound, notably in Heller's cinematography and Mischa Spoliansky's eloquently moody score, draws eclectically but fruitfully from other genres and styles in a search for greater textural richness.

Romantic melodrama: *Portrait of Clare*

The film that marked the end of Lance Comfort's run as a director of comparatively expensive 'A' films is a long slow saga based on an even longer, slower saga by the wildly prolific middle-brow novelist, Francis Brett Young.[62] The film is, however, worth examining in some detail because it marks such a watershed in Comfort's career. The novel surges on for nearly 900 pages, as the curiously under-characterised heroine goes through three generations of conflict in floridly overwrought prose, with no tremor of the heart or of the natural world, which so often mirrors her moods, unchronicled. It sketches in a social background of shifting class divisions, of international crises such as the Boer War and World War I, of changing means of transportation, and even trouble at the mines. It recalls in its length and detail such other works as Louis Bromfield's *Mrs Parkington* (filmed by Tay Garnett in 1944), Marcia Davenport's *Valley of Decision* (Garnett in 1945), Daphne Du Maurier's *Hungry Hill* (Brian Desmond Hurst in 1946), and Thomas Armstrong's *The Crowthers of Bankdam* (Walter Forde in 1947, as *The Master of Bankdam*). Perhaps the undoubted taste for such lengthy fictions predates the television age when one would expect the generational conflicts to be dealt with less time-consumingly in several lushly-produced episodes of a mini-series. Long novels are still to be found, of course, but this particular *kind* of long novel, love and heartbreak against a panorama of world events is no longer generally the stuff of which bestsellers are made, as it may well have been in the between-wars period, though the devoted following for writers such as Barbara Taylor Bradford partly contradicts this assertion. Francis Brett Young was extremely popular from the time of his winning the James Tait Memorial Prize in 1927 for *Portrait of Clare*, and several of his best-remembered novels, including *Clare* and *My Brother Jonathan* (1928), in which he drew on his own medical experiences are set in the West Midlands. One commentator has written, 'He is often long-winded and sometimes platitudinous; nevertheless his leisurely novels possess a certain quiet charm.'[63] Three of his novels were filmed in postwar Britain: *A Man About the House*, directed by Leslie Arliss in 1947, *My Brother Jonathan*, directed by Harold French in 1948 (it was the top money-making film in Britain that year) and *Portrait of Clare* in 1950. When one wonders what drew Lance Comfort to this kind of romantic melodrama, somewhat at odds with his preceding films, one should remember that Young's name, forgotten today, would have been well-known to film-makers then, and his star, Margaret Johnston, had won acclaim for her performance in the earlier Young adaptation, *A Man About the House*. Sadly the film did little for either Johnston or Comfort.

The intertextuality of the film is not limited to other hefty romantic novels, filmed or not in the decade, or even Young's filmed works. *Portrait of Clare* has purely cinematic affiliations with the romantic melodrama genre which included, in the 1940s, such titles as those above which trace family fortunes over several generations and the then quite common practice of telling a whole film in one protracted flashback. In this respect, *Portrait of Clare* recalls such films as *The White Cliffs of Dover* (Clarence Brown, 1944), *Margie* (Henry King, 1946), *Enchantment* (Irving Reis, 1948), *Letter from an Unknown Woman* (Max Ophüls, 1948), *Edward My Son* (George Cukor, 1949) and, in other ways as well, *Mrs Parkington*. Like the latter, its dramatic structure is dictated by a woman in old age telling her life story to a grand-daughter or great-grand-daughter as a kind of cautionary tale. Whatever the dramatic structure, there are other common cinematic functions evinced which ally the film to others of its time: as a lead-in to the flashback, there is usually a change in musical score, the camera moves in slowly for a close-up of the narrator, the voice takes on a special 'reminiscent' tone, and there is often either a blurring at the edges of the image and/or the use of a dissolve, these acting jointly as signifiers of a return to an earlier period. Structurally and stylistically, then, in this matter at least, Comfort is working within a genre that had been popular for some time, if not one in which he had previously shown any interest. In Britain in 1950, the year of *Clare*'s release, the only really comparable film was Anthony Bushell's *The Angel with the Trumpet*, a remake of a 1948 Austrian film about a family of Viennese piano-makers from 1888 to 1946, focusing on a lady who marries for security and lives unhappily ever after. It was no more popular than *Portrait of Clare*, so perhaps Comfort had misjudged the market, but his own previous record had shown only a perfunctory interest in romance. The romantic pairs in *Hatter's Castle* (James Mason and Deborah Kerr), *When We Are Married* (Barry Morse and Lesley Brook), *Hotel Reserve* (Mason and Clare Hamilton) and the conventional triangle (Sheila Sim, Philip Friend and Walter Fitzgerald) in *Great Day* are arguably the least interesting aspects of their respective films.

How then do Comfort and his screenwriters (Adrian Arlington and producer Leslie Landau) deal with so indigestible a slice of romance as they have inherited from Francis Brett Young? Though it is not, overall, a successful film, it should be said at the outset that, like several of Comfort's films, it considerably tightens and sharpens its precursor literary text. Further, the work of Don

Ashton (art director), Elizabeth Haffenden (costume designer) and Gunther Krampf (cinematographer), reinforced by Leighton Lucas's score which draws on Schumann (much eloquent use of *Dedication*), Chopin and Brahms, gives the film a stylish sheen that replaces and greatly improves on Young's interminable and over-lush descriptive writing. The following is a sample, taken at random from the novel:

> The straggling September borders spent their opulence of old gold against a hazel hedge with cobs in clusters. Beyond it an orchard, knee-deep in aftermath, in which moon-pale apples lay where they had fallen. The trees were haggard and twisted with age. It seemed as if the hoary lichen that made the house ethereal had spread its bloom on everything, so silvery, so unreal was the light. (p. 129)

This kind of adjectival excess is applied to everything: not just to the natural world, but to the interiors of houses and the interiors of mind and heart.

Comfort's film, though it certainly does seem like (as one reviewer noted) a 'Leisurely drama of middle-class life in late Victorian and Edwardian days',[64] shears away great chunks of the novel's cluttered narrative. Clare is already a young woman in love when the film's chronology begins, and the film dispenses with the pre-history of her mother's romantic marriage and early death. She marries Ralph Hingston (Ronald Howard), scion of the neighbouring nouveau riche industrialist Sir Joseph Hingston (Lloyd Pearson) and his domineering wife (Mary Clare). Following Ralph's early death by drowning (in the novel, he escapes a near-drowning to be carried off shortly after by the Boer War), Clare gives birth to his son, and, out of loneliness, some years later marries Dudley Wilburn (Robin Bailey), the family's dry stick of a solicitor, whose oppressive routines and dislike for her spoilt son Steven (Jeremy Spenser) finally lead her to seek divorce. She then marries Dudley's cousin Robert Hart (Richard Todd), though the film shows nothing of this except Clare's remark, 'My years with Robert have been the happiest years of my life'. In broad outline this is the shape of the novel as well as the film.

The major structural difference is that the film's story is told in one extended flashback. Clare arrives at what was once the

Hingstons' family mansion, now fifty years later the home of
Clare's son, Steven, Lord Wolverbury (Bruce Seton), who has
inherited Sir Joseph's title. His daughter Sylvia (Ann Gunning)
has lost her young husband in World War II and is about to marry
a man she doesn't love, on the grounds that 'A love like mine and
Johnny's doesn't happen twice.' Since he was shot down, she
'couldn't care less about anything', and, in answer to this postwar
problem, the camera moves in on the gently listening, white-
haired Clare who tells her own story to show that it is unwise to
marry without love *and* that love can happen twice. This framing
device really does no more than signpost the significance of Clare's
three marriages, which the film treats with some perfunctoriness.
Ralph is killed off very early, before his child is born, so that the
film gives little sense of what the marriage is like (the novel is
more interesting in exploring the limitations of the handsome,
likeable but superficial Ralph), or why Ralph's mother behaves so
venomously to Clare. A few bursts of indulged bad behaviour on
Steven's part and it is clear to Clare's Aunt Cathie (Marjorie
Fielding) that 'It's a man's handling he needs', and she warns
Clare, in another cautionary tale, not to throw her life away as she,
Cathie, once did. The marriage with Dudley turns Clare into a
victim of his patriarchal views and stifling routines. Comfort
handles this section of the film well. When Steven returns from
boarding-school to find his mother married to Dudley whom he
dislikes, the camera homes in for a moment on the neat line-up of
Dudley's coat and hats on the hall-stand as a mute signifier of his
being established in Clare's house. (In the novel she removes,
more probably, to his suburban terrace.) The camera discreetly
passes Clare's and Dudley's twin beds, leading Steven to ask 'Where
does Mr Wilburn sleep?', alerting us to the Oedipal problems
ahead, Steven having lost his father long before he can think of
taking his place and resentful of any other replacement in his
mother's life. (There is a touch of *David Copperfield* in the heavy
stepfather's unsympathetic dealings with the child.) Halfway
through the film, Robert Hart enters, shows himself sympathetic
to Clare's stifling marriage to Dudley, is a success with Steven,
and promises to wait for Clare to be free from her marriage. 'I was

wrong to marry without love,' she says, summarising her message for Sylvia. The film then returns to the present day.

This tale of love and marriage is certainly tighter than Young's novel, reducing its supporting characters and the number of significant settings, but it also removes a good deal of the novel's motivation.[65] In particular, Lady Hingston's outbursts are presumably rooted in parvenu aspiration and a ruthless nature, but the film spends no time in accounting for her behaviour. For instance, is it just a matter of not getting her own way that leads her to berate Clare for not wearing to a party the dress she has chosen for her? Is it social ambition that explains her fury at Clare's decision to marry Dudley ('It's time you started to think of what you owe to our name')? These and other matters are accomplished in very brief scenes which come to the boil too quickly to be fully convincing. The scenes between Lady Hingston and her mild husband are among the film's sharpest, culminating in his accusing her of social climbing, to which she replies, confirming what he has said, 'Don't call me lass, I don't like it' (because it suggests their humble origins). Nearer to the centre of the film, none of Clare's three marriages is treated in the sort of detail that would make her situation more involving. There are some good touches in the way Dudley's narrow routine is established: hanging his dressing-gown behind the door in exactly the same way every night before quoting his bedtime verse about the weary labourer and his rest. It is in moments like these, Clare's face reflected pensively in the mirror as she brushes her hair and looks into herself and what has become of her youth, rather than in managing the somewhat shapeless narrative, that one notices Comfort's directorial hand.

There are others too. The character of Aunt Cathie, played with her usual firmness by Marjorie Fielding, exercises much less control over the narrative and is allowed to die earlier than in the novel, but the episode of her death is beautifully managed. Her female modesty has caused her not to call a doctor early enough to act on a diagnosis while something might be done about it. Too late for help, Dr Boyd (Anthony Nicholls) lies to her about her condition, and she, unknowing, tells Clare later, ' I should hate a doctor who hedged about his diagnosis'. The camera pans gently from her weary face, as she puts to one side her book and glasses, to the window open on the night sky. There is a dissolve as the window now lets in daylight and the camera pans back to the now-made bed, signifying her death. The fluency and conciseness of this moment of mute cinematic story-telling are characteristic of Comfort at his best. Elsewhere, the distinction between the grandeur of the Hingston's mansion, Stourford, and Clare's older, inherently more dignified family house, Pen House, is made in two early long shots, and the skilful production design as the camera moves inside the two houses is underlined in Dudley's comment about how 'The old gentry will never get used to the new aristocracy'. The contrast recalls Comfort's similar use of the mise-en-scène for a socially discriminating purpose: that between the self-made Rawley's house and Lord Clandon's dignified but shabby manor in *The Silent Dust*.

That remark of Dudley's is perhaps an echo of the postwar period of the film's production. If it is such an echo, it is a rare one. The film shears away most of the novel's social background and for the most part seems uninterested in finding contemporary significance in Clare's story. Whereas the Gainsborough melodramas contained a sub-textual discourse on the conflicts of women in wartime Britain, *Portrait of Clare* seems to be operating in a time warp as far as this is concerned. Clare's marriage into the 'new aristocracy' is cut tragically short; the marriage she makes for security is a backward step, into the arms of a man approved by her aunt who has *dis*approved of the Hingstons; Robert Hart may be intended as the man for the future, combining the best qualities of his predecessors, but he is too sketchily drawn for us to make such a point with any confidence. The novel tells us more (a great deal more) about this sensitive, manly paragon, chastely loved by Clare for 300 pages, before a dying Dudley releases her from a state of moral bondage. It is a pity that Clare's situation – a woman whose roles in life are circumscribed by her relations to men – was not made to bear a greater significance. Sue Harper has written: 'The film's poster was tactless. It showed a giant female holding three homunculi in her hand, but this was inappropriate for the sexual politics of 1950.'[66] Yes, and furthermore the film doesn't really show Clare as a manipulator of men *or* as a major victim of their brutalities. In other words, Clare is neither 'wicked lady' nor Fanny by Gaslight. There was praise for Margaret Johnston as Clare: 'sympathetically attractive';[67] 'an intelligent, poised performance';[68] 'the intelligent performance of Margaret Johnston in the title-role';[69] but *Variety* felt that 'Miss Johnston, whose performance dominated the plot, is an accomplished actress worthy of much better material'.[70] A press release during production wondered whether this film would be her big chance, recalling how, after her two previous successes, *The Rake's Progress* (1945) and *A Man About the House* (1947), she was left languishing by producers.[71] In the event, hers remained a sporadic career: she made no more than ten further films, only two or three of much interest, in the ensuing twenty years, finally leaving the screen to run the agency established by her late husband, Al Parker. She recalled with pleasure working with Lance Comfort who, in relation to a contretemps over a piece of music she was meant to play, 'was big enough to let it happen my way because I had worked so hard on it', and she felt it 'was quite a graceful film'.[72] Perhaps she was an actress in a role that needed a star to impose personality on a somewhat ill-defined characterisation; perhaps the writing doesn't give her enough scope; or perhaps the amiable Comfort needed to be more demanding. Of the rest of the cast, only Robin Bailey as the unprepossessing Dudley among the men has the material to make much of an impression. Richard Todd, by then a well-known star, must surely have been forced to take the small role of Robert as part of his contract with Associated British, since it offers almost nothing for the actor to work on. His cheerful attempt to smoke in a non-smoking carriage, his recognising a quotation from Dickens which passes quite over Dudley's head, and his matey dealings with the youthful Steven are typical of the minor ways in which the film signifies his fitness to be a more compatible husband for Clare.

Only the always-dominant Mary Clare, as Lady Hingston, has the forceful, single-minded approach to her role that the film needed to turn it into a strong romantic melodrama. She represents one half of a dichotomy which doesn't find anything potent enough to react against. Comfort's flair for melodrama surfaces just often enough to remind one of what he might have made of the film. As in *Hatter's Castle*, *Bedelia* and *Daughter of Darkness*, he uses a storm scene to bring matters to a head: Dudley has locked the offending Steven in his room on a night of wild rain, and while Clare is playing the piano below to an appreciative Robert and a bored Dudley, Steven escapes from his upper-storey window, and heads for his *arriviste* grandparents' house and away from the hated Dudley. This brings to a head the relationship between Clare and Dudley and a two-shot of her and Robert aligns them sympathetically in opposition to Dudley's narrow harshness. But this is too little too late to convert an attractive but straggling tale into the fervent romantic melodrama that might have seriously exercised Comfort's talents and assured his future.

Film historian Allen Eyles writes that the film 'opened in July 1950 at the prestigious Warner Leicester Square to very unfavourable press reviews and died a box-office death, having to be removed after one week when it had definitely been booked for longer (a three-week run would have been normal). Being produced by Associated British, it still obtained a full release through the Corporation's subsidiary ABC circuit a few weeks later.'[73] The film's failure undoubtedly harmed Comfort's reputation, though it is hard to see that particular kind of melodrama as offering him much prospect in the way British cinema was moving at the turn of the decade. Further, it makes one wonder if Comfort's characteristic slant on the melodramatic mode – more obviously serious but, in hindsight, not necessarily more resonant than the commercially successful Gainsborough films half a decade earlier – was likely to displease equally those who wanted more flamboyance and those who wanted more realism. *Portrait of Clare* has a certain quiet appeal, but it lacks the waywardness of, say, *Daughter of Darkness* or the moody realism of *Temptation Harbour*. In August 1950, when it went on general release, it was quite overshadowed by the wartime escape film *The Wooden Horse*, which ushered in a very popular 1950s genre, and the Boultings' *Seven Days to Noon*, which drew much of its strength from engagement with a contemporary fear. In matters of setting and theme, both are very far from Comfort's film. Romantic melodrama had virtually no role to play in either popular or critically approved British cinema at this time, as the failure of Michael Powell's *Gone to Earth* (since reclaimed), released in September, or the Phyllis Calvert vehicle, *Woman with No Name*, released October, suggests. In British cinema in 1950, *Portrait of Clare*, whatever its virtues, may be considered as a dead end for its director, fallen victim to the preceding decade's tension between the privileged mode of realism and the more richly expressive modes which always had to fight for notice with everyone but the public, whose preferences had now changed.

Notes

1 See Peter Brooks, *The Melodramatic Imagination: Balzac, Henry James, Melodrama, and the Mode of Excess* (New Haven & London, Yale University Press), 1976; Robert Bechtold Heilman, *The Iceman, the Arsonist, and the Troubled Agent: Tragedy and Melodrama on the Modern Stage* (London, George Allen & Unwin), 1973; Thomas Elsaesser, 'Tales of sound and fury: observations on the family melodrama', *Monogram*, 4 (1972), reprinted in Christine Gledhill (ed.), *Home is Where the Heart Is: Studies in Melodrama and the Woman's Film* (London, BFI Publishing), 1987, pp. 43–69.

2 Sue Harper, *Picturing the Past: The Rise and Fall of the British Costume Film* (London, BFI Publishing) 1986; Robert Murphy, *Realism and Tinsel, Cinema and society in Britain 1939–1948* (London & New York Routledge), 1989.

3 Jean Anouilh, in *'Antigone' and 'Eurydice'* (London, Methuen and Co), 1951.

4 Heilman, *Iceman*, p. xvi.

5 *Ibid*, p. 46.

6 *Ibid*, p. 22.

7 David Quinlan, *The Illustrated Guide to Film Directors* (London, B. T. Batsford), 1983, p. 57.

8 *Daily Worker*, 14 April 1945.

9 *Lady*, 19 April 1945.

10 *Spectator*, 20 April 1945.

11 K. F. B., *Monthly Film Bulletin*, 12:136 (30 April 1945), p. 45.

12 RKO press book, p. 3.

13 C. A. Lejeune, 'The Films', *The Observer*, 15 April 1945.

14 *The Observer*, 13 May 1945. Reprinted in *The C. A. Lejeune Film Reader* (Manchester, Carcanet Press), 1991, p. 216.

15 Vera Caspary, *Bedelia* (London, White Lion Publishers Ltd.), [1945] 1972, p. 5.
16 *Bedelia – Press Book*.
17 *Daily Herald*, 7 June 1946.
18 Ernest Betts, 'She shouldn't always be wicked', *Daily Express*, 6 June 1946.
19 *Bedelia – Press Book*.
20 Marcia Landy, *British Genres: Cinema and Society, 1930–1960* (Princeton: Princeton University Press), 1991, pp. 229–30.
21 *News Chronicle*, 7 June 1946.
22 Author's interview with Elaine Shreyeck, September 1998.
23 'Duchy Film Invasion', *Western Independent*, 6 July 1947. LCC.
24 'Honor Blackman' in Brian McFarlane, *An Autobiography of British Cinema* (London, Methuen), p. 63.
25 Edith Nepean, 'Round the British studios', *Picture Show*, 51:1324 (20 September 1947), p. 11.
26 Author's interviews with John Comfort, October 1997, and Elaine Schreyeck, September, 1998.
27 Mikhail Bakhtin, *Rabelais and his World*, trans. Hélène Iswolsky (Bloomington, Indiana University Press), 1984, p. 222.
28 Michael Holquist, *Mikhail Bakhtin* (Cambridge, Mass, Harvard University Press), 1984, p. 301.
29 *Sunday Times*, 26 January 1948.
30 Lionel Collier, 'Shop for your films', *Picturegoer*, 17:703 (28 February 1948) p. 12.
31 *Daily Mail*, 23 January 1948.
32 *Sunday Times*, 26 January 1948.
33 *Daily Graphic*, 23 January 1948.
34 *News Chronicle*, 24 January 1948.
35 *Daily Mail*, 23 January 1948.
36 Lionel Collier, 'Shop for your films', *Picturegoer*, 18:730 (26 February 1949), p. 14.
37 This idea is more fully discussed in Brian McFarlane, 'Losing the peace: some British films of postwar adjustment', in Tony Barta (ed.) *Screening the Past* (Westport, Connecticut, Praeger), 1998, pp. 93–108.
38 Virginia Graham, *Spectator* (date not given). LCC.
39 *Tatler* (date not given). LCC.
40 'A variety of moods', *The Times*, 27 February 1949. LCC.
41 Unidentified clipping in LCC, possibly the *New Statesman*.
42 *Ibid.*
43 C. A. W., *The Cinema*, 26 January 1949. LCC.
44 'The blind man – and the Independent!', 'The Cinema Studio', supplement to *The Cinema*, 26 May 1948. LCC.
45 T. M. P., '*Silent Dust*', 13 February 1948.
46 Roland and Michael Pertwee, *The Paragon* (London, English Theatre Guild), 1948, p. 7.
47 *Torbay Herald*, 7 February 1948; also reported in the *Exeter Express*, 9 February 1948. LCC.
48 *The Cinema*, 26 May 1948. LCC.

49 F. Maurice Speed, *What's On* (quoted in Campaign Book for Pathé Pictures, date not given).

50 Campbell Dixon, 'Good thriller and two comedies', *Sunday Telegraph* (date not given). LCC.

51 Robert Murphy, *Sawdust and Tinsel: Cinema and Society in Britain 1939–48* (London and New York, Routledge), 1989, p. 185.

52 *Punch*, 2 April 1947. LCC.

53 'The Cinema', *Spectator*, 28 March 1947.

54 C. A. Lejeune, 'The films', *The Observer*, 23 March 1947.

55 Review (*The Observer*, 9 May 1948) reprinted in Anthony Lejeune (ed.), *The C. A. Lejeune Film Reader* (Manchester, Carcanet), 1991, pp. 229–32.

56 'Authentic scenes in *Temptation Harbour*', Campaign Book, Pathé Pictures (pages not numbered).

57 Hubert Cole, 'Strawberry wallop', *Picturegoer*, 15:669 (12 October 1946), p. 10.

58 Author's interview with Elaine Schreyeck, September 1998.

59 Murphy, *Sawdust and Tinsel*, p. 185.

60 B. J. M., *Monthly Film Bulletin*, 14:160 (April 1947), p. 47.

61 William Whitebait, *The New Statesman*, 29 March 1947.

62 Francis Brett Young, *Portrait of Clare* (London, William Heinemann), [1927] 1940 (Severn edition).

63 Stanley J. Kunitz and Howard Haycraft (eds) *Twentieth Century Authors: A Biographical Dictionary of Modern Literature* (New York, The H. W. Wilson Company), 1942.

64 *Picture Show*, 55:1443 (25 November 1950), p. 10.

65 The print of the film available for this study runs only 86 minutes instead of the original 99. This may account for something too precipitate in the development of certain scenes.

66 Sue Harper, *Picturing the Past: The Rise and Fall of the British Costume Film* (London, BFI Publishing), 1994, p. 178.

67 Lionel Collier, 'Coming your way', *Picturegoer*, 20:799 (26 August 1950), p. 16.

68 *Picture Show*, 55:1443 (25 November 1950), p. 10

69 C. A. W., *Today's Cinema*, 75:6043 (21 July 1950), p. 7.

70 Myro, *Portrait of Clare*, *Variety*, 9 August 1950.

71 'Third time lucky?' *Evening News*, 3 September 1949. LCC.

72 'Margaret Johnson', in McFarlane, *Autobiography of British Cinema*, p. 334.

73 Letter to author, 1998.

6

Interlude: where to, now?

By the end of the 1940s, Lance Comfort had established a solid record of achievement in 'A' features, primarily in the melodramatic mode. He had shown a gift for pacy, fluent storytelling, for visual flair that complemented his dealings with colourful, obsessive protagonists, for the integration of some impressive talents across a range of film-making skills, and for eliciting memorable performances from some vivid, even idiosyncratic, players. However, even if his last 'A' film, *Portrait of Clare*, had been a success, he was, as a melodramatist, working in a vein which was not likely to attract critical attention (symbolic capital) and one which was no longer such a potent force at the box-office (economic capital could no longer be counted on from such product).

Towards the end of the 1940s and into the early 1950s, the dominant figures in the British cinema's corner of the field of cultural production were those whose output could be seen as having literary or social realist affiliations. This was the period of the ascendancy of Carol Reed, David Lean and Anthony Asquith, all of whom enjoyed critically privileged positions in postwar British cinema, of Laurence Olivier's Shakespeare films, of Powell and Pressburger, then less critically secure but arguably more cinematically exciting than any. Reed's situation would founder over *Outcast of the Islands* (1951), far less popular than his great triumphs of the late 1940s (especially *The Third Man*, 1949) but subsequently given its due, *The Man Between* (1953), seen as a less exciting re-play of *The Third Man*, and the sentimental fantasy *A*

Kid for Two Farthings (1955). He never again enjoyed the critical
esteem of the late 1940s, but had one more burst of commercial
success with *Oliver!* (1968). The dominant places in the field of
production had changed at the end of the 1950s, with the 'new
realism' ushered in by *Room at the Top* and new directors, writers
and actors were now occupying the privileged positions, positions
in the field which they (Lindsay Anderson, Tony Richardson,
Karel Reisz, for example) had identified and had the disposition to
fill. Lean responded differently to this change and embarked on
the full-scale international phase of his film-making career, a
phase that had been adumbrated in *Summer Madness* (1955) and
The Bridge on the River Kwai (1957). His triumphant dealings with
Dickens (*Great Expectations*, 1946, and *Oliver Twist*, 1948) and
Coward (*In Which We Serve*, 1942, *This Happy Breed*, 1944, and,
above all, *Brief Encounter*, 1945) had given him a critical cachet
which carried him into the next decade. Whatever one's views of
his long, visually arresting films from *Lawrence of Arabia* (1962)
on, it must be allowed that he negotiated the shifting field with
commercial success, even when critical opinion was divided.
Asquith's name was made with discreet, fluent adaptations of
Shaw (*Pygmalion*, 1938, for example), Wilde (*The Importance of
Being Earnest*, 1952) and, especially, Terence Rattigan (from *French
Without Tears*, 1939, through such popular successes as *The Way
to the Stars*, 1945, *The Winslow Boy*, 1948, and *The Browning
Version*, 1951). Like Reed, he floundered somewhat after the mid-
1950s, and he ended his career in all-star portmanteau productions like *The Yellow Rolls-Royce* (1964), which seemed a long way
from the perceptive chamber pieces of the 1940s. The rehabilitation of Michael Powell was still a couple of decades in the future;
at the end of the 1940s and into the early 1950s, there was still a
wariness in the critical approach to his (that is, his and Emeric
Pressburger's) work, as if it might suddenly be booby-trapped by
some arty conceit that would show it didn't really belong securely
in the privileged area of the field as defined by the largely middle-
class critics. Others such as Thorold Dickinson (*Queen of Spades*,
1948) and Olivier (*Henry V*, 1945, and *Hamlet*, 1948) had won
acclaim for isolated films. The other important player, the habitus

that would make itself felt as it bridged the decades and claimed a firm bit of territory in the field, with critics and public alike, was Ealing Studios, especially for its notable series of comedies initiated by *Hue and Cry* (1947), comedies often celebrating eccentricity but rooted in the minutiae of everyday life. The directors associated with these – Robert Hamer, Charles Crichton and Alexander Mackendrick – would all continue productively into the 1950s, but they too would be superseded in the latter half of the decade by the popularity of different genres (the horror film, for example) and the emergence of new directors.

In a field dominated by the likes of those sketched above, a number of directors who had made some mark in the 1940s were to find difficulties in conducting careers at the same level in the succeeding decades. Among those who, like Comfort, had made their names and their most attractive films in the melodramatic mode were Leslie Arliss, Bernard Knowles, Arthur Crabtree and Lawrence Huntington. Arliss and Huntington had worked as screenwriters in the 1930s and Knowles and Crabtree had been notable cinematographers, before, like Arliss, making their marks as Gainsborough directors. These four names are relevant in relation to the trajectory of Lance Comfort's career for a number of reasons.

First, they each have several highly successful 1940s melodramas to their names. Crabtree made something significant out of the tosh potential of *Madonna of the Seven Moons* (1944), as well as directing *They Were Sisters* (1945) and *Caravan* (1946); Knowles fashioned *A Place of One's Own* (1944) into a delicate blend of ghost story and melodrama, praised by C. A. Lejeune, no less, as 'a fine piece of work ... beautiful, lovely and different',[1] and went on to make *The Man Within* and *Jassy* (both 1947); and Arliss directed the sensationally popular *The Man in Grey* (1943), *Love Story* (1944) and *The Wicked Lady* (1945), all of these under the Gainsborough banner during the period of their greatest success, embracing 1943 to 1946. As noted earlier, Comfort all but misses this vogue. Huntington, who had directed ten 'quota quickies' in the 1930s, had, like Comfort, a good melodramatic run in the latter half of the 1940s, including films with two of Comfort's leading men, Robert Newton (in *Night Boat to Dublin*, 1945) and Eric Portman (obsessed by his hangman grandfather, in the grim thriller, *Wanted for Murder*, 1946), and, best of all, *Mr Perrin and Mr Traill* (1948), an all-stops-out version of Hugh Walpole's story of love and jealousy in a boarding-school setting. Huntington, like Comfort, was too late to catch the melodrama wave which swelled up from Gainsborough.

Second, all four of these directors who did their best work in the 1940s[2] were forced into much more modest, less flavourful entertainments in the next decade. Crabtree made a small come-back in the late 1950s with a couple of stylish horror films, *Fiend Without a Face* (1957) and *Horrors of the Black Museum* (1959); Knowles made no film of interest after *The Reluctant Widow* (1951), itself a pale shadow of the palmy days of Gainsborough; Arliss made only two feeble films after 1950; and Huntington, after two minor pieces with Dulcie Gray and Michael Denison, settled for nondescript 'B' films, as did the other three. The 'B' film was a staple of 1950s British film production, comprehending a range of genre films, mostly thrillers, with some comedies and musicals, destined for the bottom half of the double-bill. This latter was then the common exhibition pattern, as indeed it had been since the 1930s, when it is said patrons wanted three hours of entertainment for their money. Comfort contributed to this situation by directing and/or producing nearly twenty such films, some of which contain work excellent by any standards.

Third, all of these directors found work in the 1950s in the fast-growing television sector of the field. In fact, they and Lance Comfort directed and/or produced dozens of half-hour films for such programmes as *Douglas Fairbanks Presents*, *Crown Theatre*, *Assignment Foreign Legion* and *Ivanhoe*. It is not the intention of this book to examine Comfort's work in television, and indeed it is difficult to see most of it, but it is interesting to note how many of those directors who were associated with 'A' features in the preceding decade found steady work in this area of which little has been written. Between television and keeping up the supply of supporting films which exhibition demanded, careers were maintained, even if this kind of work brought the film-makers little in the way of symbolic capital. In Bourdieu's terms, they were now working in dominated positions in the field; they were the 'most heteronomous cultural producers',[3] their only 'principle of legitimacy' being that of the 'popular, that is, the consecration bestowed by the choice of ordinary consumers'.[4] One will search largely in vain for any serious critical consideration of work done merely to fulfil a popular demand: neither television nor 'B' movies would then have attracted such attention, though there are some signs of later attempts to come to terms with what was produced in such circumstances.[5] At the time, it must have been discouraging for directors who knew that, however good their work was in these areas, it would be unlikely to enhance their reputations through critical notice or, in the case of 'B' movies, to bring them much economic profit because their films were sold to distributors for a flat fee. The likelihood of a 'sleeper' emerging from such production and exhibition circumstances was slim; the wonder of it is that, in them, some directors still managed to produce good work. It is a contention of this book that Lance Comfort took these changing conditions, adjusted to the idea of the 'field of cultural production [as] the site of struggles',[6] with more confidence than any of his peers and, on low budgets and against daunting schedules, produced work which is due for reappraisal, because it is lively, inventive and generically knowing, often drawing on the zest for melodrama which had made his 1940s films so attractive.

Comfort did not direct another feature film for three years, possibly because he was not contracted to Rank or to Associated British or to London Films, the three leading production players at the turn of the decade; or because his major genre affiliation was now seen as out of step with popular taste just as it had usually been with critical approval; or because the wartime and postwar surge in British film-making had largely spent itself. When he did direct again, it was clear that he had lost what ascendancy he had enjoyed in the 1940s; what he did for the rest of his life was to make the best of what came his way.

Notes

1 Quoted by David Quinlan, *The Illustrated Guide to Film Directors* (London, B. T. Batsford), 1993, p. 167.
2 There are others, too, whose names could be adduced here and whose careers similarly tailed off in the 1950s: they include Vernon Sewell, Maurice Elvey and Montgomery Tully, who scarcely ever made an 'A' film again after 1950.
3 Pierre Bourdieu, *The Field of Cultural Production: Essays on Art and Literature*, edited and introduced by Randal Johnson (Cambridge, Polity Press), 1993, p. 41. See Chapter 1 for use of these and other of Bourdieu's terms.
4 Bourdieu, *Field*, p. 50.
5 See, for example, Dave Rogers, *The ITV Encyclopedia of Adventure* (London, Boxtree), 1988; Peter Pitt, 'A reminiscence of Elstree', *Film and Television Technician*, February 1989, pp. 8–9; Pitt, 'The men who called "Action"', *The Veteran*, 75 (1995), pp. 13–15; Pitt, 'Elstree's Poverty Row', *Films and Filming*, September 1984, pp. 16–17; Mike Murphy, 'The undead: the early years of Hammer films', *Dark Terrors*, 9 (1994), pp. 45–50; Brian McFarlane, 'Pulp fictions: the British B film and the field of cultural production', *Film Criticism*, XXI:1 (1996), p. 48–70.
6 Bourdieu, *Field*, p. 42.

The double-bill: filming in the 1950s and 60s

7

> In the past the British Film Industry has produced many great film directors: Sir Carol Reed, Michael Powell and David Lean, to name but three. These top directors will not be forgotten in the future; for, apart from their films, much has also been written about them. At the same time as these directors were making their classy films, there were many other directors churning out for the cinema, a staple diet of workmanlike, entertaining pictures.[1]

The author of this comment goes on to 'pay tribute' to several 'B' film-makers of the 1950s, including Maclean Rogers and John Harlow, concluding with a reference to Lawrence Huntington and Lance Comfort who 'fared better [than the others named] ... as they were working right up until their death'.[2] The 'B' film area, which sustained these careers, has its own hierarchy, but at all levels it was the product of exhibition patterns set in place during the 1930s. In their book about US 'B' movies, Charles Flynn and Todd McCarthy wrote: 'It was the Depression-era moviegoer who first insisted on a complete three-hour-plus program for his or her money, and the practice is a logical outgrowth of the Depression state of mind.'[3] Though their book is specifically about American 'B's and their reception, the general situation was paralleled in Britain: it was not immune to the effects of the Depression and the double-bill did take root there as well.

Unfortunately for the repute of the British 'B' film, the 'quota quickies' of the 1930s, films made very cheaply to fulfil exhibition requirements relating to the screening of a certain percentage of

British film, were often of a standard so slipshod that the very notion of the British supporting film acquired such a bad odour that it never recovered, in critical appraisal at least. These films were often the product of Hollywood studios, 'produced or financed by the British subsidiaries of the American companies at a low cost, and then distributed in Britain along with the parent company's American films',[4] thus fulfilling their quota obligations, whether or not the films were actually *seen* by regular audiences. The 'B' film in Britain declined almost to nothing during World War II, 'a symptom of the shrinkage of the whole industry (in all but quality), as a result of the shortage of film stock, the recruitment of film-making personnel into the armed services, and the requisitioning of studio space.'[5] Postwar, Rank made a positive effort at its Highbury Studios to produce low-budget films showcasing new talents[6] (for example, directors such as Terence Fisher, actors such as Susan Shaw and Christopher Lee), but it was in the 1950s that the production of 'B' movies gathered steam in the British film industry, with companies such as Danzigers, Merton Park, (pre-horror) Hammer, ACT Films, Group 3, Tempean and many others, turning out dozens of titles regularly throughout the decade. The quality of the work was often of the most perfunctory kind, but threading its way through a horde of undistinguished thrillers and comedies destined for rapid consumption and early oblivion was a thin but steady stream of films that showed what could be achieved on small budgets and tight schedules if the film-makers cared enough and had the disposition to make the most of what was available to them. Lance Comfort, no longer an autonomous cultural producer, was certainly one of these. Those who continued their film-making careers in the 'B' movies of the 1950s and 1960s included those mentioned above, plus Maurice Elvey, Vernon Sewell, David MacDonald, John Baxter, Dan Birt and Compton Bennett. There were others whose names appear on 'B' films as a step to more ambitious projects and larger budgets: these include Terence Fisher, John Gilling, Clive Donner, Guy Green and Peter Graham Scott, who all went on to direct 'A' films of varying distinction. There were still others – Ernest Morris, Francis Searle, Charles Saunders and others – who worked busily and more or less exclusively in the 'B' film corner of the production field. Comfort obviously belongs in the first of these three groupings; it is one of the ironies of his career that it is now clear that some of his best work was done in this often unregarded area of British film-making.

The hierarchy in 'B' film-making referred to above is partly explained in terms of studios and companies, partly in terms of a distinction made between 'second features' and 'co-features', on the basis of cost, concept, length and billing. As to the former criteria, Group 3 seems to have had pretensions to a kind of sub-Ealing quality, verging on 'A' film production with Philip Leacock's mining drama, *The Brave Don't Cry* (1952); Tempean made highly proficient thrillers, often with American stars to further distribution in the USA; ACT Films was formed essentially to provide work for members of the technicians' union, and broke out of its second feature programme only twice with Anthony Asquith's *The Final Test* (1953) and Don Chaffey's *The Man Upstairs* (1958); while at the bottom end of the 'B' production hierarchy were studios such as Merton Park ('Terrible! [It] was a small house and in the garden was an old bus garage with great pillars up the middle, so all your sets had to be hinged to fit around the pillars!' recalled Peter Graham Scott)[7] where facilities were strictly limited to match the budgets. It seems that, if 'B' films were made in unwanted corners, either spatially or in terms of scheduling (just before Christmas, for example), at larger studios such as Pinewood of Twickenham, at both of which Comfort often worked, there was the chance for an ingenious director to make use of superior sets,[8] costumes and properties and thus to make second features or co-features with some of the physical gloss of 'A' film-making.

Second features were usually between fifty-five and sixty-five minutes in length, were shot in two to three weeks, and, according to several sources, cost between about £12,000 and £20,000.[9] According to Tempean producer, Robert S. Baker, 'The actors would have been the most expensive component, and then studio costs'.[10] This was borne out by director Francis Searle ('artistes would be the main item') who went on to distinguish between co-features and second features: 'It would have been a bit of all three [length, budget, billing]. 'A co-feature would have a bigger concept, a bigger budget (not much bigger!), be more ambitious and in all probability have a star of some sort, usually one from America ... Having an American star was the bankable part.'[11] The co-feature would cost upwards of £20,000, Searle recalls. The billing was perhaps the most clearcut means of distinguishing between these two levels (there was a still 'lower' one which consisted of half-hour features): whereas co-features would share the billing on a fifty-fifty basis, the second feature would be lucky to get twenty per cent of the billing space in newspapers, magazine ads, or outside theatres. In the pages of the British fan magazine, *Picturegoer*, one finds Universal being commended for the 'shrewd planning'[12] that packaged two middle-range 'A's as co-features (*Johnny Dark* and *Tanganyika*, a racing melodrama and an African adventure respectively), with stars (Tony Curtis and Van Heflin) to appeal across a wide age range. Most British 'B' films did not look like even modest 'A's, though a couple of Lance Comfort's do fall within this description. It was more common, drawing again on *Picturegoer*, to find much more characteristic British double-bills advertised. In the advertisement for *The Seekers* (Ken Annakin, 1954) and *Delayed Action* (John Harlow, 1954),[13] for example, it is made plain that the supporting film, given ten-to-twenty per cent of the space, is a clear 'B' film, a second feature, not one of a pair of lesser 'A' films.

The returns from 'B' films were strictly limited. In terms of economic capital, they were usually sold to exhibitors for a flat fee, so that, however good the film might prove to be, its makers were not likely to earn any more for their work. Essentially, the 'B' film fulfilled an industrial function (that is, filling the bottom half of the double bill) as long as the demand was there, and for which it was modestly rewarded. However, director Michael Winner, who made several 'B's before graduating to main features, recalls them as 'very commercially viable ... they not only got their rental from the cinemas, but they also got a bigger share of the Eady fund[14] ... they were an industry – a wonderful training ground'.[15] Their value as a 'training ground' obviously depended on what stage of his career the director was at; for a number, as has been suggested, they represented a descent from bigger things. As to symbolic capital, the pickings were likely to be slim. Asked about the critical coverage such films received, Robert Baker said: 'You'd get it from the trade magazines like *Cinema* and *Kinematograph Weekly* which would review all the pictures made; the exhibitors would look at the reviews and tend to favour the good reviews when they were booking second features.'[16] The only other notices that 'B' films could expect were in the fan magazines, *Picturegoer* and *Picture Show*, and a characteristically snooty line or two in the *Monthly Film Bulletin*. The daily and Sunday paper reviewers never reviewed them, nor would journals such as *Sight and Sound*. Even allowing for a more democratic approach to film culture in the last two decades, it is still noticeable how little attention they have attracted. If you had made a name in 'A' films as Lance Comfort had done, you must have felt yourself in a changed cultural climate – that is, if you had time to notice such things, as Comfort may not have. From 1951 until 1965, the year before his death, he made twenty films as director (and sometimes as producer), several more as producer only, and dozens of television half-hour films.

While the 'A' picture was devoting itself to war films, Technic-oloured comedies set in the Home Counties and outpost-of-empire adventures, in none of which genres is it easy to imagine Comfort's dark talent being seen at its best, some of those directors responsible for the melodramatic panache of the 1940s were forced to look elsewhere. The field of cultural production as it affected British film-making and Comfort in particular had changed radically in the 1950s, but he seems to have had the energy, foresight and proficiency to carve out areas of fruitful activity for himself. Of Comfort's subsequent directorial output, at least half are co-features by virtue of length, stars, budget or billing, or of a combination of one or more of these factors. In genre terms, most of Comfort's supporting films are crime stories of one kind or other, often with a strong melodramatic flourish, but he also made a couple of cheerful minor musicals (*Live It Up*, 1963 and *Be My Guest*, 1965) and two comedies (*The Ugly Duckling*, 1959 and *Make Mine a Million*, 1959). The co-features also include a drama of postwar malaise, a courtroom drama, a kidnap thriller and a Gothic horror piece. If melodrama is the continuing strain through most of Comfort's work, it needs to be said that he was able to ring changes on it and that he was, in addition, proficient across a range of genres, with an eye to what was acceptable to distributors and exhibitors.

In adapting himself to the demands of 'B' film production, Comfort continued to surround himself with recurring collaborators, whose presence perhaps helps to account for the efficiency of many of these films, both in production and as purveyors of genre entertainment. He was no longer under contract to a studio – he had this luxury/bondage only for a few years with RKO-British in the early 1940s – so it seems likely that this kind of community of personnel was important to him. Among the production companies for which he worked in this latter part of his career, he made three films for Butcher's Film Service and five for Blakeley's Films. These were not prestige names in British film production, any more than was the Mancunian Film Corporation, which distributed five of the 1960s films, but they had offered a guarantee of financial backing and of the films actually being seen. Tom Blakeley was, by several accounts,[17] not a creative producer, but rather one with an eye to making one pound do the work of two; however, some of the other names associated with Comfort in these films made real contributions to the creative side of production. These included screenwriter Lyn Fairhurst (four films), cinematographer Basil Emmott (ten), editors John Trumper (seven) and Peter Pitt (five), and production designer John Earl (eight), as well as actors such as Derek Farr (four), David Hemmings, Veronica Hurst (three each), Christina Gregg, William Sylvester, Nanette Newman and William Lucas (two each). Comfort tended to surround himself with familiar personnel in the way that a contract director in a differently organised field might once have had access to the studio's roster.

It is no longer a matter of importance whether a film was regarded as a second feature or a co-feature, but it no doubt mattered at the time when budgets and schedules and distribution deals were being set up, and in consequence it will have influenced the quality of the production values or the status of the stars who

could be hired. Of the twenty films Comfort directed in the 1950s
and 1960s, nine are, on one or more grounds, certifiably co-
features. In regard to length, nine run for 80 or more minutes: *Eight
O'Clock Walk* (1954) and *Devils of Darkness*[18] (1964) are, arguably,
minor 'A's; others such as *Bang! You're Dead* (1954), *Tomorrow at
Ten* (1962) and *Be My Guest* (1965) would have been assigned fifty
per-cent of the advertising for the double bills on which they
appeared. It is now hard to find precise evidence for this, other
than the recollections of those who were associated with the
productions or in display advertisements in such magazines as
Picturegoer. The latter also divided its review section into 'Main'
and 'Double Bill', adjusting its length of review in line with this
distinction of status: it lists *Eight O'Clock Walk* (87 minutes) as
'Main',[19] though elsewhere[20] one reads of its being double-billed
with *Devil On Horseback* (1954), which runs for 88 minutes, but
which *Picturegoer* lists as 'Double Bill'.[21] Clearly there is more at
stake here than just length, but with Richard Attenborough
starring in the former and Googie Withers and John McCallum in
Devil on Horseback, star power was about even; the latter was,
however, made for Group 3, the avowed intention of which was to
make superior supporting films.[22] *Bang! You're Dead* (88 minutes),
reviewed under *Picturegoer*'s 'Double Bill' heading, appears to
have provided the bottom half of a double bill with *An Inspector
Calls* (1954), though the latter ran only 79 minutes. One can only
speculate that Alastair Sim, star of the latter, was considered a
bigger draw than even popular Jack Warner, star of the Comfort
film, or perhaps it had to do with the cachet attaching to Priestley's
name as author of the original play. Star drawing-power, then as
now, was an important factor in the cinematic equation, and a
number of Comfort's 'B' films make use of reliable stars not quite
of the first magnitude but still names widely known. These include
Derek Farr who appeared in *Bang! You're Dead*, *Eight O'Clock
Walk* and *The Man in the Road*, co-starring with US 1940s favourite,
Ella Raines. Arthur Askey (plus a number of 'guest stars') was the
recognizable name on *Make Mine a Million*; William Sylvester,
who had starred in a mixture of 'A's and 'B's, appeared in *Blind
Corner* and *Devils of Darkness*; and John Gregson (a major star of

the 1950s) and the fast-rising Robert Shaw starred in *Tomorrow at Ten*. Comfort made excellent use of second-string stars and such character players as William Hartnell and Renee Houston (in *Tomorrow at Ten*) and Donald Wolfit and Cyril Cusack (in *The Man in the Road*) to give a texture of character, especially – but not only – in his co-features. There are excellent performers such as Kenneth Griffith (in *Rag Doll, The Painted Smile*) and William Lucas (in *Touch of Death*) in what are, in terms of length and production values, clearly second features. Several of these twenty films have been unavailable for this study: the comedy, *The Ugly Duckling* (1959, 84 minutes); two thrillers *A Face in the Night* (1957) and *At the Stroke of Nine* (1957), both with stronger-than-usual 'B' film leads, Stephen Murray and Griffith Jones respectively, and both running for over 70 minutes so that their status as 'B' films is not quite clear, and the second feature, *The Girl on the Pier* (1953, 65 minutes).

It is not my intention to discuss all the 'B' features one by one, but to group them in ways which may suggest the sorts of qualities Comfort brought to them. The first group consists of the half-dozen minor thrillers, minor in the sense of being short and of not having lavish production values or major stars; the second comprises the comedies and musicals which reflect less Comfort's own tastes than an urge to meet a market demand; and third the solid achievement of the more varied co-features in which some of Comfort's most incisive work is to be found. Though this is not intended as an *auteur* study so much as an attempt to trace a career trajectory (and a symptomatic one at that) against the background of a changing industry, certain recurring stylistic and thematic preoccupations do emerge even in these straitened circumstances that point to an individual creative talent.

Short and snappy: second-feature thrillers

Of the minor thrillers, those obviously aspiring to no more than second-feature status for one or more of the reasons suggested above, probably the most efficient is *Touch of Death* (1962). It is also a good illustration of the ways in which Comfort was able to bring a touch of individuality to a workaday project: it is fast-moving, setting up its basic plot with no waste time; it complicates this plot in ways which give it a greater sense of reality than is usual at this level of film-making; it does not shy away from the enjoyable excesses of melodrama; it imbues its characters with enough sense of motivation and individuality to avoid the merely formulaic; and it makes excellent use of locations.

The film opens on a fast forward-tracking shot from the point of view of a car speeding along suburban streets until it pulls into a garage, where petrol pump attendant Len (David Sumner) tells the driver Pete (William Lucas) and his accomplice Nick (Thomas Kyflin) that plans have changed and that they must steal the £17,000 in the garage safe now, as it won't be left there overnight. They knock out the middle-aged mechanic Fred, blow open the safe (tension tightened by the arrival of a customer) and Pete and Len drive off, while Nick is knocked over by a passing lorry and killed. All this is executed swiftly and for maximum suspense, in plain but tightly controlled film-making, with some moments of sharp surprise, as, for instance, when Fred comes to consciousness just in time to grab Nick as he is about to run off. It is an admirable opening sequence which recalls Vernon Sewell's fine thriller, *Strongroom*, in the same year, which begins with the arrival of three thugs at a bank. The reactions of Pete and Len to Nick's death are used to distinguish the experienced criminal from the nervous neophyte, and this distinction (very well developed in Lyn Fairhurst's screenplay and the clearly differentiated performances and physical types of Lucas and Sumner) will have a bearing on what follows.

The robbery scenario then undergoes some texturally enriching complications. First, Inspector Maxwell (Ray Barrett), leading the police investigation, which proceeds in alternation with the escape of the thieves, learns that the notes have been contaminated by potassium cyanide. This had been left in the safe by a medical researcher after his car had crashed, and the effect is to expose anyone who touches the notes to the gravest danger. (In this matter, the film has echoes of those thrillers where disease-bearing persons unwittingly threaten whole communities, such as *Panic in the Streets* 1950, *The Killer Who Stalked New York*, 1950, *80,000 Suspects*, 1963, and *Outbreak*, 1995.) Second, the garage owner, Baxter (Geoffrey Denton), is involved in some undefined way with the large sum of money in the safe, and when his wife (Mary Jones) urges him to go to the police and 'tell them everything', he replies that 'Everything in the safe was destroyed', implying that there had been evidence there that might have implicated him. (The *Daily Cinema* reviewer was right to draw attention to how this thread of plot remains undeveloped, possibly the result of 'its modest footage'.)[23] Third, the confused young Len seriously injures his leg when he rescues a small child from the river at a campsite they stop at as they flee the city. His greater vulnerability is signified by this episode as well as his reaction to later developments, such as when he hears on the radio that Nick is dead. Fourth, the two men board a houseboat tied up on the river and hold hostage the attractive young woman, Jackie (Jan Waters), who owns it and is trying to sell it. Again, Len urges gentler treatment of her than Pete is prepared to consider. The film then takes on an element of the woman-in-peril thriller genre, and this is intensified when Pam (Roberta Tovey), the young daughter of the local boathouse keeper, brings Jackie a message, and Pete refuses to let her leave. Running alongside these plot threads is the police investigation itself, conducted by Inspector Maxwell (a typically authoritative sketch from Ray Barrett).

So, it is a busy little film which moves briskly towards a climax on the river when Pete falls to his death from the platform above a weir, the contaminated notes floating on the water, the swirling current and Johnny Douglas's highly charged music coming up on the soundtrack reminding the viewer that Lance Comfort was not a director to shrink from the full panoply of melodramatic effect. He has controlled tension throughout in a series of economically written and trimly edited sequences: for example, in two instances when Jackie's intentions are foiled, first in a close-up of her preparing hot soup in the boat's galley with a view to hurling it at Pete, and second in the boathouse where, following Pete's instructions, she is taking a phone call from her boyfriend and is trying to scrawl a message for help. Both these moments are well directed for tension which snaps when Pete intervenes. The tension related to the spread of the contaminated notes grows through the police difficulties in getting the truth from Baxter, from their unwillingness to make a public announcement because this will lead the criminals to get rid of the notes. The camera watches intently as the notes claim their first known victim, Jack (Lane Meddick), the boathouse keeper, when Pete buys petrol with the money to escape in the boat. Minutes later his wife calls Jack from the balcony of their house and the camera cuts to him lying unconscious below. Such moments are handled with unfussy effectiveness.

The whole film is strengthened by the relationships between the hardened Pete and the callow Len and between Len and Jackie. In her own interests, Jackie seeks to undermine Len's reliance on Pete, but she also comes to recognise his gentler instincts and he to value her spirited resistance in the face of danger. One does not want to make unsustainable claims for what is essentially modest film-making but the care that has been taken in such matters lifts *Touch of Death* well out of the 'B' movie rut. The review in *Films and Filming* is right to say 'the characters and their relationships are developed to an unusually convincing degree',[24] adding 'These are clichéd figures, perhaps, but sharp-edged portrayals give them here depth and authenticity.' Comfort's characteristic use of locations is another key element in the film's sense of authenticity. He makes sharply observed use of the garage, a supermarket, a gym, a rural campsite, the houseboat and the boathouse and the river generally, so that the film avoids that stultifying, studio-bound look of many British second features. *Kinematograph Weekly* noted that 'the backgrounds are realistic';[25] *The Daily Cinema* wrote: 'the riverside setting is deftly used to add to the tension';[26] and *Films and Filming* praised 'A great deal of location work which forestalls the "B" film's major hazard, the cardboard studio set.'[27] As matters of fact, the film was made at Twickenham and the river settings and the weir were filmed at nearby Teddington on the Thames, as recalled by both star, William Lucas, and screenwriter, Lyn Fairhurst.[28] Comfort in this period of his career was not able to afford distant locations, but, making the best of what was readily available, he clearly liked to get his films out of the studio and into real settings, whether suburban streets or the Thames valley or the quarry near Shepperton Studios where he made *The Break* (1962).

It was fairly unusual for the monthly journal, *Films and Filming*, to review second features, so that the mere fact that *Touch of Death is* noticed there, and at some length, suggests qualities out of the ordinary. Comfort is described as 'one of the few directors whose "B" picture work is worth keeping an eye on' and the review praises 'the director's observation of natural human behaviour'.[29] Even the *Monthly Film Bulletin* commended it: '[It] creates a nice sense of urgency, and the direction, though not particularly original, keeps the action going at a lively pace',[30] praising the characterisation of 'this able little second feature'. It must have been a rare reward for a director working in this part of the field to have had noticed those touches that make a difference between threadbare perfunctoriness and a real 'feeling for the game'.

If none of the others of this half-dozen minor pieces is as compelling as *Touch of Death*, they are generally well above the level of 'B' film production. Structurally, the other five in this group – *The Man from Tangier, The Breaking Point, Rag Doll, The Pit of Darkness* and *The Painted Smile* – have in common a protagonist who, for reasons of naivety or other sorts of disadvantage, is made vulnerable to criminal intentions. In *The Man from Tangier*, US actor Robert Hutton (well past his minor Hollywood stardom of the mid-1940s) plays Chuck Collins, a film stunt man who inadvertently becomes involved in a passport-forging racket when, in a barber's shop, he mistakenly takes an overcoat belonging to Armstrong, one of the crooks. The complications mount when Armstrong is hurled from a hotel window and Collins meets the attractive Michele (Lisa Gastoni, who made several films with Comfort). In Hutton's relaxed performance, Chuck is clearly just a nice guy entangled in circumstances that are none of his making. *The Breaking Point* opens with a young man, Eric Winlatter (Peter Reynolds), arriving for work at his uncle's printing and engraving company in a sleek sports car and several hours late. To the secretary he makes a series of smart-alec remarks about his uncle (Jack Allen) who emerges from his office just in time to hear. Eric is not a likeable character, and Reynolds' slick and shifty persona is neatly used to sketch the sort of second-rate smoothie who always has a cigarette lighter ready for a lady. In trying to finance his luxurious tastes, he quickly gets out of his depth as he engages with a foreign legation which offers him the chance to make money by drawing on his knowledge of his uncle's firm to print money with which to flood the economy of the foreign country. His vulnerability is also fuelled by the extravagance of his wife, Cherry (Joanna Dunham), and he will eventually pay for his naivety with his life. Carol (Christina Gregg), the heroine of *Rag Doll* (1961), a somewhat glum cautionary tale, runs away from her drunken stepfather's (Patrick Magee) roadhouse to London, where she falls in with a dubious café owner, Mort Wilson (Kenneth Griffith), resists his advances but succumbs to the charms of Joe (Jess Conrad), a singer with criminal tendencies. This is a cut-price version of Peter Graham Scott's more ambitious 1963 feature, *Bitter Harvest*, in which a provincial girl falls prey to the allurements of London. The vulnerability of safe-designer Richard Logan (William Franklyn), protagonist of *Pit of Darkness*, derives from the amnesia (a narrative device Comfort had used in his 1956 co-feature, *The Man in the Road*) which has blotted out the events of the three weeks preceding the film's opening scene when he is found unconscious in a bomb-site off Wapping High Street. His situation is made more difficult by the initial disbelief of his wife Julie (Moira Redmond) and the fact that the private investigator she has employed to find him has been murdered. The narrative is thus based on his efforts to gain control over his life. In *The Painted Smile*, three young men, polytechnic graduates, are at a nightclub celebrating the winning of a prize by one of their number, Tom (Tony Wickert), who goes off drunk and euphoric with one of the 'hostesses', Jo (Liz Fraser). As a result, he becomes implicated in the murder of her lover (Peter Reynolds). He is the archetypal nice young man who gets in above his head and in the final frame walks away soberly from the body of Jo who has been shot by the club-footed nightclub owner, Kleinie (Kenneth

Griffith), for whom she has worked.

Chuck, Eric, Carol, Logan and Tom: each of these is catapulted into circumstances perilously beyond their control; and each, even Tom who sails close to the legal wind, is treated sympathetically by director Comfort. As in his major films, his sympathies are for life's victims, even when their own weakness helps to expose them to danger. One recalls Captain Ellis in *Great Day*, Emmy Baudine in *Daughter of Darkness*, Mallinson in *Temptation Harbour*: whatever wrong they do, they are in some sense victims, albeit of their own natures. None of the five in the second features under discussion is characterised in any depth or detail, but they are sufficiently well directed in terms of how they are placed in the frame and in relation to the other characters, and they are well enough acted, for their plight to impel the narrative which hangs on their unwitting descent into a spiral of threatening events. In particular, Tony Wickert, of whom nothing further seems to have been heard, plays Tom in *The Painted Smile* in a way which quite touchingly evokes a decent boy who pays dearly for a momentary indulgence, and his interpretation has the advantage of bouncing off a finely drawn study in tough opportunism from Liz Fraser, who 'proves that she can act as well as wiggle',[31] as one reviewer noted. Christina Gregg, who would star again for Comfort in *The Break*, also manages to imbue the provincial runaway in *Rag Doll* with a certain poignancy, despite an accent that seems wrong by several classes and a script which stretches the possibilities of naivety. Indeed, scattered through these films are performances of easy authority from actors such as Fraser, Kenneth Griffith (twice), Hermione Baddeley as a fake fortune-teller in *Rag Doll* (a film omitted from her autobiography,[32] though she need not be ashamed of it), Jack Allen (the drunk in *The Man from Tangier* and the respectable printer in *The Breaking Point*), and, as the amnesiac Logan, William Franklyn, who remembered Comfort as 'absolutely unpretentious, very gentle ... he'd choose something about you he wanted, and then mine that'.[33] In fact, the *Monthly Film Bulletin* praised Franklyn's performance, declaring him 'unbeatable in suggesting solid virtues behind a rakish, smooth exterior', in a film 'made plausible by effective writing and direction'.[34]

In all of these unremarkable, but not unenjoyable, programme-fillers, which represent the most straitened circumstances in which Comfort as a director for the cinema would work, there are recurring incidental pleasures. On all except *The Man from Tangier* (photographed by veteran Geoffrey Faithfull), the cinematographer was Basil Emmott, whose career stretched back to the late 1920s and included the famous documentary *Drifters* (1929). Emmott was a respected black-and-white cameraman and he gives all four of these films – he also lensed *Touch of Death* among several others for Comfort in the 1960s – a properly moody, *noir*-on-a-shoestring look that serves well their sombre plots and beleaguered protagonists. Comfort always knew when a close-up – a dropped hat in a field or a club foot on the stairs – would act as either narrative shorthand or suspense-tightener, and Emmott's unobtrusive but fluent camera articulated this under-standing acutely. Further, each of these films makes the use noted in the discussion of *Touch of Death* of locations, chosen for verisimilitude, certainly, but also for slightly disorientating effect on a particualar occasion, as in the Wapping bombsite (the child's involvement here in *Pit of Darkness* recalls Comfort's skilful juxtaposition of a young boy and inimical circumstances in the earlier *Bang! You're Dead*), or the use of a large railway terminal ('efficient location work at St Pancras Station', wrote the *Monthly Film Bulletin*)[35] and the chillingly used quarry as the camera pans round its walls in the final moments of *The Painted Smile*. At the end of *Rag Doll*, when Carol is running across a hillside field at night after the wounded Joe, the film dissolves to early morning with a long overhead shot of a village with a church whose bells begin to peal: the effect is one of those ironic pastoral touches found in such 'A' films as *Great Day* and *The Silent Dust*, in which the pastoral serenity of setting seems to mock the reality of human strife. These are journeyman films but Comfort always moves them along through exposition and development to dénouement with a no-nonsense speed that carries them over some desultory plotting and meagre motivation. Above all, his feeling for the gratifications of melodrama and his old visual perspicuity keep them fresher than most at this level of British film-making.

Sturdy co-features

The most unusual of Comfort's co-features is *Bang! You're Dead*, the title[36] of which is taken from a record played constantly by a simple-minded boy Willy (Sean Barrett) on a gramophone he has salvaged from a former wartime US army base in Southern England. This is a strange film in several ways, above all in its setting. The widowed Perce Bonsell (Jack Warner) and his small son Cliff (Anthony Richmond) live in one of several abandoned Nissen huts in what has become a sort of shanty town after the Americans have left. The men mostly work as woodsmen in the neighbouring forest, resorting for leisure to a distinctly uncosy pub. The film gives the impression of looking at the underside of English society, not criminal but just bleak, and once again Comfort uses the pastoral beauty of trees and sky to comment on the drabness of the human lives involved. Whereas, say, Anthony Asquith's beautiful, elegiac *The Way to the Stars* (1945) pays tribute to the US presence during the war, this film takes a clear-eyed look at the detritus left in its wake. Almost all the reviews of the film commented on its unique location: 'Backgrounds of secluded country community and surrounding woods are agreeably fresh';[37] 'The atmosphere of a squatters' colony is finely sustained throughout';[38] 'The background to the picture will be completely unfamiliar to most cinemagoers but is, I am assured quite authentic';[39] and another writes of 'the paint-fresh use it makes of a background most directors wouldn't look at twice ... And all the time the breathless, heavy summer feeling, hangs over the squalid oasis among the trees.'[40] Only the *Monthly Film Bulletin* cavilled about this aspect of the film, saying that 'the woodland settings might have been employed to better account',[41] without glossing this criticism in any way. As a result of the collaboration of cinematographer Brendan Stafford's oddly sultry lighting and Norman Arnold's uncompromising art direction which does nothing to prettify the makeshift community, Comfort ensures that the film *looks* genuinely strange, the works of nature and those of man in uneasy contrast. The social setting is as unusual in British cinema as the physical setting: one reviewer described it as depicting 'an England left untidy in the aftermath of war',[42] in ways which will become apparent.

The film is unusually structured too. Its opening recalls what has been said of Emeric Pressburger's approach to his screen-plays: 'The beginnings were like little films in themselves, which drew the audience into the story and gave them clues as to what was to come.'[43] It opens, as a number of Comfort's 1950s films do, with a pre-credits sequence, a practice maybe legitimated at the time by the Hollywood film, *The Desert Fox* (1951), when it was much praised, and used by Comfort in *The Man in the Road, The Break, Be My Guest* and *Devils of Darkness*, as well as in *Bang! You're Dead*. In the latter's opening sequence, the camera pans the woodland, picks out a small boy who 'holds up' a man on a bicycle, Ben Jones (Philip Saville),[44] and takes his watch, then tilts up to the branches of trees, before returning to the ground where the bicycle wheel is spinning and the man is lying beside it. Through-out this sequence, the title song is heard and the singing (by Edmund Hockridge) proves to be diegetic as the camera reveals the gramophone record turning. This is a very astutely handled, enigmatic start, leaving the audience to wonder if the boy has killed the man and alerting it to the literalness of the child's under-standing of the world – and the song's insistent words. Then, some time into the film, after Jones has fought with fellow forester Bob Carter (Michael Medwin) over the favours of barmaid Hilda (Veronica Hurst), Jones comes cycling down the woodland path and meets Cliff who shoots him with the loaded revolver he has found in a derelict American army hut. This time, Bob rides by, stops and picks up the revolver, while the title song reiterates its inane lyric and the camera executes the same movement as that in the pre-credit sequence. The film now becomes a murder investigation piece as Detective Grey (Derek Farr) arrests Bob. Ironically, Perce Bonsell, not knowing his son's involvement, says, 'When they lay their hands on Ben's watch, they'll know who did it.' In hindsight, the pre-credits sequence takes on the function of precursor and warning in relation to the main action of the film, and also confers on the film a curiously reflective tone, forcing the viewer to consider what this tragic circumstance means in terms of the child's view of the world. The *Variety* reviewer wrote that 'The gradual tracking down by the police and the terror of the hunted boy is tensely unreeled',[45] and that is true enough, but the real fascination of the film is in the discrepancy between the ways in which the child and the adults view the world. For the child, Ben Jones' death is a game which, in some dreadful way, has gone wrong; for the adults, it is a criminal matter in which another man's life, Bob Carter's, is now imperilled. The investigation is conducted with a low-key conviction: 'For once in a while here is a film which presents an authentic true-to-life police officer', said one reviewer,[46] and Derek Farr plays him with easy conviction and no hint of patronage for either lower orders or children. However, the main interest is in Cliff's reactions to the chain of events his playful act has set off. Comfort's recurring interest in obsessive protagonists is in evidence again in the two boys: the slow-witted, older boy with his record, the younger one's liking for synchronising its title words to actions. (There is an echo of *Of Mice and Men* in this relationship between the perky little boy and the slow older one.) The pre-credits sequence, set against sunny skies, assumes then the role of grim warning of what such obsessions among semi-neglected children might lead to. Seen this way, one is not likely to accept one reviewer's opinion that 'it seems unnecessary to give the climax before the credit titles'.[47]

In the event, the actual investigation assumes the status of background to matters of greater thematic interest. 'Nothing's right around here since we lost your Mum', says Perce Bonsell, echoing Mallinson's sense of loss in *Temptation Harbour*, and placing too much responsibility on a child (again like Mallinson). With Comfort's characteristic lack of sentimentality, he undermines the kindly persona associated with Jack Warner, so that Perce Bonsell's affection for his son, though undoubted, is also negligent. Not only does he talk carelessly, as does the pubkeeper (Gordon Harker), about 'that Ben Jones always running after what's not his' and 'That kinda man's no good to nobody', but he also comes home to their Nissen shack more than a little drunk, so that the child (as in *Temptation Harbour*) seems almost to 'parent' the father, just as he parents a stray cat, whose kittens he has been forced to surrender. The postwar climate has lost all euphoria by now and the society represented looks distinctly shabby. The pubkeeper talks critically about people working fiddles as he grabs a poached bird from a local who makes a living from such theft. Bob Carter is another postwar casualty: *his* parents have 'cleared off' and Jones appears to have got a job during the war which should have gone to a local like Bob. The slow-witted Willy is also parentless and is looked after in the neighbouring Nissen hut by his hard-working grandma (Beatrice Varley, of course). When Grey finally learns the truth about Jones's death, Perce says, 'It's me to blame', but Grey corrects him with: 'We might as well start with the GI who left the gun lying around or the bomb or the war that smashed up so many lives'. It is a sober resonance to find in what is after all a modest film. The film ends sombrely as Perce picks up his exhausted son and carries him home, with Grey's final words ringing in his ears: 'Do what all parents should do – look after him.' On the soundtrack in a minor key is 'Greensleeves', a traditional air associated with an older, very different England, dating back at least to Shakespeare's time.

Bang! You're Dead is one of the most visually rewarding of Comfort's post-1950 films. He uses closeup and editing to very tense effect in a scene on the boys' tiny wooded island, where he cuts between Cliff's agitated face and the incessantly-playing record, finally releasing his fear in smashing the disc. But the film's most striking episode is the search for the terrified Cliff, who fears he will be blamed for the death not of Jones but of his friend Willy, who has fallen from a tree. It is shot with a near-lyrical quality in a long sequence without dialogue, with a melancholy undertow to the soundtrack, as the camera picks out the child secretly observing those who are searching for him, crossing a railway track just in front of a passing train, and finally climbing to shelter through a hole in the roof of an unused hut. Comfort's control of visual narration is finely in evidence here as he alternates between the child's terror and exhaustion and the rallying and conduct of the search party, creating a montage of mounting anxiety since we know the ending cannot, in any circumstances, be a conventionally happy one. It would have been easy merely to make this sequence the melodramatic climax of the story's events, but Comfort imbues it as well with a strong sense of the differences between adult and child's ways of seeing the world. Again, one wonders what the *Monthly Film Bulletin* had in mind, when it wrote of this sequence: 'Scenes such as Cliff's flight through the woods appear to be used to win sympathy from the audience by emphasising the child's terror, and, where the story is as contrived as it is here, the effect is slightly unpleasant.'[48] Such perfunctory, unsubstantiated dismissiveness is typical of the kind of critical desuetude with which most 'B' films had to contend, though for the most part *Bang! You're Dead* attracted more critical attention than most, perhaps an indicator of its unusual qualities.

The film has, of course, a melodramatic story but its peculiar richness resides in its frightening conflation of play and reality. It was probably too unusual to be very popular, though it garnered some good notices, despite some qualifications. The *Sunday Express* concluded its notice with: 'From this naive-sounding excursion into child psychology, director Lance Comfort has rescued a sometimes thrilling, sometimes intensely moving film which stings with sincerity and has more than the usual share of magic.'[49] *Variety* commended 'the production [as] directed with equal sense of drama and pathos.'[50] Another reviewer wrote: 'Director Lance Comfort has, with great imagination, not only succeeded in putting across a first-class piece of child psychology, but compiled a pretty brisk and shrewd picture of an adult postwar generation and their influences on the young.'[51] Elsewhere, there was attention to the film's cautionary element: '[It] warns parents of the danger of casual talk in front of youngsters';[52] 'The film is a plea for parents to try to understand the often misguided interpretation children make of their elders' careless conversations and to give more thought to the importance of a child's training.'[53] There is an element of moralising in such comments but they nevertheless help to define a hybrid genre: part thriller, part love story, part family problem drama, with traces of *film noir*'s visual style. It is not an exercise in sheer tension as the somewhat similar US 'sleeper', Ted Tetzlaff's *The Window* (1948), was. It is by turns leisurely and reflective; an exercise in unsettling pastoral in which the woodland has been invaded (as Hardy, fifty years earlier, knew it would be) by forces inimical to its quiet beauties; an evocative study in postwar malaise, suggesting a world grown tired and shabby; a haunting study in child terror; and a murder story to which we have always known the answer – but not how this could be dealt with. Without wanting to make too much of what is essentially an unassuming piece of work, it is no hyperbole to describe it as one of the most individual films of the early 1950s – at any level of production.

None of the other co-features is quite so distinctive or quite so difficult to categorise, but several offer real rewards. Perhaps best of all is the 1962 kidnap thriller, *Tomorrow at Ten*, made at the MGM studios, Borehamwood, which displays Comfort's narrative skills at their tautest, though it was thrown away as support to the box-office draw, *Hud*, and, according to film historian Allen Eyles was not shown to the press.[54] This suggests a lack of clout on the part of its recently formed (minor) distributor, Planet, or maybe a failure to recognise the film's unpretentious merits. Like so many of Comfort's later films, it begins with an excellent, teasing pre-credits sequence. A car pulls into the drive of a large house; a solidly-built man gets out and lets himself in. The house is large and quite grandiose but empty and derelict. The man, Marlow (Robert Shaw), goes to the topmost room which is set up as a sort of bedsitter, where he unpacks milk and food, then unwraps a gollywog[55] as he sings 'Pop Goes the Weasel', pausing over the line, 'That's the way the money goes'. He then slits the doll open at the back, pulls out the wadding and puts in an explosive device as he whistles, and then re-sews the doll and props it up on what is obviously a child's bed. At this point the credits begin, to the accompaniment of Bernie Fenton's ominous score. All this is economically and enigmatically done, with a striking close-up of Marlow's eyes, a shot that recalls how Comfort had filmed Nigel Patrick in *The Silent Dust* as the returned deserter skulking in his father's house. From here the film cuts to another, more imposing house in Hampstead with a small boy, Jonathan (Piers Bishop) playing with his city-gent father, Chester (Alec Clunes), just as the driver arrives to take him to school. The nanny, Robbie (Helen

Cherry), is briefly disconcerted to see that it is not Tom, the usual driver, but not as apprehensive as the audience who recognise his replacement as the man with the golliwog in the opening sequence. In a series of shots very unsettling because of the way they play on the child's trust, Marlow now drives Jonathan to the earlier house, phones Chester and demands £50,000 in return for the child's safety, while Jonathan clutches the golliwog. Marlow locks him in and leaves the house, turning for a striking low-angle shot of the top window which stresses the child's dangerous isolation.

After these very tensely executed opening sequences, the film's narrative proceeds by a series of well-timed twists in Peter Miller and James Kelly's screenplay. Marlow explains the situation to Chester, warning against calling the police, but Robbie phones them and the drama changes course when Inspector Parnell (John Gregson) arrives at Chester's home. He refuses to allow Chester to pay the money, because he believes in the law and believes he can break Marlow down. He has been shown doing just that with a small-time crook, Smiley (Harry Fowler), in an inserted sequence, the only function of which is to establish Parnell's tenacity and psychological acuity. In a crisp visual alternation between them, Parnell is on the verge of breaking Marlow's resolve, when Chester re-enters and pulls rank and class by over-riding Parnell and calling his friend, Chief Inspector Bewly (Alan Wheatley), an arrogant social-climber from Scotland Yard, who succumbs to influential pressure. The most crucial turn of the plot takes place when Chester knocks Marlow down; he suffers a serious concussion and dies in hospital before regaining consciousness – and before revealing the child's location. The film then becomes a race against time, until, in 'a tremendously exciting twist ending',[56] the child actually and unwittingly saves himself just before ten o'clock the next morning.

After the death of Marlow the screenplay becomes more routine,[57] until the final moments, including the suave Bewly's appropriation of credit and photo opportunities with the rescued child. Tension has been admirably maintained through cross-cutting which links the imperilled child with the adults who are dicing with his life. There are two long dialogue sequences – first, between Chester and Marlow, then between Marlow and Parnell, when the latter is trying to find the source of Marlow's psychological disorder – but these are well enough written to avoid the debilitating static talkiness of so many poor British 'B' films. They are also so admirably acted, especially by Robert Shaw, whose flat, affectless tones contrast with Clunes's upper-class accent and with Gregson's quiet, insistent probing, as not to drag. The action is furthered through the class and temperamental clashes among the men. The psychological underpinning of Marlow's behaviour, rooted in an unsatisfactory relationship with his mother, is simple stuff but it serves its function. This is, after all, a thriller, not a family melodrama, and Comfort compels attention to the way Marlow is transfixed by a portrait of the child's mother, as he talks about his own careless mother who once gave him a gollywog. There are echoes here of those earlier Comfort films, *Bedelia* and *The Silent Dust* in which an obsessive personality, which Marlow is, is signified by a portrait, and there is an astute cut between Marlow's eyes and those of the woman in the portrait. As well as the writing and acting in these sequences, the camerawork, without being fussy, makes use of some unusual angles to articulate further the conflict of wills between Parnell and Marlow.

The main function of *Tomorrow at Ten* is to 'put the audience through it' in Hitchcock's famous statement of his intentions, and it does so with the utmost efficiency. However, it is worth reflecting on what makes it so superior an example of British 'B'-film-making. Above all, it starts with a screenplay that has more in mind than merely a series of events, understanding that to put the audience through it involves more than this. It characterises its key figures sufficiently in terms of motivation and class and temperament to ensure a level of concern beyond that of the conventional 'B' thriller. An example of this is the way in which Parnell is allowed to make his point about how the law functions and how to give in to Marlow's demands would be to undermine this without even guaranteeing the safety of the child. What if, he puts to Chester, you pay Marlow the £50,000 and he flies to Rio De Janiero, but his plane is delayed or crashes before he can phone you to reveal the child's location? It's not just that there is a point to be made here, but also that it anticipates the film's major turn of the screw when Marlow does in fact die before giving the crucial information. Further, Parnell is not interested in suppressing a crime just because the wealthy, patrician Chester wants him to and can afford to meet Marlow's demands. Parnell's professional life, including his relationships with his superior Bewly, for whom he has ill-disguised contempt, and with Grey, his younger sidekick, is created in enough detail to provide a context for his handling of the present crisis; and, in two brief inserts, his home life, in a pleasant ordinary suburb, is sufficiently glimpsed to allow the audience to see him as an individual, not just a cog in the narrative wheel. As for Marlow and Chester, it is suggested above how the contours of their characters are filled out to a degree unusual in co-feature production.

The usual virtues of Comfort's films are in evidence here too: the sense of place, whether derived from location work or from sets, is securely established as the film moves among several houses, the streets in which life goes on mundanely as if there were no crisis afoot, the hospital where Marlow lies in a coma, and the police station where the sheer tedium of much of the work is sharply suggested. (In passing, one notes that the police hierarchy is much less benignly presented than it was over a decade earlier in *The Blue Lamp*, 1950.) As well, the editing, rightly seen as crucial to the establishing of tension, cuts between Bewly threatening to remove Parnell from the case and the boy, who will suffer from this, heedlessly kicking the gollywog, and later, with time running out, between the police car hurtling through the suburbs and the child washing himself and the gollywog. With John Trumper as his editor and Basil Emmott as his cinematographer, Comfort had on hand two of the major collaborators of his last years, and they serve him exceptionally well, making of *Tomorrow at Ten* a film that thinks its narrative in visual as well as verbal terms.

Critical antennae were apparently so desensitised in regard to possible value among 'B' films that Comfort seems to have had almost no notice for this fine example of the melodramatic thriller genre. *Sight and Sound* of course failed to review it or even to list it in its guide to current films; and it received no critique in the normally more comprehensive and democratically-inclined *Films and Filming*. A year later, the name of Robert Shaw, having made his mark in *From Russia with Love*, might have attracted reviewers; in 1962, the other star, John Gregson, was past his *Genevieve*-induced box-office prime. Such matters may well help to determine how a film is received and perceived. The trade press was moderately pleased with it: '*Tomorrow at Ten* has its moments of routine excitement and was agilely directed by Lance Comfort';[58] *Kinematograph Weekly* praised it comprehensively as a 'Very good British programmer' and 'well above the average quota "double bill"', commending the acting and 'the widely varied interiors and exteriors [which] are finely photographed';[59] while *Film Daily*, praising Shaw's 'particularly outstanding acting job', found the film as a whole 'perfectly suitable for general commercial runs and ... a contribution to any twin bill'.[60] Such comments may have helped ensure the film's distribution, but they scarcely constitute the symbolic capital that might have encouraged a serious film-maker. They were, however, pretty much what a 'B' film director, whether of co-features or supporting films, had to be content with.

Of the remaining co-features, *Eight O'Clock Walk*, is the most up-market in terms of its credentials, possibly a minor 'A' film, according to its exhibition. It is essentially a courtroom drama and would be a tighter film if it concentrated its energies more on its central action. Often, Comfort has shown himself adept at juggling several plotlines in the one film, as he does in *Bang! You're Dead*, but in *Eight O'Clock Walk* the subsidiary actions are too underdeveloped to make a serious impact. The central action involves a newly and happily married young couple, Tom and Jill Manning (Richard Attenborough and Cathy O'Donnell), whose life together is torn apart when Tom is wrongfully accused of killing a little girl. On April Fool's Day she had led him into a bombsite with a tearful tale about her lost doll; when he realises he has been hoaxed, he raises his hand in mock anger, then goes off to work. Circumstantial evidence points to him as the murderer, though the audience has known from the start that someone else, represented only by a menacing shadow which hovers over the little girl at play, is responsible. The same shadow effect recurs at the Old Bailey trial and is finally identified as belonging to one of the witnesses, Clifford (Maurice Denham), who is seen giving sweets to another little girl by Tom's counsel (Derek Farr). The actual mystery is not the film's main interest, though the use of the repeated shadows recalls Comfort's skills of visual narration, and its solution is the result of a lucky coincidence.

However, Comfort narrates this strand of the plot swiftly and unaffectedly, so that it creates and retains its tension. What is particularly effective is the evocation of the processes of justice themselves and the use of the locations and settings in relation to these, conferring an authenticity on the film that its sometimes contrived plotting doesn't achieve. On this matter, the *Monthly Film Bulletin* writes: 'The film's main point of interest is the attempt to build up a convincing picture of the Old Bailey and the legal procedure attending a murder trial.'[61] The *Financial Times* claimed that: 'After the necessary preliminaries which show how an innocent man may find himself in this terrible predicament, the piece settles down into a fairly absorbing Old Bailey trial drama and a consoling demonstration of the clear-sightedness of justice.'[62] The *Sunday Times* praised 'the director and his writers (Guy Morgan and Katherine Strueby) for [having] made effective use of the physical preparations for the trial',[63] and indeed there is some well-judged detail involving cleaners, gallery regulars and laconic attendants swopping racing tips, all of whose detachment is used to heighten the drama as it affects Tom and Jill. This is not courtroom drama on the level of Billy Wilder's *Witness for the Prosecution* (1958), but, lacking Wilder's pyrotechnics, it is in some ways more quietly convincing about its procedures.

There was praise, too, for the realism with which Comfort had represented postwar London life (as there had been for his depiction of postwar rural life in *Bang! You're Dead*): 'It's London streets are truly London, its people are the kind that walk them, its delightful children are the variable and unpredictable fruit of our Welfare State, and its dialogue is right on key.'[64] As a police officer says, 'These derelict bomb sites just ask for trouble'. The film doesn't stress this aspect, but in small touches such as this Comfort places his film in a recognisable society. There is talk about the murdered child's truancy and how common this is in the neigh-bourhood, as if to suggest that control is defective and that children are being inadequately supervised (another echo of *Bang! You're Dead*). Neither Irene, the murdered child, nor Ernie, who is a witness in the trial, appears to have a father (there are two sharp sketches of over-stretched working-class mothers from Eithne Dunne and Grace Arnold): the implication may be of further postwar casualties. The quiet realism with which the film's milieu is sketched carries over into the characterisation of the young lower-middle-class couple, whose aspirations – a home, children, Tom to own his taxi – are convincingly realised in the dialogue and the performances of Attenborough and the US star O'Donnell. And Tom is, too, a victim of war in the sense that, as a pilot, he suffered a head-wound which has caused occasional blackouts, during one of which, the police wonder, did he kill Irene Evans?

While the film sticks to the frightening situation in which the Mannings find themselves, it is compelling enough. However, it goes off at two tangents which partly dissipate the tension. First, there is the situation of the trial judge (Harry Welchman), whose wife is to be operated on for cancer on the morning of the trial during which news comes of her death under the anaesthetic. The screenplay doesn't do enough to establish any kind of interest in him or his situation; the function of this particular side-issue is presumably to stress the ways in which personal problems are not allowed to hinder the processes of justice. The other tangent involves the rival court appearances of Geoffrey Tanner Q. C. (Ian Hunter) and his son, Peter (Farr), who makes his debut in court as the Manning's defence counsel when the barrister appointed for the purpose is unable to appear. These two exchange a number of 'my learned friend' and other conventional legal ripostes in court and go off arm in arm at the end. In fact, the film's last image is of them walking away from the camera. Their camaraderie is in the West End theatre's jocular mode, and the only discernible point of spending time on them is again to suggest the incorruptibility of British justice: whatever their feelings for one another, they are perfectly able to carry out the necessary legal procedures on opposite sides of the case. The relatively stereotyped rendering of these two sets of characters is made more obvious by comparison with the sharper observation of the central action.

With his usual discreetly kinetic style, Comfort moves the camera about streets and corridors, making neat connections, such as that between the shots that signify the child's threatened innocence by the pond and Tom's when the police come to question him at his landlady's home. His style does not draw attention to itself, but there is some adroit editing between the carefree dance attended by Tom and Jill and the police investigation which, unknown to them, is about to blight their innocent pleasure in life. In prison later on, there is a poignantly composed shot of the way the grille separates Jill from Tom, but such moments are not lingered over: they serve their function briefly and the narrative moves on. Comfort rarely made a film without some visual distinction, but this is not one in which the *look* of the film stays powerfully in the mind as it does with, say, *Great Day* or *Bang! You're Dead*. The film's real interest is in the processes of the judicial system and the dangers of circumstantial evidence. Considering the debate that was raging at the time about capital punishment, it is only weakly polemical ('If we're wrong, nothing can bring him back', says one juror). The film is enjoyable co-feature fare, but it is a shade too tidy to excite Comfort's most imaginative efforts.

There are three other co-features which one may class as thrillers, though they are, within that broad generic category, quite distinct from each other. *The Man in the Road* mixes kidnapping, amnesia and Cold War espionage; *The Break* is a moody crime melodrama, centred on an escaped convict; and *Blind Corner* is a melodrama of sexual betrayal. All are structured around major deceptions. While none of these is an especially distinguished film, they are all solidly entertaining examples of their kind: the co-feature designed to fill a market demand, without aspirations to art and yet often as watchable several decades later as some of the more highly touted 'A' films of their period. Often, too, such films are revealing of what was widely acceptable at the time of their production. In matters of sexual candour, for instance, there is a palpable liberalising of mores between the semi-facetious banter of *The Man in the Road* in 1956 and the love-making of either *The Break* or *Blind Corner* in, respectively, 1962 and 1964. Such films were not intended to shock their audiences (not beyond certain clearly defined and acceptable points, at any rate) and thus provide peripheral interest as barometers of social change. In *The Man in the Road*, the hero laid low in hospital and the nurse have this exchange:

> 'You're a wonderful nurse. You've only got to lift your little finger and compound fractures get up and ...'
> 'And what?'
> 'When I'm mobile I'll show you'

This mildly saucy exchange, and a little scene later on, in which the hero watches the open doorway as the heroine changes her clothes and hurls blouse and jodphurs across the gap till they land on the bed, signify what was permissible in what is after all a conventional entertainment in 1956. In the later two films, there are beds which have obviously been used and women in semi-undress. Small points, but the kind which give even much less efficient films than this some socially revealing value.

The Man in the Road depends on a record of Western distrust of the Soviet Union, though not many British films, at co-feature or higher levels of aspiration, took the Cold War threat seriously. Mario Zampi's *Top Secret* (1952; US title: *Mr Potts Goes to Moscow*) and Anthony Asquith's *The Young Lovers* (1955) exploited it for, respectively, comedy and tender tragic romance, but there was not the recurring incidence of Russian villains who became so common in Hollywood films of the late 1940s and the 1950s. A historian might find a congruence between these differential film-making figures and the socio-political reality that was part of their production contexts. *The Man in the Road* is by no means a political film in any overt sense: its political interest lies in the attitudes that it assumes it will find in its audiences. Scientist James Paxton (Derek Farr) is kidnapped on a country road at night and wakes to find himself in a private nursing home presided over by Professor Cattrell (Donald Wolfit), one of those suavely cultured types who are invariably up to no good in British 'B' films. Paxton is suffering from a range of injuries and from amnesia,[65] and Cattrell has manufactured a new identity for him as 'Ivan Mason', an accountant who had been planning to visit Moscow to see his seriously ill mother. Of course it is his services as a scientist that the Russians are after, and the villains – Cattrell, the entire staff of the nursing home and Dmitri Balinkev (Karel Stepanek, all-purpose foreign villain in British films for thirty years) – plan that he will not return to Britain. A young American woman, Rhona Ellison, who writes crime stories pluckily joins cause with him and the police round up the conspirators at the end – except for the Russian who falls from a helicopter. This is no more than a thriller with a romantic interest, with a faded American star (Ella Raines, in her last film) to help with US distribution.[66] It was perceived by reviewers as proficient popular fare: 'it is all done with some gusto and played with appropriate seriousness';[67] 'A very soundly made and acted quota subject, thoroughly safe double-bill booking anywhere';[68] and 'Good spy thriller for better-half booking in the popular halls'.[69] It is pacy enough to maintain audience attention: experienced screenwriter Guy Morgan[70] varies the tone from sinister to jocular, moves the action from rural settings to the streets of London to the private hospital, and introduces several ambiguous characters. The most notable of the latter are the alcoholic ex-doctor, who, at Cattrell's bidding, has been forced into the conspiracy, and the genteel Mrs Lemming, whom Cattrell has persuaded to pose as Paxton's landlady, two roles vividly filled by Cyril Cusack and Olive Sloane. Careful casting in small roles is as much a recurring feature of Comfort's work as the way in which he refuses to be confined by studio sets. Here, he makes use, as he often does, of areas of London one doesn't often see on the screen (including Mrs Lemming's shabby middle-class Victorian terrace) and of a very unusual rural retreat ('delightfully photographed amid countryside backgrounds')[71] where Rhona gives Paxton sanctuary when he escapes from the private hospital. If, as was commonly held, Lance Comfort at this stage of his career never engaged in distant, expensive location work, it is certainly true to say that he made vivid use of what was near at hand.[72]

The deception which impels the narrative in *The Man in the Road* is that which is practised on Paxton, made to believe he is someone other than his real self. In *The Break*, a party of three people arrives at a Dartmoor farmhouse, nursing secrets/deceptions of various kinds. Before this notably bleak exterior scene, there has been a pre-credits sequence in which a man has leapt from a moving train at night apparently grappling with another man, whom he kills. He is then picked up in a landrover and a close-up reveals him to be wearing handcuffs. Accompanying this brisk, baffling opening, and indeed recurring throughout the film, is a very attractive theme tune (composed by music director Brian Fahey, and 'of no little importance during the more climactic moments'),[73] which continues through the credits. This provides a bridge with the sequence depicting the arrival of Pearson (Robert Urquhart), a jocular bore who is actually a private detective, Greg Parker (Tony Britton), an embittered author, whose wife has engaged Pearson, with divorce in mind, and a young woman Sue (Christina Gregg), who proves to be the sister of the criminal Jacko Thomas (William Lucas) who leapt from the train. She is unwillingly following her brother's instructions in coming to the farmhouse, run as a hotel by Judd Tredgear (Eddie Byrne) and his dissatisfied wife, Jean (Gene Anderson), who are also engaged in a smuggling racket with Jacko. As this cast is assembled – a religious fanatic handiman, Moses (Edwin Richfield), and his devoted mute sister, Sarah (Sonia Dresdel), the cook, complete it – the film assumes the feel of a conventional three-act play of earlier decades, and it retains some of this in the interior scenes in the cosily chintzy farmhouse.

What distinguishes the film is not its somewhat contrived plotting but its exceptionally well-staged action sequences, especially the chase in which the murderous Jacko in the jeep pursues Parker across the moors in the direction of a lime quarry, and the use Comfort makes of a genuinely strange location, which was actually Woking Common, not two miles from Shepperton Studios, where the interiors were shot.[74] Most of the meagre reviews drew attention to this aspect of the film. '[A] first-rate example of what can be done with a well-thought-out script, deft characterisation, full use of available locations and a cast of good players who pull their weight',[75] said the *Daily Cinema* of *The Break*. '[F]ilmed on the British moors',[76] claimed the US *Motion Picture Herald* erroneously. 'Gaunt exteriors heighten key situations, and the dialogue is slick',[77] praised *Kinematograph Weekly*. The other two main action sequences, involving a shoot-out between Moses and Jacko in an outhouse of the farm and the final moments in which Sarah, seeking revenge for Moses's death, shoots Jacko as he is about to kill Parker, are also staged and edited to make the best use of the grim locations. At heart, this is a conventional thriller, but those aspects which lift it well above most of its kind belong to Comfort: his eye for locations and for a camera angle which will both clarify and comment on the action, his speed in getting the narrative under way, and his use of an ensemble of competent actors. In this case, he gets sharply observed performances from William Lucas (so chilling in *Touch of Death*), Eddie Byrne, Christina Gregg (the waif-at-risk in *Rag Doll*), Tony Britton, Gene Anderson and the grim-visaged Sonia Dresdel. None of these was, in 1962, a major player, but Comfort draws on their individualities to give life to some hectically plotted melodramatic action. One trade press reviewer summed up the film with: 'If all second features were as entertaining as this, the top-liners would really have to look to their laurels.'[78]

The message to be drawn from such films, and from *Blind Corner* (made at Pinewood), is that Comfort, even when working in areas of the production field which attracted little prestige criticism, was still able to invest routine assignments with the deftness that had marked his major work – and which separated him from those who had never been involved in more demanding assignments, never been anywhere near the dominant end of the production field. The protagonist of *Blind Corner* is a blind composer of pop music, Paul Gregory (William Sylvester) whose luxury-loving wife, Anne (Barbara Shelley), is deceiving him sexually with his manager, Mike Williams (Mark Eden), and also deceiving her artist lover, Rickie Seldon (Alex Davion), who is no more than a dupe in Mike's and her plan to murder Paul. The other point of the quincunx is Paul's adoring secretary, Joan (Elizabeth Shepherd), who wants him to get on with writing his concerto and will be around to pick up the pieces at the end of a nicely knotty drama of sexual machinations. As co-features go, this is a reasonably compelling piece, with Paul obsessively adoring the faithless Anne, his blindness acting as a signifier of his obsession as it had for Robert Rawley in *The Silent Dust* fourteen years earlier; Paul similarly insists on everything having its exact place in his dark world. The comparison with the earlier film comes to a head when Ricky comes to murder Paul, in anticipation of life with £500,000 and the treacherous Anne, and there is the scuffle with the blind man and the threat of a balcony with a too-low parapet.

There are other echoes of the earlier films too: Anne is a *femme fatale* who shares Bedelia's passion for money and what it can buy (and thereby pressuring Paul into writing cheap music easily); and, as in *Bedelia*, much is made of Anne's portrait being painted by the gullible Ricky as part of a deceitful scheme, as Bedelia's was by Chaney, the insurance investigator posing as an artist. In the sexual passions she arouses in three men, and its dangerous potential, Anne recalls Emmy Baudine in *Daughter of Darkness*. In the portrait of Paul painted after he went blind, and hanging in his plush flat, there are other echoes of *Bedelia* and *The Silent Dust* in which a portrait assumes a watchful, potentially destructive identity (a portrait is used to different effect in *Tomorrow at Ten*). This reference to the 1940s films is apposite because *Blind Corner*, at least in generic terms, harks back to the mode in which Comfort had made his name in 'A' features: that of romantic melodrama with a strong sense of sexual danger and betrayal. The resonance is reinforced too by Brian Fahey's score whose stirring romantic strains are first heard as the camera pans over a night cityscape before the shot dissolves to the interior of the flat. Here the blind composer Paul is playing the piano and is interrrupted by Anne who sets the drama of deceit in motion by borrowing money from Paul, ostensibly for her friend Margot, but actually for her lover Ricky, who is waiting below in her car and to whom she says, 'Let's have dinner on my generous husband.' From this point, the film is in familiar genre territory, the contours of which it fills in with some surprising narrative twists (that Mike is Anne's real object of love is the main one: 'the convulsions of the later sequences and the final twist largely compensate for weaknesses elsewhere',[79] one reviewer grudgingly allowed), a lot of talk (generally quite smart talk in James Kelly and Peter Miller's screenplay, and delivered with some relish by the cast, especially Shelley and Sylvester), and some moments of imaginative visual relish in the cinematography of Comfort's regular collaborator, Basil Emmott. Three such moments come to mind because they are not merely decorative but inherently dramatic in their context. First, there is a sudden, surprising high-angle shot of the courtyard below the apartment, made telling because it represents Anne's point-of-view while she looks reflectively over the shoulder of Paul who is embracing her on the balcony – the glimpse of the courtyard reaffirms her murderous intentions. Second, the moment at which Mike is revealed as Anne's true lover is very astutely shot and framed so as to keep the audience wondering who has come into the cottage and put his hands on her bare shoulders. (Comfort favoured this visual approach to the creation of suspense about matters of identity on other occasions, as in the stealthy ascent of the stairs by the murderous Kenneth Griffith in *The Painted Smile*.) Third, when the hapless Ricky comes to kill Paul, the whole episode is inventively filmed: 'Who is it?' asks Paul seated at the piano as the camera, affecting to be precisely in Ricky's place, glides forward in a manner to underline the threat to the blind man; and there is a very imaginative shot of the whisky decanter and ice bucket on the bar, suddenly highlighted to look like a photographic still life and to stress the semi-drunken state in which Ricky has expected to find Paul. As well as such effects, Comfort wisely realises that Sylvester is a good enough actor to sustain a very long medium close-up as he gives Ricky a verbal flash-forward of what his fate will be when Anne deserts him and puts on her grieving-widow performance in court. As one trade reviewer suggested, 'the improbable yarn is carried off with dash and style';[80] its moments of visual flair lift it well above mere execution of twisty plot; and a more recent commentator has written: 'The transfer of his [Paul's] affections from Barbara Shelley, his selfish, malevolent wife, to Elizabeth Shepherd, his stoically loving secretary, charts a satisfying path from indulgence and obsession to creativity and respect.'[81]

Light and lively

One of the recurring characteristics of Comfort's later films is his use of the popular music of the day, not because he had any special interest in it but because, according to his son and other colleagues,[82] he felt it helped to make co-features more acceptable to wider audiences. In several of his crime melodramas, there is a guest spot for a singer (for example, Ronnie Carroll in *Blind Corner*, Jess Conrad in *Rag Doll* and Ronnie Lovell in *Pit of Darkness*), there is the insistent title song in *Bang! You're Dead*, there are guest stars such as Dennis Lotis in the 1958 comedy *Make Mine a Million*, and there are young people dancing to pop music in the 'Gollywog' bar in *Tomorrow at Ten*. It was perhaps inevitable he would try his hand at the musical genre and the result was two cheerful teen movies, *Live It Up* (1963) and *Be My Guest* (1965).

Preceding them, *Make Mine a Million* has a parade of guest stars, some of whom sing (Denis Lotis, Dickie Henderson, Leonard Weir, Patricia Bredin), some who do not (Evelyn Laye, Tommy Trinder, Raymond Glendenning). This is not a musical, but a broad and often very funny satire on the habits of television, both 'commercial' and 'National' (for which read 'BBC'). Not since *Old Mother Riley Detective* back in 1943 had Comfort tried his hand at fast-moving, unsophisticated comedy, and, just as the earlier film had relied on popular star comedians, Arthur Lucan and Kitty McShane, so this one depends on Arthur Askey and Sidney James. (Recalling the earlier comedy, *Make Mine a Million* also ends by rounding up crooks in a farmyard, and employing a pitch-fork to help do so. Tonally, the two films have a lot in common.) In narrative terms it is structured on the time-honoured theme of the little man triumphing against all odds. In this case, Arthur Ashton (Askey), is the make-up man for National who falls victim to the wiles of Sid Gibson (James) for whose washing powder product, Bonko, Arthur inserts an advertising card during a tasteful National musical programme. In order to bring his products to yet wider audiences, Sid involves Arthur in the televising of Ascot and the Edinburgh Festival, including his making a bespectacled appearance as one of the huntsmen during *Swan Lake*.

To call it satire is to suggest a level of sophistication to which the film does not aspire, but it manages some amusing swipes at both commercial and National television, to both of whom Ashton is a threat: the commercial channel is afraid of his effect on its advertising because of the huge publicity his appearances on National have garnered, while National is appalled at the effect on its cultural image ('It will take three poetry readings and a visit to Glyndebourne to reclaim our audiences', wails its chairman after Arthur's first eruption on to its screen). The film good-naturedly satirises the then-burgeoning television culture and the audiences who fed on it: 'It can't be much good, it hasn't been advertised on the telly,' says a housewife about the suggestively-named Bonko (made with 'a high concentration of supercilious acid'); 'A triumph of good taste, unmarred by unsavoury interruptions,' says the National chairman about his channel's programmes. In fact, it is the National/BBC which comes in for most of the satire, for its high-cultural aspirations to respectability which it clearly sees as rubbing off from its dealings with ballet and other art forms. No, it is not really satire: it is not serious enough: as one writer says simply, it 'pokes fun at the world of television'.[83]

The brunt of the comedy is borne by the two stars, with Askey repeating his inept little guy-taken-for-a-ride routine and James as the incorrigible, fast-talking con-man. Askey even dons drag in the Ascot sequence in which he is dressed as a nurse for the role he is to play in James's plan for publicity. 'You're not the usual nurse,' says someone. 'No, as a matter of fact I'm very unusual,' he tosses back. His background in variety, on stage and radio, enables him to make the most of all the gags that come his way. Old jokes are trotted out as new or at least so brazenly that one accepts and laughs at them, especially in the patter Askey engages in with his landlady (Olga Lindo, who did several Comfort films): as he is going to the laundry she asks him to take 'Just a few of my smalls' [He holds up bloomers.] 'If these are your smalls, I'd hate to see your bigs.' And so on. This is not dialogue meant to be read coldly on the page but to be heard delivered by those who know how. James would of course go on to perfect his persona in the *Carry On* series, but its chief elements – an eye to the main chance, a capacity to manipulate the gullible, a leering appreciation of girls – are already in place. The film's use of guest stars varies from walk-ons – Evelyn Laye failing to recognise Arthur who has boasted of his intimacy with the stars – to singing favourites of the period, but it does not present the latter in the uncritical way that the two later musicals do. Here, though Lotis and Henderson, Weir and Patricia Bredin are allowed to sing their romantic ballads, there is an underlying suggestion that the National's idea of the popular is decidedly old-hat. The film was viewed as undemanding fare but efficiently handled within its modest parameters. *The Daily Cinema* considered it 'a happy comedy, full of laughs and with a long parade of popular TV personalities ensuring easy selling and warm reception with mass audiences',[84] while the *Monthly Film Bulletin* pronounced it 'wholesome family entertainment set firmly in the tradition of British pantomime.'[85] In view especially of Askey's costume changes as he assumes several roles and the kind of formula patter he is so at home with, this is a fair comment.

Live It Up and *Be My Guest* were both written by Lyn Fairhurst and both starred the clean-cut young David Hemmings. John Trumper, who edited *Live It Up*, may be right when he claims that 'the thing about pop music of the time is that it dates a film so that it can never be revived',[86] unless of course the singers become a phenomenon like the Beatles, whose films have continued to appeal in ensuing decades. Nevertheless, pop stars of the period such as Kenny Ball and Patsy Ann Noble in *Live It Up* and American Jerry Lee Lewis in *Be My Guest* no doubt helped the films' quest for audiences in the early 1960s, and, if today they seem extraordinarily wholesome, or even staid, they are instructive about what might have appealed to young people in the pre-Rolling Stones era. Even if they were not his personal cup of tea, Comfort doesn't patronise his guest singers, but gives them uncluttered access to the camera, putting the narrative on hold while they do their turns.

The central characters of these two cheap and cheerful pieces are teenage Dave Martin (a pre-*Blow Up* David Hemmings, who had already appeared in a small role in Comfort's *The Painted*

Smile), his mates Ricky and Phil (Stephen Marriott and John Pike), and his parents. In each film Dave is bent on being a success in the pop scene. In *Live It Up* he and his mates (plus a third, Heinz Burt, the singer of the group) work as Post Office messengers and share the expense of getting one of their numbers professionally taped, but Dave loses the tape, which, in the happy manner of such films in which young hopefuls seek to make their way, turns up in a film studio. After a series of mishaps, the teenagers, now styling themselves 'The Smart Alecs' (having toyed briefly with the idea of 'The Maggots'), make good through being discovered by the producer of a pop musical. The basic outline of the plot will be familiar from a hundred musicals, and it works in, on some very flimsy pretexts, half a dozen pop stars or groups of the day. Comfort stages these numbers unfussily, obviously expecting them to succeed on the basis of songs and singers, rather than on elaborate production, for which no doubt he would not have had the resources. As a background for the music, there is a simply but sympathetically sketched family situation: father (Ed Devereaux), hall porter at a big hotel, is tired of Dave's obsession with pop music and gives him a month to make good; mother (Joan Newell), on the other hand, has had a minor background in variety and encourages him. There are two good little scenes involving Dave with his parents. In the first, his mother sharply rejects Dave's criticism that his father hasn't 'got on'; this scene was written when the film was already in production, because screenwriter Fairhurst felt 'I made the mother too sweet, too nice, and I thought, She's becoming a bore',[87] so Comfort agreed that he should write a scene in which 'she berates the boy for not appreciating what his father's been doing for him' (see Plate 15). The second scene takes place in the back garden, with the father making clear that he really backs Dave's initiative. *Films and Filming* commended this 'finely played little scene' in which '[the director] integrates the location into the scene without comment taking it as would the characters themselves'.[88] Not for the first time was one of Comfort's features reviewed in this journal which did not, as a rule, review 'B' films. It is in small, discreetly handled sequences such as these two (and a few funny swipes at pop music idols and their fans) that Comfort shows how a director (and writer) willing to exercise a little extra care can give distinction to a basically conventional scenario.

Be My Guest is a sort of sequel to *Live It Up*. Bert, the father (now played by Ivor Salter), and Margaret, the mother (now Diana King, playing like a younger, slightly more middle-class Kathleen Harrison), have inherited a guest house in Brighton which they decide to take over and run, with the glum assistance of Mrs Pucil (Avril Angers), as cook. The central action again involves Dave, now assistant on the *Brighton Herald*, and his friends, Ricky and Phil, entering the title song in an amateur competition run by an opportunist US entrepreneur Milton Bass (David Healey), and exposing the machinations of the stage manager of the Brighton theatre, Artie Clough (Tony Wager), who has rigged the show. It is of course considerably more complicated than this, but not in any way that matters. There are, for instance, three innocent brushes with the Brighton police; there is a glamorous singer (Joyce Blair) who tries to vamp Dave into selling the rights of the song; and there is Erica (Andrea Monet), from Texas, whose hopes of break-ing into show business are finally gratified by the big-hearted Bass. In most respects, it follows the lines laid down by *Live It Up*: youthful aspirations are encouraged and rewarded after compli-cations are ironed out; this element is embedded in a background which is well-enough observed to give a certain reality to the proceedings; each has a pre-credits sequence which sets the light-hearted tone; each moves along briskly enough, both in terms of story events and of Comfort's easy kinetic approach to film-making; the guest artistes in each are introduced with minimal but adequate diegetic motivation and are allowed to do their turns without interruption; and the casts of each generously surround the kids with older players who give a little bite to proceedings. (It must be said, though, that Veronica Hurst as a caustic publicity woman in *Live It Up* is no substitute for Eve Arden.) Subsequent shifts in musical tastes probably mean that these films would be derided by youth audiences of later decades, as might the US *Rock Around the Clock* (1956), but they provide a record of what was popular in their time and they are both, as *Variety* said of *Be My*

Guest, 'a cut above many program film fillers'.[89] Both, too, deserve
the *Monthly Film Bulletin*'s praise for *Be My Guest* as a 'tremendously good-humoured teenage frolic'.[90] Comfort was answering
an exhibition demand of the period, both in content and in
relation to the double bill, and, as, say, in his charming use of
Brighton locations in *Be My Guest*, adding just that little extra that
a perceptive film-maker could do within the limits of a constrained
budget. If he was not likely to reactivate the prestige of his 1940s
reputation, he was unlikely to alienate the audiences at whom
these genre pieces were aimed.

Going gothic

In the early 1960s, new directors such as Karel Reisz, Tony
Richardson, John Schlesinger and Lindsay Anderson were winning critical plaudits for the exemplars of what came to be called
the 'new realism'. They were achieving, in Bourdieu's words 'the
establishment of an unprecedented relationship between the body
of interpreters and the work of art … [D]iscourse about a work is
not a mere accompaniment … but a stage in the production of the
work, of its meaning and value.'[91] It was these 'realist' (the term is
misleading) directors who were enjoying the symbolic capital that
had once been the reward for, say, Carol Reed, Anthony Asquith
and David Lean and which, in future retrospective writings would
be the happy lot of Michael Powell. Certainly the Hammer
phenomenon had then nothing to do with critical attention: as
David Pirie in his study of the British Gothic tradition says, 'at the
time outraged critics fell over each other to condemn it [*The Curse
of Frankenstein*, the first in the Hammer horror series].'[92] In the
case of Hammer only the audiences were happy, and they made
Hammer, 'In commercial terms, the most successful film company in the British cinema'.[93] Since then, of course, the Hammer
(and related) oeuvre has been subjected to the serious critical
appraisal largely denied it at the time. In British film criticism,
realism was for decades the favoured mode, and achievements in
popular genres were rarely given serious attention, unless, as in

the case of the horror genre, to revile and dismiss them. In 1965, in his second last film, Lance Comfort was working not in a critically privileged arm of British film production but in one which was enjoying remarkable commercial success.

However, two major critical works on the British horror film have nothing positive to say of *Devils of Darkness* (1965), Lance Comfort's one foray into the genre. Peter Hutchings writes: '*Devils of Darkness* was the first British-made vampire film with a contemporary setting (and, other than that, it is insignificant in terms of the influence it has wielded over the genre).'[94] For David Pirie, 'The fact that it was one of the first vampire movies in a modern setting gives this otherwise uninteresting film a certain curiosity value.'[95] There had been Gothic elements in some of his earlier films – in *Hatter's Castle* and *Daughter of Darkness* – but *Devils of Darkness* is the only one which mixes Gothic with horror. No doubt Comfort saw the success of the Hammer horror cycle as suggesting another generic path he might follow, just as he had done with the teen musicals, and *Devils of Darkness*, his only colour film, was actually a return to 'A' territory, at least in terms of production values and running time (90 minutes). It was not much liked at the time, and by comparison with the best of the Hammer cycle, such as *The Brides of Dracula* (1960) and *The Devil Rides Out* (1967), it is lacking in style and resonance. The genre scarcely attracted critical attention in the 1960s, but it was certainly popular with audiences, and it seems likely Comfort would have felt to work in it might have given his career a fillip. To invoke Bourdieu again, it seems like the case of a disposition for film-making's constantly needing to find a position in the field of production as it was constituted at the time.

Lyn Fairhurst's screenplay for *Devils of Darkness* opens on a very literary note: 'Through the low-lying ground mist, gravestones are etched at crazy angles against the night sky. Overgrown with weeds, this black "plague spot" where the Vampire and his victims lie buried is a picture of evil. The flickering light from a candle bobs in the background.'[96] The narrative is constructed about several oppositions common to the horror genre: the occult and the everyday; science and superstition; the rational and the fantastic. Two others also add to the film's texture: the old and the contemporary and the indigenous and the foreign. It has a long, vivid pre-credits sequence set in Brittany in 1800, when a gypsy wedding celebration (recalling the unsettling 'carnival' element in such other Comfort films as *Daughter of Darkness* and *Temptation Harbour*) goes seriously wrong. As the bride, Tanya (Carole Gray), dances, her red skirt flashes against the lush green of the Breton woodland (Pinewood standing in quite convincingly); an elder interrupts with a knife to carry out a ceremonial mingling of the blood of bride and groom, at which point she faints, and a bat flies out of a grave. A bat then hangs in large close-up as the camera moves to show Tanya being raised from her grave at the behest of Sinistre (Hubert Noël), the 'Devil of Darkness', who holds before her the 'talisman', a bat entwined with a serpent, and who promises her, 'You will follow me till the end of time.' So far, there is little to distinguish the film from even the best of the Hammer films; it is in its representation of the contemporary world that it is curiously bland. Even so, the early post-credits sequences set in Brittany have some genuinely alarming moments. Two young men go off on a caving expedition, while Anne (Rona Anderson), the sister of one of them, and writer Paul Baxter (William Sylvester) watch the 'All Souls Eve' procession. Comfort (and his regular editor John Trumper) cut suspensefully between the underground exploration, in which a hand emerges from a coffin and one of the boys is grabbed from behind, and the woodland hocus-pocus, with an old gypsy warning that 'the Black Death has struck'. Paul and Anne stand for normality, for common sense and for the limitations of both, and Anne pays with her life when a suave Frenchman offering her sympathy on the death of her brother proves to be the vampire Sinistre. Her fate is sealed in a moment when he and she stand on a bridge and only her reflection is seen in the water below. When the film moves to London, it loses a good deal of the atmosphere it has built up in its first movements set in Brittany. Though cinematographer Reg Wyer (replacing Comfort's usual collaborator at this time, Basil Emmott, who had no colour experience) differentiates well in terms of lighting, and John Earl, of art direction, between the everyday world in which Paul lives and the dark world in which Sinistre and his followers practise their satanic rites, the film fails to imbue the clash of good and evil with the same elemental power that, say, Terence Fisher achieves in *The Devil Rides Out*. This film makes an instructive comparison in several ways: both are centrally concerned with the attempts of outsiders to rescue innocent young people from the purveyors of devilish corruption and perversion, though the Hammer film also stresses 'a paternalist ideology'[97] that has no place in *Devils of Darkness*. Both use a stately home as the setting for devil worship, one having an observatory with a symbolically figured floor, the other a specially appointed cellar; in each there are people who sound 'ordinary' but are involved in satanic rites; Fisher's film makes much of the sign of the winged serpent, Comfort's of the bat-and-serpent talisman; and each engages in woodland rituals. That *The Devil Rides Out* is the more compelling experience is partly explained by the fact that its stars, Christopher Lee and Charles Gray, as representatives of good and evil, are far more charismatic than William Sylvester and Hubert Noël in Comfort's film; and as the female victim, Nike Arrighi as Tanith in *The Devil Rides Out* strikes a genuinely strange and alarming note of anguish while her counterpart, Tracy Reed (Karen), is too inexpressive to excite much concern for her situation, when she is about to become Sinistre's next victim.

This is not, however, to dismiss Comfort's film, as happened in the critical accounts referred to above. For one thing, the supposedly intractable opposition of science and superstition is handled with exemplary and unsettling subtlety. Paul goes to visit his scientist friend, Dr Kelsey (Eddie Byrne), who is also an expert on superstition and witchcraft, to explain his fears of what has happened to Anne and her brother in Brittany. When Paul has left Kelsey's laboratory, the caged animals, including snakes and bats, begin to be disturbed and the cages rock. There is a close-up of mounting panic on Kelsey's face and the camera cuts to the Chelsea party to which Paul has been invited. The party is a stereotyped version of a 1960s 'orgy' with an elderly colonel making passes at young women and with two lesbians (Avril Angers and

Marianne Stone) smoking long thin cigars to signify their deca-
dence, but the preceding scene in the laboratory, which enforces a
blurring of the line between the scientific and the supernatural
has real imagistic power. There is, too, an unusual blending of the
motif of sexual jealousy with the function of diabolic possession in
the way Tanya comes to resent Sinistre's interest in Karen, who is
taken to the manor house to be inducted into the ways of
darkness, and, in a striking visual trope, her blood falls on a thick
white rug. In his determination to find out what has become of the
bodies of the pair murdered in Brittany and to rescue Sinistre's
next victim (Reed), Paul exhibits some of the obsessive quality so
characteristic of Comfort's protagonists, though Sylvester brings
only easy authority to a role which might have benefited from
more suggestion of a man urgently possessed of an idea. As with
The Devil Rides Out, Comfort's film ends with the rescue of an
innocent, but it lacks the disturbing power of the later film in
which innocence is felt as a more potent force and the final rescue
scarcely reassures one about the lasting victory of good over evil.
Of course, the elaborate special effects available to the Hammer
film are outside the scope of *Devils of Darkness*, though Comfort's
old visual flair reasserts itself in the way he drenches the screen in
yellow (an effect recalling the red dissolve in Powell and Pressburger's *Black Narcissus*, 1947) as Sinistre falls at the sign of the
cross and then disintegrates before our eyes. If *Devils of Darkness*
is not a remarkable horror film, it is not without merits. The
reviewer in the *Monthly Film Bulletin* may have found it 'disagree-
able but never in the least alarming';[98] however, *Films and Filming*
claimed that 'everything is made "plausible", with a few imaginative
touches';[99] *Kinematograph Weekly* felt that 'it pulled out all the
stops to keep [the] audience in a state of tension and has met with
a considerable amount of success';[100] and *The Daily Cinema* wrote
that 'director Lance Comfort and writer Lyn Fairhurst whip up a
gripping suspense, blending traditional shocks with contemporary kinks, sacrificial orgies with cliff-hanging climaxes'.[101]

It is hard to know how Comfort would have coped with the
industry changes which overtook British cinema in the late 1960s,

when the days of the 'B' film were over as part of exhibition patterns, and when the withdrawal of US financial support made production difficult at any level. He was 58 when he died in 1966, perhaps too old to embrace the 'new realism' that won favour in the early 1960s, but part of the interest of examining his career is in noting how he kept finding positions in one of the most insecure production fields – the cinema, a high-risk, large-scale enterprise even at its lower levels as distinct, say, from painting or publishing a book. He had shown some proficiency in adapting to the needs of television and perhaps that would have engaged him further if he had lived.

Notes

1 Peter Pitt, 'The men who called action!', *The Veteran*, 75 (Autumn 1995), p. 13.
2 Huntington died in 1968, Comfort in 1966.
3 Todd McCarthy and Charles Flynn (eds), *Kings of the Bs: Working within the Hollywood System* (New York, E. P. Dutton & Co), 1975, p. 15.
4 H. Mark Glancy, 'Hollywood and Britain: MGM and the British "quota" legislation', in Jeffrey Richards, *The Unknown 1930s: An Alternative History of the British Cinema, 1929–1939* (London, I. B. Tauris), 1998, p. 60.
5 Brian McFarlane, 'Pulp fictions: the British B film and the field of cultural production', in *Film Criticism*, XXI:1 (1996), p. 51.
6 See a series of brief articles on Highbury's 'B' film project in the trade paper, *Kinematograph Weekly*, 358:2070 (18 December 1947), pp. 71–9.
7 'Peter Graham Scott', in Brian McFarlane, *An Autobiography of British Cinema* (London, Methuen), 1997, p. 521.
8 Producer Roy Baird who, at the start of his career, worked several times with Comfort as assistant director or production manager, recalls making use of the Pinewood 'scene dock' for *Devils of Darkness* (1964). Author's interview with Roy Baird, October 1998.
9 See interviews with 'Robert S. Baker', 'Francis Searle' and 'Peter Graham Scott', in McFarlane, *An Autobiography of British Cinema*.
10 Baker in *Ibid*, p. 43.
11 Searle in *Ibid*, p. 524.
12 Ronald Morris, 'Backbone of the Business', *Picturegoer*, 28:1018 (6 November 1954), p. 8.
13 *Picturegoer*, 28:1008 (28 August 1954), p. 26.
14 A levy imposed on every cinema ticket bought with a view to helping film production in Britain.
15 'Michael Winner', in McFarlane, *Autobiography of British Cinema*, p. 600.

16 Baker, in *Ibid*, p. 43.

17 Author's interviews with John Trumper and Lyn Fairhurst, September 1998.

18 There seems to be some doubt as to whether this film was a co-feature or an 'A', according to interviews with assistant director Roy Baird and editor John Trumper, September 1998.

19 *Picturegoer*, 27:987 (3 April 1954), p. 27.

20 '"Real people" in this murder drama', in *Brighton Evening Argus* (undated). The *Sunday Times* review (21 March 1954) begins: 'The London Pavilion has two British films in its programme, both of them with good qualities.' LCC.

21 *Picturegoer*, 27:989 (17 April 1954), p. 17.

22 See film historian, Charles Oakley, *Where We Came In: Seventy Years of the British Film Industry* (London, George Allen & Unwin), 1964, p. 199.

23 M. H., '*Touch of Death*', *The Daily Cinema*, 8701 (17 December 1962), p. 8.

24 Ian Johnson, *Films and Filming*, 9:5 (February 1963), p. 41.

25 *Kinematograph Weekly*, 2881 (20 December 1962), p. 15.

26 *The Daily Cinema*, 17 December 1962, p. 8.

27 *Films and Filming*, February 1963, p. 41.

28 Author's interviews with William Lucas and Lyn Fairhurst, September 1998.

29 Johnson, *Films and Filming*, p. 41.

30 *Monthly Film Bulletin*, 30:349 (February 1963), p. 25.

31 'Reviews', *Kinematograph Weekly*, 2845 (12 April 1962), p. 19.

32 Hermione Baddeley, *The Unsinkable Hermione Baddeley* (London, Collins), 1984.

33 Author's interview with William Franklyn, October 1998.

34 *Monthly Film Bulletin*, 28:335 (December 1961), p. 171.

35 *Monthly Film Bulletin*, 29:340 (May 1962), p. 68.

36 Hitchcock used the same title to tell a story similarly involving a child and a gun in one of the episodes he himself directed in the 1962–64 series, *Alfred Hitchcock Presents*.

37 J. G. W., *Cinema*, 82:6967 (10 March 1954), p. 19.

38 Paul Holt, 'At the films', *Daily Herald*, 12 March 1954. LCC.

39 'Wardour', 'This new British child star is a fully-formed personality already', *The Citizen*, 18 March 1954. LCC.

40 Peter Wilsher, 'At the cinema', *Sunday Chronicle* (Manchester), 14 March 1954. LCC.

41 *Monthly Film Bulletin*, 21:243 (April 1954), p. 55.

42 Grace Conway, 'It was a danger to men at work', *Catholic Herald*, 12 March 1954. LCC.

43 Kevin MacDonald, *Emeric Pressburger: The Life and Death of a Screenwriter* (London, Faber and Faber), 1994, p. 248.

44 Saville later became a film and television director.

45 Clem, *Variety*, 24 March 1954.

46 Peter Burnu, 'The New Films', *News of the World*, 14 March 1954. LCC.

47 Wilsher, 14 March 1954.

48 *Monthly Film Bulletin*, 21:243 (April 1954), p. 55.

49 'Bang! It's good!', *Sunday Express*, 14 March 1954. LCC.

50 Clem, *Variety*, 24 March 1954.

51 *Kensington Post* (date obscured). LCC.

52 Josh Billings, 'Reviews for showmen', *Kinematograph Weekly*, 2437 (11 March 1954), p. 15.

53 Maud Hughes, 'Previews', *Picture Show*, 62:1619 (10 April 1954), p. 2.

54 Letter to author, 1998.

55 The film's original title was *The Golliwog*, the new title being the idea of editor John Trumper. Author's interview with Trumper, September 1998.

56 *Kinematograph Weekly*, 2903 (23 May 1963), p. 20.

57 The *Monthly Film Bulletin* considered that, by killing off Marlow 'relatively early on, this film robs itself of its prinicipal asset' (i.e., Shaw's 'intelligent performance'), 30:355 (August 1963), p 122.

58 Richard Gertner, *Motion Picture Herald*, 231:9 (29 April 1964), p. 42.

59 *Kinematograph Weekly*, 23 May 1963, p. 20.

60 E. L., *Film Daily*, 124: 86, p. 6.

61 *Monthly Film Bulletin*, 21:242 (March 1954), p. 39.

62 Quoted in David Castell, *Richard Attenborough: A Pictorial Film Biography* (London, The Bodley Head), 1984, p. 52.

63 Dilys Powell, *The Sunday Times*, 21 March 1954. LCC.

64 'The power of applied observation', *Sussex Daily News*, 9 April 1954. LCC.

65 A not-uncommon narrative complication in films of the period, whether romantic drama such as *Random Harvest* (1942) or thriller *Somewhere in the Night* (1946).

66 It was distributed in the USA by Republic.

67 *Monthly Film Bulletin*, 23:268 (May 1956), p. 62.

68 *Today's Cinema*, 86:7484 (20 March 1956), p. 12.

69 Leslie Wood, *The Daily Film Renter*, 7088 (20 March 1956), p. 8.

70 He wrote several other films for Lance Comfort, including *The Girl on the Pier* and *Eight O'Clock Walk*, and several short television films produced by Comfort for Douglas Fairbanks Productions, including *Tony* and *Street of Angels* in 1956.

71 *Picture Show*, 66:1728 (12 May 1956), p. 10.

72 This was borne out in several interviews, including those with Lyn Fairhurst (screenwriter), son John Comfort (production manager), Roy Baird (assistant director) and Peter Miller (screenwriter), and actors William Franklyn and William Lucas. Author's interviews, September and October, 1998.

73 Allen M. Widem, *Motion Picture Herald*, 230:8 (18 September 1963), p. 891.

74 Information given in author's interviews with editor Peter Pitt and assistant director Roy Baird, October 1998.

75 M. H., *The Daily Cinema*, 8771 (7 June 1963), p. 6.

76 Widem, *Motion Picture Herald*, p. 891.

77 *Kinematograph Weekly*, 2904 (30 May 1963), p. 92.

78 M. H., *Daily Cinema*, p. 6.

79 *Monthly Film Bulletin*, 31:366 (July 1964), p. 105.

80 M. H., *The Daily Cinema*, 8917 (25 May 1964), p. 3.

81 Robert Murphy, *Sixties British Cinema* (London, BFI Publishing), 1992, p. 213.
82 Author's interviews with John Comfort (October 1997) and Lyn Fairhurst (September 1998).
83 Geoff Brown with Tony Aldgate, *The Common Touch: The Films of John Baxter* (London, BFI Publishing), 1989, p. 121.
84 F. J., *The Daily Cinema*, 8116 (11 February 1959), p. 8.
85 *Monthly Film Bulletin*, 26:302 (March 1959), p. 34.
86 Author's interview with John Trumper, September 1998.
87 Lyn Fairhurst explained making this change in interview with the author, September 1998.
88 Richard Whitehall, *Films and Filming*, 10:4 (January 1964), p. 28.
89 Rich., *Variety*, 21 April 1965.
90 *Monthly Film Bulletin*, 32:376 (May 1965), p. 74.
91 Pierre Bourdieu, *The Field of Cultural Production: Essays on Art and Literature*, edited and introduced by Randal Johnson (Cambridge, Polity Press), 1993, p. 110.
92 David Pirie, *A Heritage of Horror: The English Gothic Cinema 1946–1972* (London, Gordon Fraser), 1973, p. 40.
93 Gilbert Adair, 'The British tradition', in Adair and Nick Roddick, *A Night at the Pictures* (Bromley, Columbus Books), 1985, p. 63
94 Peter Hutchings, *Hammer and Beyond: The British Horror Film* (Manchester, Manchester University Press), 1993, p. 132.
95 Pirie, *Heritage*, p. 179.
96 Lyn Fairhurst, Screenplay for *Devils of Darkness*, held by the BFI.
97 Hutchings, *Hammer and Beyond*, p. 153.
98 *Monthly Film Bulletin*, 32:381 (October 1965), p. 149.
99 Robin Bean, *Films and Filming*, 12:2 (November 1965), p. 30.
100 *Kinematograph Weekly*, 3021 (26 August 1965), p. 18.
101 M. H., *The Daily Cinema*, 9106 (20 August 1965), p. 6.

Conclusion

8

The answer to the question with which this study opened, 'Why Lance Comfort?' has, I hope, emerged during the preceding chapters. Apart from the purely personal matter of *liking* his films, I hope also to have shown other reasons for wanting to write about him. First, he has been shamefully neglected in the standard histories of British cinema, which have tended to be dominated by the work of major figures to an extent which obscures beguiling work being done in less obviously prestigious areas of the field. Unlike, say, the Gainsborough or the Hammer oeuvres, Comfort's work has not yet been the subject of reappraisal. Second, his work exhibits strengths in categories that have been habitually under-valued in the discourse on British cinema: melodrama, genre film-making and the 'B' film have only very recently been given overdue attention. Third, he offers a very instructive example of what it was to be a working director in the context of an industry where there is incessant jostling for places, among the producers of its artefacts and among those who constitute its assessors. This study was never intended as an auteurist paean or as a fiercely theorised analysis of the artist and his field, though it has been prepared to draw on such approaches where they seemed likely to illuminate the career of a film-maker who, in one way or another, remained busy for forty years.

If he had been a Hollywood director, he might well have been taken up by the likes of Andrew Sarris in his archaeological work on the studio years,[1] perhaps finding a place in Sarris's category of

'Expressive Esoterica', for his on-going preoccupation with the melodramatic mode and with obsessive personalities. As the present study has argued, Comfort was for most of his career involved in work unlikely to bring him much critical kudos or much of Bordieu's symbolic capital. As a director whose 'A' films were predominantly melodramas, sometimes touched with the Gothic, he was not making the sorts of films which would have attracted much contemporary critical attention. If he had been a Gainsborough director, he might have at least had a period of major commercial success, but even in those circumstances his work would have looked darker than the films to which audiences flocked in the mid-1940s. Characteristically, his films do not end with the automatic handing out of heterosexual rewards to the good while the bad end unhappily, to paraphrase Wilde's famous definition of what fiction means.[2] Even in his later 'B'-movie career, the final upbeat clinch was never to be relied on. Also, as one whose work was almost entirely within generic categories, he was less likely to win critical acclaim than those whose films seemed to transcend such classification: when he was not making melo-dramas of one kind or other, he was making thrillers or comedies or musicals, rather than one-off pieces or distinguished works of realism or adaptations of literary classics. The 'respectability' of genre, a by-product of its intelligent theorisation by the likes of Steve Neale and Thomas Schatz,[3] was several decades down the track from Comfort's heyday. It is not that all Comfort's work in any genre is notable; at its best, though, it deserved more attention than it has ever received. Genre work in British 'B' movies was, of course, doomed to obscurity from the outset by the very fact of its position on the double bill. There is virtually no history of sharp-eyed British reviewers showing anything like the alertness of, say, James Agee in the USA to the possibilities of a 'sleeper' in the bottom half of the bill. As a rule, only the trade press or the fan magazines would refer to such films, and though a favourable notice there might have increased distribution prospects, where these were not part of a pre-determined arrangement, it did little to outweigh the critical neglect that was routinely the lot of the 'B' films among newspaper reviewers and the 'quality' journals.

It is not hard to establish that Lance Comfort's work has been neglected, nor, this study contends, to make a case for its reappraisal. Actually, the word 'reappraisal' is a misnomer since Comfort has never had serious appraisal, even when he was the 'busiest film director' in Britain in the early 1940s. In trying to do justice to a comparatively unknown film-maker it is important not to overstate one's claims. No service is done to Comfort's reputation to imply that he combined the story-telling acumen of David Lean with the soaring pictorialism of Michael Powell, or that, to quote the source of one of Comfort's titles, 'Some Heart once pregnant with celestial fire' has gone unsung into the 'silent dust'.[4] The truth is that his directorial oeuvre of nearly forty films reveals an attractive talent and a more than competent craftsman, who can legitimately make claims on our serious attention. His greatest strength, revealed in his first major success, *Hatter's Castle*, was for the mode of melodrama in full cry: he – and his collaborators – took A. J. Cronin's tiresomely downbeat, bogusly 'realistic' novel and made a work of melodrama that is fascinated by the power of monomaniacal tyranny and feels compassionately for its victims. It is probably fair to say that all his best work recalls the polarisations of this early triumph, though some such as *Temptation Harbour* complicate the mode with a brooding intensity and a rueful sense of life's endemic difficulties. All these films, at least up to *The Silent Dust*, and in a number of the modest works of the subsequent decades, reveal too a flair for visual story-telling, sometimes leading to delirious effects of montage-created ellipsis or audacious juxtapositions, to a panache which recall the Hollywood likes of Jacques Tourneur or John Brahm. To call such films melodramas is not, as the critical habit so often was at the time, to disparage but to point to a fascination with a particular way of interpreting and ordering the world. His work in other genres is less exhilarating, though the best of the thrillers, *Tomorrow at Ten* or *Touch of Death*, make use of melodramatic structures and excesses, and the comedies, especially *When We Are Married*, and the good-natured teen musicals, *Live It Up* and *Be My Guest*, have the charm of a film-maker who warms to his characters and never patronises or sentimentalises them.

His strengths, though, are primarily melodramatic and he had the advantage of cinematographers such as Max Greene, Erwin Hillier, Freddie Young, Gunther Krampf and, in all but one of his last eleven films, Basil Emmott, who could give visual expression to what often seems a dark vision of human behaviour. He also had at his service music directors such as William Alwyn, Mischa Spoliansky and Clifton Parker, whose scores made swirling contributions to the emotional power of these films. Not for nothing does the word 'darkness' occur three times in his titles: the most haunting films of this most amiable-sounding of film-makers *are* shot through with dark insights about dark passions. He seems also to have been an actor's director, not in the George Cukor or William Wyler sense of seeking minute variations through dozens of takes, but from the point of view of casting carefully and then giving actors room to move, sometimes allowing the more flamboyant ones to have their showy heads. Robert Newton, for example, was rarely more effective than in the contrasted roles of the domestic bully in *Hatter's Castle* and the conscience-tormented signalman in *Temptation Harbour*; others, such as Eric Portman, Stephen Murray, Siobhan McKenna and Robert Shaw responded to Comfort's melodramatic demands with appropriately large-scale performances, while Jack Warner was rarely allowed to be so subtly, ordinarily flawed as he was in *Bang! You're Dead*. Comfort gave the celebrated comic Sydney Howard the opportunity to create a memorable figure of the sozzled cameraman in *When We Are Married*, and such character actors as Beatrice Varley, Charles Victor, Irene Handl and Seymour Hicks were all encouraged to endow their stock figures with a rewarding touch of verisimilitude.

Comfort had no place in the British 'quality film adventure' (to quote the title of a recent article)[5] of the war and postwar years. His imagination was not fired by the quotidian realities or by a sense of alignment with great literature, those key strands which critics identified and extolled in 'the idea of the "quality film" they were constructing ... as something they passionately hoped the wide public would recognize and appreciate'.[6] Perhaps *Temptation Harbour* would have come nearest to acceptance as part of this enterprise on the grounds of its realism and in spite of its

melodramatic core, for 'Documentary versus extravagant entertainment defines the difference between quality and prestige
films for most critics'.[7] It is also the difference between quality
and the popular mode of melodrama, though, as we have seen,
Comfort for the most part was too late to enjoy even this popularity. The rehabilitation of his critical reputation may depend on
further work in melodrama and on an openness to the possibility
of finding rewards in the too-often dismissed category of the 'B'
film. The enjoyment his films have to offer is not that of a powerfully original style or the commitment to some vaguely appre-
hended notion of quality, but that of a craftsman who hurdled the
shifting aesthetic requirements and industrial conditions of
British cinema with unassuming skill and a sympathetic awareness of human conflicts in a changing society. Like too many
other film-makers of his time – and in many ways his career is
paradigmatic – he has been overlooked as a result of unduly
preclusive criteria. He was an unpretentious craftsman who was
also at best an artist, and in exploring his career trajectory the
viewer is rewarded by the spectacle of one who responded
resiliently to the challenges of a volatile industry. Lance Comfort
may be a purveyor of essentially modest pleasures, but these are
none the less pleasurable for being modest.

Notes

1 Andrew Sarris, *The American Cinema: Directors and Directions 1929–1968*
  (New York, E. P. Dutton & Co), 1968.
2 Oscar Wilde, *The Importance of Being Earnest*, Act Two.
3 Steve Neale, *Genre* (London, BFI Publishing), 1980; Thomas Schatz,
  Hollywood Genres (New York), 1981.
4 Thomas Gray, 'An Elegy Written in a Country Churchyard'.
5 John Ellis, 'The quality film adventure: British critics and the cinema
  1942–1948', in Andrew Higson (ed.), *Dissolving Views: Key Writings on
  British Cinema* (London, Cassell), 1996.
6 *Ibid*, p. 69.
7 *Ibid*, p. 71.

Filmography

Early career

The titles covering the period 1925–39 are taken from a typed document in the possession of John Comfort and, where possible, checked against the credits of surviving prints. The list is incomplete: Lance Comfort had been involved in films since 1925, but details of the functions he fulfilled in his first two years are no longer available.

This Marriage Business 1927, 6,206 ft.

Production company: Film Booking Offices
Producer: F. A. Enders
Director: Leslie Hiscott
Screenplay: Leslie Hiscott
Leading players: Estelle Brody (Annette), Marjorie Hume (Pat), Owen Nares (Robert)
Lance Comfort (LC) Stills photographer

The Constant Nymph 1928, 10,600 ft.

Production company: Gainsborough
Producer: Michael Balcon
Director: Adrian Brunel, Basil Dean
Screenplay: Basil Dean, Alma Reville
Leading players: Ivor Novello (Lewis Dodd), Mabel Poulton (Tessa Sanger), Frances Doble (Florence), Mary Clare (Linda Sanger), Benita Hume (Antonia Sanger)
LC Trick cameraman

Blockade 1928, 88 min.

Production company: New Era
Producer: Gordon Craig
Director: Geoffrey Barkas, Michael Barringer
Screenplay: Michael Barringer
Director of photography: Sydney Blythe
Leading players: J. P. Kennedy (Admiral Sims), Roy Travers (Captain von
   Haag), Johnny Butt, Val Gielgud
LC Chief recordist

Piccadilly Nights 1930, 86 min.

Production company: Kingsway General
Producer: Albert H. Arch
Director: Albert H. Arch
Screenplay: Arch, Roger Burford
Leading players: Billie Rutherford (Billie), Elsie Bower (Elsie), Julian
   Hamilton (Jackson), June Grey (Dolly)
LC Lighting

The Ghost Train 1931, 72 min.

Production company: Gainsborough (Islington Studios)
Producer: Michael Balcon
Director: Walter Forde
Screenplay: Angus Macphail, Lajos Biro, Sidney Gilliat (uncredited),
   based on the play by Arthur Ripley
Director of photography: Leslie Rowson
Editor: Ian Dalrymple
Art director: Walter W. Murton
Leading players: Jack Hulbert (Teddy Deakin), Cecily Courtneidge
   (Miss Bourne), Donald Calthrop (Saul Hodgkin), Ann Todd
   (Peggy Murdock), Cyril Raymond (Richard Winthrop), Angela
   Baddeley (Julia Price), Allan Jeayes (Dr Sterling)
LC Trick cameraman

Spare Room 1932, 34 min.

Production company: PDC (Cricklewood)
Director: Redd Davis

Screenplay: G. Marriott Edgar
Leading players: Jimmy James (Jimmy), Ruth Taylor (Mrs James), Charles Paton (Mr Webster), Charles Farrell (Boxer)
LC Chief recordist

The New Hotel 1932, 49 min.

Production company: PDC (Cricklewood)
Music: Marc Anthony
Lyrics: Bruce Sievier
Leading players: Norman Long, Dan Young, Al Davidson and his band
LC Chief recordist

Smilin' Along 1932, 38 min.

Production company: Argyle Talking Pictures
Producer, Director, Screenplay: John Argyle
Leading players: Rene Ray (Teresa), James Benton, Margaret Delane
LC Chief recordist

Account Rendered 1932, 35 min.

Production company: PDC (Cricklewood)
Director, Screenplay: Leslie Howard Gordon, from play by Michael Joseph
Leading players: Cecil Ramage (Barry Barriter), Reginald Bach (Hugh Preston), Marilyn Mawm (Barbara Wayne)
LC Chief recordist

Partners Please 1932, 34 min.

Production company: PDC (Cricklewood)
Director: Lloyd Richards
Screenplay: Charles Bennett
Leading players: Pat Paterson (Angela Grittlewood), Tony Simpson (Archie Dawlish), Ronald Ward (Eric Hatington), Binnie Barnes (Billie), Ralph Truman (CID man)
LC Chief recordist

Callbox Mystery 1932, 73 min.

Production company: Samuelson
Producer: Gordon Craig
Director: G. B. Samuelson
Screenplay: Joan Wentworth Wood
Director of photography: Desmond Dickinson
Leading players: Harold French (Inspector Layton), Warwick Ward (Leo Mount), Wendy Barrie (Iris Banner)
LC Chief recordist

Here's George 1932, 64 min.

Production company: Thomas Charles Arnold (Cricklewood)
Producer: Thomas Charles Arnold
Director: Redd Davis
Screenplay: G. Marriott Edgar, from his play, *The Service Flat*
Director of photography: Desmond Dickinson
Art director: Edward Delaney
Leading players: George Clarke (George Muffitt), Pat Paterson (Laura Wentworth), Marriott Edgar (Mr Wentworth), Merle Tottenham (Perkins), Rene Ray (telephonist)
LC Chief recordist

The Wonderful Story 1932, 72 min.

Producer, Director, Screenplay (from a novel by I. A. R. Wylie): Reginald Fogwell
Director of photography: Henry Harris
Leading players: Wyn Clare (Mary Richards), John Batten (John Martin), Eric Bransby Williams (Bob Martin), Moore Marriott (Zacky Richards), Sam Livesey (Doctor)
LC Chief recordist

Perfect Understanding 1933, 80 min.

Production company: Gloria Swanson British (Ealing, Cannes)
Producer: Gloria Swanson
Director: Cyril Gardner
Screenplay: Miles Malleson and Michael Powell, from a story by Powell

Director of photography: Curt Courant
Art director: Edward Carrick
Leading players: Gloria Swanson (Judy Rogers), Laurence Olivier (Nicholas Randall), Genevieve Tobin (Kitty), John Halliday (Ronnson), Nigel Playfair (Lord Portleigh), Nora Swinburne (Lady Stephanie Fitzmaurice), O. B. Clarence (Dr Graham), Mary Jerrold (Mrs Graham)
LC Chief recordist

The Love Wager 1933, 64 min.

Production company: Anglo-European
Producer: E. A. Fell
Director: A. Cyran
Screenplay: Moira Dale
Leading players: Pat Paterson (Peggy), Wallace Douglas (Peter Neville), Frank Stanmore (Shorty), Moira Dale (Auntie Prue), Morton Selton (General Neville)
LC Chief recordist

Karma 1933, 68 min. (bilingual versions)

Production company: Himansu Rai Indo-International Talkies and Indian and British Film Productions (Stolls, India)
Producer: Himansu Rai, John L. Freer-Hunt
Director: Freer-Hunt
Screenplay: Rai, Freer-Hunt
Leading players: Devika Rani (Maharani), Abraham Sofaer (Holy Man), Himansu Rai (Prince)
LC Chief recordist

Daughters of Today 1933, 74 min.

Production company: FWK (Cricklewood)
Producer, Director: F. W. Kraemer
Screenplay: Michael Barringer
Director of photography: Desmond Dickinson
Art director: Oscar Werndorff
Leading players: George Barraud (Forbes), Betty Amman (Joan), Marguerite Allan (Mavis), Hay Petrie (Sharpe), Marie Ault (Mrs Tring)
LC Chief recordist

Love's Old Sweet Song 1933, 79 min.

Production company: Argyle Talking Pictures (Cricklewood)
Producer: John Argyle
Director: Manning Hayes
Screenplay: Lydia Haywood
Director of photography: Desmond Dickinson
Art director: Hugh Gee
Leading players: John Stuart (Paul Kingslake), Joan Wyndham (Mary
    Dean), Ronald Ward (Eric Kingslake), Moore Marriott (Old Tom),
    Barbara Everest (Nurse)
LC Chief recordist

The Commissionaire 1933, 72 min.

Production company: Granville (Cricklewood)
Producer: Edward G. Whiting
Director: Edward Dryhurst
Screenplay: Herbert Ayres
Director of photography: Desmond Dickinson
Leading players: Sam Livesey (Sgt George Brown), Barrie Livesey (Tom
    Brown), George Carney (Sgt Ted Seymour), Betty Huntley-Wright
    (Betty Seymour)
LC Chief recordist

Dick Turpin 1933, 79 min.

Production company: John Stafford (Cricklewood)
Producer: Clyde Cook
Director: John Stafford, Victor Hanbury
Screenplay: Victor Kendall, from the novel, *Rookwood*, by Harrison
    Ainsworth
Director of photography: Walter Blakeley, Desmond Dickinson
Leading players: Victor McLaglen (Dick Turpin), Jane Carr (Eleanor
    Mowbray), Frank Vosper (Tom King), Cecil Humphries (Luke
    Rookwood), Gillian Lind (Nan)
LC Chief recordist

Song at Eventide 1934, 83 min.

Production company: Argyle Talking Pictures

Producer: John Argyle
Director: Harry Hughes
Screenplay: John Hastings Turner
Director of photography: Desmond Dickinson
Leading players: Fay Compton (Helen d'Alaste), Lester Matthews (Lord Belsize), Nancy Burne (Patricia Belsize), Leslie Perrins (Ricardo), Tom Helmore (Michael Law)
LC Chief recordist

Josser on the Farm 1934, 63 min.

Production company: Fox-British (Cricklewood)
Producer, Director: T. Hayes Hunter
Screenplay: Con West, Betty Sargent
Director of photography: Alex Bryce
Leading players: Ernie Lotinga (Jimmy Josser), Betty Astell (Betty), Garry Marsh (Granby), Muriel Aked (Mrs Savage), [Wilfred] Hyde White
LC Chief recordist

Irish Hearts 1934, 69 min.

Production company: Clifton-Hurst (Cricklewood, Ireland)
Producer: Harry Clifton
Director, Screenplay (from Dr Johnson Abrahams' novel, *Night Nurse*): Brian Desmond Hurst
Director of photography: Eugen Schufftan
Leading players: Nancy Burne (Norah O'Neale), Lester Matthews (Dermot Fitzgerald), Molly Lamont (Nurse Otway), Patric Knowles (Pip Fitzgerald), Sara Allgood
LC Chief recordist

Danny Boy 1934, 83 min.

Production company: Panther Pictures (Cricklewood)
Producer, Director: Oswald Mitchell, Challis Sanderson
Screenplay: Mitchell, H. Barr-Carson, Archie Pitt
Director of photography: Desmond Dickinson
Leading players: Dorothy Dickson (Jane Kaye), Frank Forbes-Robertson (Pat Clare), Cyril Ritchard (John Martin), Archie Pitt (Silver Sam), Fred Duprez (Leo Newman)
LC Chief recordist

Romance in Rhythm 1934, 73 min.

Production company: Allied Film Productions (Cricklewood)
Producer, Director, Screenplay: Lawrence Huntington
Director of photography: Desmond Dickinson
Editor: Challis Sanderson
Music: Carroll Gibbons and his orchestra
Leading players: Phyllis Clare (Ruth Lee), David Hutcheson (Bob Mervyn), David Burns (Mollari), Queenie Leonard
LC Chief recordist

A Real Bloke 1935, 70 min.

Production company: Baxter and Barter Productions
Producer: John Barter
Director: John Baxter
Screenplay: Herbert Ayres
Director of photography: Desmond Dickinson
Editor: Winifred Cooper
Art director: J. Elder Wills, H. Fraser Passmore
Leading players: George Carney (Bill), Mary Clare (Kate), Diana Beaumont (Mary), Peggy Novak (Lil), Mark Daly (Scottie)
LC Chief recordist

The Small Man 1935, 72 min.

Production company: Baxter and Barter Productions (Stoll, Cricklewood)
Producer: John Barter
Director: John Baxter
Screenplay: Con West, with additional dialogue by E. C. Reed
Director of photography: Desmond Dickinson
Editor: Sam Simmonds
Art director: John Bryan
Music: Haydn Wood
Leading players: George Carney (Bill Edwards), Minnie Rayner (Alice Roberts), Mary Newland (Mary Roberts), Ernest Butcher (Arthur)
LC Chief recordist

Strictly Illegal 1935, 69 min.

Production company: Leslie Fuller Pictures (Cricklewood)
Producer: Joe Rock
Director: Ralph Cedar
Screenplay: Syd Courtney and Georgie Harris, from the play, *The Naughty Age*
Director of photography: Desmond Dickinson
Leading players: Leslie Fuller (Bill the Bookie), Betty Astell (Mrs Bill), Georgie Harris (Bert the Runner), Glennis Lorimer (The Girl)
LC Chief recordist

Barnacle Bill 1935, 90 min.

Production company: City (Cricklewood)
Producer: Basil Humphreys
Director: Harry Hughes
Screenplay: Aveling Ginever, from a story by Archie Pitt
Director of photography: Desmond Dickinson
Leading players: Archie Pitt (Bill Harris), Joan Gardner (Jill Harris), Gus McNaughton (Jack Barton), Sybil Jason (Jill, child), O. B. Clarence (Uncle George)
LC Chief recordist

Variety 1935, 86 min.

Production company: Argyle Talking Films (Cricklewood)
Producer: John Argyle
Director: Adrian Brunel
Screenplay: Brunel, Oswald Mitchell
Director of photography: Desmond Dickinson
Editor: Dan Birt
Leading players: Sam Livesey (Charlie Boyd), Cassie Livesey (Maggie Boyd), Jack Livesey (Matt Boyd), Barrie Livesey (Victor Boyd), George Carney
LC Chief recordist

City of Beautiful Nonsense 1935, 88 min.

Production company: Butcher's Film Service (Cricklewood)
Producer: Wilfred Noy

Director: Adrian Brunel
Screenplay: Donovan Pedelty, from a novel by E. Temple Thurston
Director of photography: Desmond Dickinson
Leading players: Emlyn Williams (Jack Grey), Sophie Stewart (Jill Dealtry), Eve Lister (Amber), George Carney (Chesterton)
LC Chief recordist

Cock o' the North 1935, 84 min.

Production company: Panther-Mitchell Films (Cricklewood)
Producer: Oswald Mitchell
Director: Mitchell, Challis Sanderson
Screenplay: Mitchell
Director of photography: Desmond Dickinson
Leading players: George Carney (George Barton), Marie Lohr (Mary Barton), Ronnie Hepworth (Danny Barton), Peggy Novak (Maggie Harris), Johnnie Schofield (Bert Harris)
LC Chief recordist

Jimmy Boy 1935, 72 min.

Production company: Baxter and Barter Productions (Stoll, Cricklewood)
Producer: John Barter
Director: John Baxter
Screenplay: Con West, Harry O'Donovan
Director of photography: Desmond Dickinson; locations shot by George Dudgeon Stretton
Editor: Sam Simmonds, Vi Burdon
Art director: John Bryan
Music: Kennedy Russell
Leading players: Jimmy O'Dea (Jimmy), Guy Middleton (The Count), Vera Sherburne (Nora), Enid Stamp-Taylor (The Star), Peggy Novak (Chambermaid)
LC Chief recordist

Men of Yesterday 1936, 82 min.

Production company: UK Films (Sound City, Shepperton)
Producer: John Barter
Director: John Baxter

Screenplay: Gerald Elliott, Jack Francis
Director of photography: Jack Parker
Editor: Sydney Stone
Art director: John Bryan
Music: Kennedy Russell
Leading players: Stewart Rome (Major Radford), Sam Livesey, Hay
Petrie, Eve Lister, Cecil Parker, Roddy Hughes, George Robey,
Will Fyffe
LC Technical supervisor

Hearts of Humanity 1936, 75 min.

Production company: UK Films (Sound City, Shepperton)
Producer: John Barter
Director: John Baxter
Screenplay: Gerald Elliott
Director of photography: Jack Parker
Editor: Sydney Stone
Art director: John Bryan
Music: Kennedy Russell
Leading players: Eric Portman (Jack Clinton), Wilfrid Walter (Rev
John Maitland), Cathleen Nesbitt (Mrs Bamford), Pamela Randall
(Ann Bamford), Bransby Williams (Mike), Hay Petrie (Alf), Fred
Duprez (Manager)
LC Technical supervisor

Song of the Road 1937, 71 min.

Production company: UK Films (Sound City, Shepperton)
Producer: John Barter
Director: John Baxter
Screenplay: Gerald Elliott, H. F. Maltby
Director of photography: Jack Parker
Editor: Sydney Stone
Art director: John Bryan
Music: Kennedy Russell
Leading players: Bransby Williams (Bill), Ernest Butcher (Farm
Foreman), Muriel George (Mrs Trelawney), Percy Parsons (Show-
man), Peggy Novak (Showman's wife), Tod Slaughter (Another
showman)
LC Technical supervisor

Talking Feet 1937, 79 min.

Production company: UK Films (Sound City, Shepperton)
Producer: John Barter
Director: John Baxter
Screenplay: H. Fowler Mear
Director of photography: Jack Parker
Editor: Ivy Swire, Michael Truman
Art director: John Bryan. Music: Kennedy Russell
Leading players: Hazel Scott (Hazel Barker), Jack Barty (Joe Barker), Davy Burnaby (Mr Shirley), Enid Stamp-Taylor (Sylvia Shirley), John Stuart (Dr Roger Hood), Ernest Butcher (Thomas), Johnnie Schofield (Doorman)
LC Technical supervisor

Stepping Toes 1938, 84 min.

Production company: UK Films/Two Cities Films (Sound City, Shepperton)
Producer: John Barter
Director: John Baxter
Screenplay: H. Fowler Mear, from a story by Jack Francis and Barbara K. Emary
Director of photography: Jack Parker, with additional photography by Erwin Hiller
Editor: Ivy Swire, Michael Truman
Leading players: Hazel Scott (Hazel Warrington), Enid Stamp-Taylor (Mrs Warrington), Jack Barty (Joe), Edgar Driver (Titch), Ernest Butcher (Stringer)
LC Technical supervisor

Old Mother Riley in Society 1940, 80 min.

Production company: British National (Nettlefold)
Producer: John Corfield
Director: John Baxter
Screenplay: Austin Melford, Mary Cathcart Borer, Barbara K. Emary
Director of photography: James Wilson
Editor: Michael C. Chorlton
Art director: Holmes Paul
Music: Kennedy Russell

Leading players: Arthur Lucan (Mrs Riley), Kitty McShane (Kitty), John Stuart (Tony Morgan), Dennis Wyndham (Tug Mulligan), Charles Victor (Sir John Morgan), Ruth Maitland (Lady Morgan), Athole Stewart (Duke), Margaret Halstan (Duchess)

LC Assistant director

Crook's Tour 1940, 79 min.

Production company: British National
Producer: John Corfield
Director: John Baxter
Screenplay: Original story by John Watt and Max Kester, adapted by Barbara K. Emary from the BBC radio series by Frank Launder and Sidney Gilliat (uncredited)
Director of photography: James Wilson
Editor: Michael C. Charlton
Art director: Duncan Sutherland
Music: Kennedy Russell
Leading players: Basil Radford (Hawtrey Charters), Naunton Wayne (Sinclair Caldicott), Greta Gynt (La Palermo), Charles Oliver (Sheik), Abraham Sofaer (Ali), Noel Hood (Edith Charters), Silvia St Claire [Patricia Medina] (receptionist)

LC Technical supervisor

Old Mother Riley in Business 1940, 80 min.

Production company: British National (Rock Studios, Elstree)
Producer: John Corfield
Director: John Baxter
Screenplay: Geoffrey Orme, based on the screenplay for *The Small Man* (1935) by Con West
Director of photography: James Wilson
Art director: Duncan Sutherland
Leading players: Arthur Lucan (Mrs Riley), Kitty McShane (Kitty Riley), Cyril Chamberlain (John Halliwell), Charles Victor, Wally Patch, Ernest Butcher, Ernest Sefton, O. B. Clarence, Edgar Driver, Edie Martin

LC Assistant director

Love on the Dole 1941, 82 min.

Production company: British National (Rock Studios, Elstree)
Producer, Director: John Baxter
Screenplay: Walter Greenwood, with Barbara K. Emary and Rollo
    Gamble, from the play by Greenwood and Ronald Gow
Director of photography: James Wilson
Editor: Michael C. Chorlton
Art director: Holmes Paul
Music: Richard Adinsell
Music direction: Muir Mathieson
Leading players: Deborah Kerr (Sally), Clifford Evans (Larry), Mary
    Merrall (Mrs Hardcastle), George Carney (Mr Hardcastle), Geoffrey
    Hibberd (Harry Hardcastle), Joyce Howard (Helen Hawkins), Frank
    Cellier (Sam Grundy), Maire O'Neill (Mrs Dobell), Iris Vandeleur
    (Mrs Nattie), Marjorie Rhodes (Mrs Bull), Marie Ault (Mrs Jike)
LC Associate director/Technical supervisor

Old Mother Riley's Ghosts 1941, 82 min.

Production company: British National (Rock Studios, Elstree)
Producer, Director: John Baxter
Screenplay: Geoffrey Orme, Con West
Director of photography: James Wilson
Editor: Jack Harris
Art director: Holmes Paul
Leading players: Arthur Lucan (Mrs Riley), Kitty McShane (Kitty Riley),
    John Stuart (John Cartwright), Bromley Davenport (Warrender),
    Dennis Wyndham (Jem)
LC Associate director/Technical supervisor

As director and/or producer

Sandy Steps Out 1938, 1,502 ft. (Children's film)

Production company: A. P. & W. Productions
Studio: Whitfield
Production manager: Michael Wilson
Director: Lance Comfort
Photography: Jack Parker
Compère: Kent Stevenson

Laddie's Day Out 1939, 1,514 ft. (Children's film)

Production company: A Comfort-Millar Production
Director: Lance Comfort
Photography: E.Graham Clennell
Compère: Kent Stevenson

Judy Buys A Horse 1939, 1,523 ft. (Children's film)

Production company: P. & W. Productions
Studio: Whitfield
Production Manager: Michael Wilson
Director: Lance Comfort
Photography: Jack Parker
Compère: Kent Stevenson

Thoroughbreds 1939, 1,570 ft. (Children's film)

Production company: A Jack Parker Production
Studio: Sound City
Director: Lance Comfort
Photography: Jack Parker
Compère: Kent Stevenson

Penn of Pennsylvania (US title: *The Courageous Mr Penn*) 1941, 77 min.

Production company: British National Films
Studios: Rock (Elstree), Denham
Producer: Richard Vernon
Director: Lance Comfort
Screenplay: Anatole De Grunwald, from C. E. Vulliamy's book, *William Penn*
Director of photography: Ernest Palmer
Editor: Sidney Cole
Art director: R. Holmes Paul
Music: William Alwyn
Musical director: Muir Mathieson
Cast: Clifford Evans (William Penn), Deborah Kerr (Guglielma Spring-ett), King Charles II (Denis Arundell), Charles Carson (Admiral Penn), D. J. Williams (Lord Arlington), Joss Ambler (Lord Mayor of

London), Edward Rigby (Bushell), Aubrey Mallalieu (Chaplain), Mary Hinton (Lady Castlemaine), O. B. Clarence (Lord Cecil), James Harcourt (Fox), Henry Oscar (Pepys), Max Adrian (Elton), John Stuart (Bindle), Maire O'Neill (Cook), Edmund Willard (Ship's Captain), Herbert Lomas (Captain Cockle), Gus McNaughton (Ship's Mate), Gibb McLaughlin (Indian Chief), Percy Marmont (Holmes), Drusilla Wills (Hannah), Rosamund Greenwood (Servant girl), Nina Alvis (King's lady friend), David Farrar (Soldier), G. H. Mulcaster, Lawrence Hanray, Amy Dalby, Manning Whiley, Arthur Hambling

Hatter's Castle 1941, 102 min.

Production company: Paramount
Studio: Denham
Producer: Isadore Goldsmith
Director: Lance Comfort
Screenplay: Paul Merzbach, Rudolf Bernaur, with scenario and dialogue by Rodney Ackland, from the novel by A. J. Cronin
Director of photography: Max Greene
Editor: Douglas Robertson
Art director: James Carter
Music: Horace Shepherd
Sound: C. C. Stevens
Cast: Robert Newton (James Brodie), Deborah Kerr (Mary Brodie), James Mason (Dr Renwick), Beatrice Varley (Mrs Brodie), Emlyn Williams (Dennis), Enid Stamp-Taylor (Nancy), Henry Oscar (Grierson), Anthony Bateman (Angus Brodie), Stuart Lindsell (Lord Winton), Mary Hinton (Lady Winton), Brefni O'Rourke (Foyle), George Merritt (Gibson), Lawrence Hanray (Dr Lawrie), Ian Fleming (Sir John Latta), Aubrey Mallalieu (Clergyman), Claude Bailey (Paxton), David Keir (Perry), June Holden (Janet Grierson)

Those Kids from Town 1942, 75 min.

Production company: British National
Studio: Rock, Elstree
Producer: Richard Vernon
Director: Lance Comfort
Screenplay: Adrian Arlington, from his novel These Are Strangers
Director of photography: James Wilson

Editor: Erwin Reiner
Art director: R. Holmes Paul
Music: Kennedy Russell
Cast: Jeanne De Casalis (Sheila), Percy Marmont (The Earl), D. J.
    Williams (Butler), Maire O'Neill (Housekeeper), Charles Victor
    (Vicar), Olive Sloane (Vicar's Wife), Felicity Watt (Glory), Bransby
    Williams (Uncle Sid), Ronald Shiner (Mrs Burns), Josephine
    Wilson (Mrs Burns), Hay Petrie (Ted Roberts), Bromley Davenport
    (Egworth), Christine Silver (Millicent), Margaret McGrath (Sheila's
    Maid), Eleanor Hallam (Georgina). The Kids: George Cole
    (Charlie), Harry Fowler (Ern), Shirley Lenner (Liz Burns), Angela
    Glynne (Maud Burns), Stanley Escane (Stan), Leslie Adams
    (Arthur), Dane Gordon (Vicar's Son)

Squadron Leader X 1942, 99 min.

Production company: RKO-British
Studio: Denham
Producer: Victor Hanbury
Director: Lance Comfort
Screenplay: Wolfgang Wilhelm, from the story by Emeric
    Pressburger; additional dialogue by Miles Malleson
Director of photography: Max Greene
Editor: Michael C. Chorlton
Art director: William C. Andrews
Music: William Alwyn
Cast: Eric Portman (Eric Kohler), Ann Dvorak (Barbara), Walter Fitz-
    gerald (Inspector Milne), Martin Miller (Mr Krohn), Beatrice Varley
    (Mrs Krohn), Henry Oscar (Dr Schultz), Barry Jones (Bruce Fenwick),
    Charles Victor (Marks), Mary Merrall (Miss Thorndike), Carl Jaffe
    (Luftewaffe Colonel), Marjorie Rhodes (Mrs Agnew), Frederick
    Richter (Inspector Siegel), John Salew (Sentry), Aubrey Mallalieu
    (Pierre), David Peel (Michel Bertelot), Cyril Smith, Ronald Shiner,
    Eleanor Hallam, Ian Fleming, David Ward, Franklyn Bennett,
    Walter Gottel, Arnold Ridley, Miki Iveria, Mavis Claire

Escape to Danger 1943, 82 min.

See Chapter Four for discussion of the confusion over producer/
    director credits for this film. In the absence of a print of the film, it
    is difficult to make definitive attributions.

Production company: RKO-British
Studios: Denham, Pinewood
Producer: William Sistrom (sometimes given as Victor Hanbury)
Director: Lance Comfort (plus, perhaps, Victor Hanbury, Max Greene)
Screenplay: Wolfgang Wilhem, Jack Whittingham, from a story by
    Patrick Kirwan
Photography: Max Greene, Guy Green
Editor: E. B. Jarvis
Art director: William C. Andrews
Music: William Alwyn
Cast: Eric Portman (Anthony Lawrence), Ann Dvorak (Joan Grahame),
    Karel Stepanek (Von Brinkman), Ronald Ward (Chessman),
    Ronald Adam (Merrick), Felix Aylmer (Sir Alfred Horton), Brefni
    O'Rourke (Security Agent), Hay Petrie (The Quisling), A. E.
    Matthews (Rear Admiral), Ivor Barnard (Henry Waud), David Peel
    (Lieut. Peter Leighton), Charles Victor (Petty Officer), George
    Merritt (Works Manager), Marjorie Rhodes (Mrs Pickles), Anthony
    Shaw (Lisbon Attaché), John Ruddock (Jim Crawley), Frederick
    Cooper (Gardener), Lilly Kann (Karin Moeller), Richard George,
    Paul Sheridan, David Ward, George Howe, G. R. Schjelderup,
    James Pirie, D'Oyley John, Norman Whitcomb

Old Mother Riley Detective 1943, 80 min.

Production company: British National Films
Studio: Rock, Elstree
Producer: John Baxter
Director: Lance Comfort
Screenplay: Austin Melford, Geoffrey Orme, with additional dialogue
    by Arthur Lucan
Director of photography: James Wilson
Editor: Jack Harris (supervising editor), E. W. White
Art director: Wilfred Arnold
Costumes: Maude Churchill, Mrs Seaman
Continuity: Joan Wyatt
Music: Kennedy Russell
Sound: James Morris
Cast: Arthur Lucan (Mrs Riley), Kitty McShane (Kitty Riley), Ivan Brandt
    (Inspector Victor Cole), Owen Reynolds (Kenworthy), George Street
    (Inspector Moresby), Johnnie Schofield (P. C. Jimmie Green),
    Edgar Driver (Bob), Hal Gordon (Bill), Valentine Dunn (Elsie),

Marjorie Rhodes (Cook), H. F. Maltby (H. G. Popplethwaite), Michael Lynd (Tony), Peggy Cummins (Lily), Nellie Bowman, Jimmy Rhodes, Eddie Stern, Pat Kavanagh, Jack Vyvyan, Gerry Wilson, Alfredo Campoli, Pat Keogh, Eve Chipman, Vi Kaley, Ernest Metcalfe, Mike Johnson, Louise Nolan, Mary Norton

When We Are Married 1943, 97 min.

Production company: British National Films
Studio: National (formerly Rock), Elstree
Producer: John Baxter
Director: Lance Comfort
Screenplay: Austin Melford, Barbara K. Emary, from the play by J. B. Priestley
Director of photography: James Wilson
Editor: Jack Harris (supervising editor), Vi Burdon
Art director: R. Holmes Paul
Costumes: Maude Churchill
Music: Kennedy Russell
Sound: James Morris
Cast: Sydney Howard (Henry Ormonroyd), Raymond Huntley (Albert Parker), Marian Spencer (Annie Parker), Lloyd Pearson (Joe Helliwell), Olga Lindo (Maria Helliwell), Ernest Butcher (Herbert Soppitt), Ethel Coleridge (Clara Soppitt), Lesley Brook (Nancy Holmes), Barry Morse (Gerald Forbes), Marjorie Rhodes (Mrs Northrup), Patricia Hayes (Ruby Birtle), Lydia Sherwood (Lottie Grady), Charles Victor (Mr Northrup), Cyril Smith (Fred Dyson), Bromley Davenport (Mayor), George Carney (Landlord of 'Hare and Hounds'), Charles Doe (Seth), Charles Mortimer, Terry Randall

Hotel Reserve 1944, 89 min.

Production company: RKO-British
Studio: Denham
Produced and directed by: Lance Comfort, Victor Hanbury, Max Greene
Screenplay: John Davenport, from the novel by Eric Ambler
Director of photography: Max Greene
Camera-operator: Arthur Ibbetson
Editor: Sydney Stone
Art director: William C. Andrews
Music: Lennox Berkeley

Music director: Muir Mathieson
Sound: J. C. Cook
Cast: James Mason (Peter Vadassy), Lucie Mannheim (Madame Suzanne Koche), Raymond Lovell (Monsieur Robert Duclos), Julien Mitchell (Monsieur Beghin), Clare Hamilton (Mary Skelton), Valentine Dyall (Warren Skelton), Martin Miller (Herr Vogel), Hella Kury (Frau Vogel), Herbert Lom (André Roux), Patricia Medina (Odette Roux), Frederick Valk (Herr Emil Schimler), Ivor Barnard (Chemist), David Ward (Henri Asticot), Anthony Shaw (Major Clandon-Hartley), Lawrence Hanray (Police Commissaire), Patricia Hayes (Jacqueline), Josef Almas (Albert), Ernest Ulman (Man in black), Mike Johnson, Hugo Schuster, Henry T. Russell, John Baker

Great Day 1945, 79 min.

Production company: RKO-British
Studio: Denham
Producer: Victor Hanbury
Director: Lance Comfort
Screenplay: John Davenport, Wolfgang Wilhelm, from Lesley Storm's play
Director of photography: Erwin Hiller
Camera-operator: Arthur Ibbetson
Editor: Sydney Stone
Art director: William C. Andrews
Music: William Alwyn
Music director: Muir Mathieson
Sound: J. C. Cook, Desmond Dew
Cast: Eric Portman (Captain Ellis), Flora Robson (Mrs Ellis), Margaret Ellis (Sheila Sim), Philip Friend (Geoffrey Winthrop), Isabel Jeans (Lady Mott), Marjorie Rhodes (Mrs Mumford), Margaret Withers (Miss Tyndale), Walter Fitzgerald (Bob Tyndale), Maire O'Neill (Mrs Walsh), Beatrice Varley (Miss Tracy), Irene Handl (Miss Tomlinson), Kathleen Harrison (Maisie), Leslie Dwyer (Her friend), Ivor Barnard (Man in pub), Joan Maude (Miss Allen), Patricia Hayes (Mrs Beale), Jean Shepherd (Mrs Riley), John Laurie (Soldier in pub), Pauline Tennant (Vicky Calder), Valentine Dunn (Beryl), American Officer (John McLaren)

Bedelia 1946, 90 min.

Production company: John Corfield Productions
Studio: Ealing
Producer: Isadore Goldsmith
Director: Lance Comfort
Screenplay: Vera Caspary, Herbert Victor, Isadore Goldsmith, additional dialogue by Moie Charles, M. Roy Ridley, from the novel by Vera Caspary
Director of photography: Frederick A. Young
Editor: Michael Truman
Art director: Duncan Sutherland
Costumes: Elizabeth Haffenden
Music: Hans May
Sound: A. E. Rudolph
Continuity: Elaine Shreyeck
Cast: Margaret Lockwood (Bedelia), Ian Hunter (Charlie), Barry K. Barnes (Ben Chaney), Anne Crawford (Ellen), Jill Esmond (Nurse Harris), Beatrice Varley (Mary), Louise Hampton (Hannah), Julian Mitchell (Dr McAfee), Vi Stephens (Mrs McAfee), Kynaston Reeves (Mr Bennet), Olga Lindo (Mrs Bennet), John Salew (Alec Johnstone), Barbara Blair (Sylvia Johnstone), Daphine Arthur (Miss Jenkins), Claude Bailey (Captain McKelvey), Ellen Pollock (McKelvey's Housekeeper), Henry de Bray (M. Martin), Marcel Poncin (M. Perry), Martin Harvey (Abbé), Aubrey Mallalieu (Vicar), Yvonne André (Chambermaid), Alice Gachet (Manageress), Oscar Nation (Police Inspector), Dermot Walsh (Doctor's chauffeur), Al Gold and Lola Cordell (Specialty Dancers), Paul Boniface (Insurance Manager), David Keir (Chemist), Sonia Sergyl, Jill Bardi, Elizabeth Maude, Malcolm Homas, Charles Paton, Paul Hardtmuth

Temptation Harbour 1947, 104 min.

Production company: Associated British Picture Corporation
Studio: Welwyn
Producer: Victor Skutezky
Director: Lance Comfort
Screenplay: Rodney Ackland, Victor Skutezky, Frederic Gotfurt, from the novel *Newhaven-Dieppe*, by Georges Simenon
Director of photography: Otto Heller
Editor: Lito Carruthers

Art director: Cedric Dawe
Music: Mischa Spoliansky
Continuity: Elaine Shreyeck
Cast: Robert Newton (Bert Mallinson), Simone Simon (Camelia), William Hartnell (Jim Brown), Marcel Dalio (Inspector Dupré), Margaret Barton (Betty Mallinson), Edward Rigby (Tatem), Joan Hopkins (Beryl Brown), Charles Victor (Gowshall), Irene Handl (Mrs Gowshall), Kathleen Harrison (Mabel), Leslie Dwyer (Reg), Wylie Watson (Fred), W. G. Fay (Porter), George Woodbridge (Frost), Kathleen Boutall (Mrs Frost), Gladys Henson (Mrs Titmuss), John Salew (C. I. D. Inspector), Edward Lexy (Stationmaster), Dave Crowley (Teddy)

Daughter of Darkness 1948, 91 min.

Production company: Kennilworth/Alliance
Studio: Riverside
Producer: Victor Hanbury
Director: Lance Comfort
Screenplay: Max Catto, from his play, *They Walk Alone*
Director of photography: Stanley Pavey
Editor: Lito Carruthers
Art director: Andrew Mazzei
Music: Clifton Parker
Music director: Muir Mathieson
Sound: George Burgess
Continuity: Elaine Scheyreck
Cast: Siobhan McKenna (Emmy Baudine), Anne Crawford (Bess Stanforth), Maxwell Reed (Dan), Mr Tallent (George Thorpe), Honor Blackman (Julie Tallent), Barry Morse (Robert Stanforth), Liam Redmond (Father Corcoran), Grant Tyler (Larry Tallent), David Greene (David Price), Denis Gordon (Saul Trevithick), Arthur Hambling (Jacob), Nora O'Mahony, Iris Vandeleur, Ann Clery (Irish village women), George Merritt (Constable), Cyril Smith, Norman Shelley, Leslie Armstrong

The Silent Dust 1949, 82 min.

Production company: Independent Sovereign Films
Studio: Warner Bros. Studio, Teddington
Producer: Nat A. Bronsten

Director: Lance Comfort
Screenplay: Michael Pertwee, from the play, *The Paragon*, by Michael and Rowland Pertwee
Director of photography: Wilkie Cooper
Editor: Lito Carruthers
Art director: C. P. Norman
Costumes: Ricardo, Rahvis
Music: Georges Auric
Music director: George Melachrino
Continuity: Peggy Singer
Sound: A. E. Rudolph
Cast: Stephen Murray (Robert Rawley), Sally Gray (Angela Rawley), Nigel Patrick (Simon Rawley), Derek Farr (Maxwell Oliver), Beatrice Campbell (Joan Rawley), Sir Seymour Hicks (Lord Clandon), Marie Lohr (Lady Clandon), Irene Handl (Cook), Yvonne Owen (Nellie), James Hayter (Pringle), Edgar Norfolk (Simpson), George Woodbridge (Foreman), Maria Var (Singer)

Portrait of Clare 1950, 98 min.

Production company: Associated British Picture Corporation
Studio: Elstree
Producer: Leslie Landau
Director: Lance Comfort
Screenplay: Adrian Arlington, Leslie Landau, from the novel by Francis Brett Young
Director of photography: Gunther Krampf
Editor: Clifford Boote
Art director: Don Ashton
Music: Leighton Lucas
Music Director: Louis Levy
Costumes: Elizabeth Haffenden
Continuity: Thelma Orr
Sound: Harold V. King
Cast: Margaret Johnston (Clare Hingston), Richard Todd (Robert Hart), Robin Bailey (Dudley Wilburn), Ronald Howard (Ralph Hingston), Mary Clare (Lady Hingston), Lloyd Pearson (Sir Joseph Hingston), Marjorie Fielding (Aunt Cathie), Jeremy Spenser (Steven Hingston), Molly Urquhart (Thirza), Anthony Nicholls (Dr Boyd), Bruce Seton (Lord Wolverbury), Anne Gunning (Sylvia), Beckett Bould (Bissell), S. Griffiths-Moss (Bates), Yvonne André

(Marguerite), Hugh Morton (Ernest Mayhew), Campbell Copelin (Detective-Inspector Cunningham), Hugh Cort (Detective-Sergeant Pike), Una Venning (Miss Pidgeon), Amy Veness (Lady on train), Lady Astill (Grace Arnold), Sir Joseph Astill (Robert Adair), Ann Codrington (Mrs Renton), Andrew Leigh (Hemus), Cameron Miller (Cabby), Charles Paton (Registrar), Scott Harrold (Farmer)

Home to Danger 1951, 66 min.

Production company: New World
Studio: Riverside
Producer: Lance Comfort
Director: Terence Fisher
Screenplay: John Temple-Smith, Francis Edge
Director of photography: Reg Wyer
Cast: Guy Rolfe (Robert), Rona Anderson (Barbara), Francis Lister (Wainwright), Alan Wheatley (Hughes), Bruce Belfrage (Solicitor), Stanley Baker (Willie Dougan), Dennis Harkin (Jimmy the One), Peter Jones (Lips Leopard)

The Girl on the Pier 1953, 65 min.

Production company: Major
Producer: John Temple-Smith
Director: Lance Comfort
Screenplay: Guy Morgan
Director of photography: William McLeod
Editor: Gerald Landau
Art director: Don Russell
Music: Ray Terry
Music director: Eric Robinson
Cast: Veronica Hurst (Rita Hammond), Ron Randell (Nick Lane), Charles Victor (Chief Inspector Chubb), Marjorie Rhodes (Clara Chubb), Campbell Singer (Joe Hammond), Eileen Moore (Kathy Chubb), Brian Roper (Ronnie Hall), Anthony Valentine (Charlie Chubb), Steve Conway (Detective-Sergeant Webb), Raymond James (Cyclist), Thorp Devereux (Man at peepshow), Diana Wilding (Girl friend)

The Genie 1953, 75 min.

This film consists of three stories which first appeared separately on television, before being spliced together for cinema release.
Production company: Douglas Fairbanks Productions
Producer: Douglas Fairbanks Jr
Director: Lance Comfort (1st story, 'The Heel', and 3rd story, 'The Genie'; other story directed by Lawrence Huntington)
The Heel
Screenplay: Noel Charles, Peter Graham Scott
Director of photography: Eric Cross
Editor: Inman Hunter
Art director: Norman Arnold
Music: Allan Gray
Cast: Bill Travers (Morgan), Scott McKay (Sellars), Patricia Cutts (Sylvia)
The Genie
Screenplay: Doreen Montgomery
Director of photography: Brendan Stafford
Editor: Francis Bieber
Art director: Norman Arnold
Music: Allan Gray
Cast: Yvonne Furneaux (Suzie), Martin Miller (Papa), Douglas Fairbanks Jr (The Genie)

The Triangle 1953, 77 min.

This film consists of three stories which first appeared separately on television, before being spliced together for cinema release.
Production company: Douglas Fairbanks Productions
Producer: Douglas Fairbanks Jr
Director: Lance Comfort (1st story, *American Duel*; others directed by Leslie Arliss and Bernard Knowles)
Screenplay: Robert Westerby, Doreen Montgomery
Director of photography: James Wilson, Brendan J. Stafford, Eric Cross
Editor: Sam Simmonds, Francis Bieber
Art director: Norman Arnold
Music: Allan Gray
American Duel Cast: Ron Randell (Sam), June Thorburn (Mitzi), Christopher Lee (Franz), Gerald Heinz (Professor), Carl Duering (Willi Schloss), Leslie Linder (Elliott), John G. Heller (Heinrich), Derek Prentice (Doctor)

Bang! You're Dead (US title: *Game of Danger*), 1954, 88 min.

Production company: Wellington Films
Studio: British Lion, Shepperton
Producer, Director: Lance Comfort
Screenplay: Guy Elmes, Ernest Bornemann
Director of photography: Brendan Stafford
Editor: Francis Bieber
Art director: Norman Arnold
Music: Eric Spear
Singer: Edmund Hockridge
Continuity: Barbara Wainwright
Sound: Buster Ambler, Red Law
Cast: Jack Warner (Perce Bonsell), Derek Farr (Detective Grey), Veronica Hurst (Hilda), Michael Medwin (Bob Carter), Beatrice Varley (Mrs Moxby), Gordon Harker (Mr Hare), Anthony Richmond (Cliff Bonsell), Sean Barrett (Willy), Philip Saville (Ben Jones), John Warwick (Sergeant Gurney), Toke Townley (Jimmy Knuckle), Fred Griffiths, Larry Burns, Arnold Bell, Leo Phillips

Eight O'Clock Walk 1954, 87 min.

Production company: British Aviation/George King Productions
Studio: British Lion, Shepperton
Producer: George King
Director: Lance Comfort
Screenplay: Guy Morgan, Katherine Strueby, from a story by Jack Roffey and Gordon Harbord
Director of photography: Brendan Stafford
Editor: Francis Bieber
Art director: Norman Arnold
Costumes: Bill Smith
Music: George Melanchrino
Continuity: Barbara Wainwright
Sound: Cecil Mason, Red Law
Cast: Richard Attenborough (Tom Manning), Cathy O'Donnell (Jill Manning), Derek Farr (Peter Tanner), Ian Hunter (Geoffrey Tanner, Q. C.), Maurice Denham (Horace Clifford), Bruce Seton (D. C. 1), Harry Welchman (Mr Justice Harrington), Kynaston Reeves (Mr Monro), Lilly Kann (Mrs Zunz), Eithne Dunne (Mrs Evans), Cheryl Molineaux (Irene Evans), Robert Adair (Jury

Foreman), David Hannaford (Ernie Higgs), Grace Arnold (Mrs Higgs), Totti Truman Taylor (Miss Ribden-White), Arthur Hewlett (Reynolds), Jean St. Clair (Mrs Gurney), Noel Dyson (Gallery Regular), Philip King (Prison Doctor), Vernon Kelso, Robert Sydney, Max Brimmell, Humphrey Morton, Enid Hewit, Dorothy Darke, Bartlett Mullins

The Last Moment 1954, 51 min.

This film consists of two stories which first appeared separately on television, before being spliced together for cinema release.
Production company: Douglas Fairbanks Productions
Production supervisors: Tom D. Connochie, Roy Goddard
Director: Lance Comfort
Screenplay: Selwyn Jepson (1st story), Paul Vincent Carroll (2nd story)
Director of photography: James Wilson, Brendan J. Stafford
Editor: Francis Bieber
Art director: Norman Arnold
Music: Alan Gray
Sound: Henry Benson, Wally Milner
The Last Moment Cast: Greta Gynt (Sarah), Paul Carpenter (Derwent), MacDonald Parke (Tom Canting), Mary Merrall (Housekeeper)
The Sensible Man Cast: Cyril Cusack (Daniel O'Driscoll, Barbara Mullen (Mrs O'Driscoll), Fulton Mackay (Paddy), Valerie Carton (Kathleen)

Port of Escape 1956, 76 min.

Production company: Wellington Films
Producer: Lance Comfort
Director: Tony Young
Screenplay: Barbara Harper, Tony Young, Abby Mann, from a story by Barbara Harper
Director of photography: Philip Grindrod
Editor: Peter Pitt
Art director: Don Russell
Music: Bretton Byrd
Cast: Googie Withers (Anne Stirling), John McCallum (Mitchell Gillie), Bill Kerr (Dinty Missouri), Joan Hickson (Rosalie Watchett), Wendy Danielli (Daphne Stirling), Hugh Pryse (Skinner), Alexander Guage (Inspector Levins), Ingeborg Wells (Lucy), Ewan Roberts (Sergeant Rutherford), Simon Lack, Carl Jaffe, Basil Dignam,

Cameron Hall, Gerald Anderson, Jack Lester, George Rose, Robert Bruce, Norman Pierce, Len Llewellyn

The Man in the Road 1956, 84 min.

Production company: Gibraltar Films
Studio: Beaconsfield
Producer: Charles A. Leeds
Director: Lance Comfort
Screenplay: Guy Morgan, from Anthony Armstrong's novel, *He Was Found in the Road*
Director of photography: Stanley Pavey
Editor: Jim Connock
Art director: Ray Simm
Music: Bruce Campbell
Music director: Philip Marshall
Continuity: Rita Davidson
Cast: Derek Farr (Ivan Mason), Ella Raines (Rhona Ellison), Donald Wolfit (Professor Cattrell), Lisa Daniely (Mitzi), Karel Stepanek (Dmitri Balinkev), Cyril Cusack (Dr Kelly), Olive Sloane (Mrs Lemming), Bruce Beeby (Dr Manning), Russell Napier (Superintendent Davidson), Frederick Piper (Inspector Hayman)

Atom at Spithead 1956

Production company: Danzigers/New Elstree
Studio: Elstree
Director: Lance Comfort
Leading players: Clifford Evans, Dane Clark, Veronica Hurst, Leslie Phillips
No further information is available on this film. An item giving the above information appeared in the 'Lance Comfort Collection', held at the BFI, and John Comfort recalled its making and especially the US star, Clark, but it seems likely that the film was never released. It does not appear in the credits for director or players.

Passport to Treason 1956

Lance Comfort began directing this film for Tempean, but became ill and co-producer Robert S. Baker took over. The film starred the American Rod Cameron and Comfort regular Clifford Evans.

Face in the Night (US title: *Menace in the Night*), 1957, 75 min.

Production company: Gibraltar Films
Studio: Nettlefold
Producer: Charles A. Leeds
Director: Lance Comfort
Screenplay: Norman Hudis, John Sherman, from the novel by Bruce
   Graeme
Director of photography: Arthur Graham
Editor: Peter Pitt
Art director: John Stoll
Music: Richard Rodney Bennett
Music Director: Phillip Martell
Sound: W. H. Lindop
Cast: Griffith Jones (Rapson), Lisa Gastoni (Jean Francis), Vincent
   Ball (Bob Meredith), Eddie Byrne (Art), Victor Maddern (Ted),
   Clifford Evans (Inspector Ford), Leonard Sachs (Victor), Joan
   Miller (Victor's Wife), Leslie Dwyer (Toby), Jenny Laird (Post-
   man's Widow), Barbara Couper (Mrs Francis), Marie Burke,
   André Van Gyseghem, Angela White

At the Stroke of Nine 1957, 72 min.

Production company: Tower Films
Studio: National
Producer: Harry Booth, Michael Deeley, Jon Pennington
Director: Lance Comfort
Screenplay: Booth, Deeley, Pennington, Tony O'Grady, from a story
   by O'Grady
Director of photography: Gerald Gibbs
Art director: Duncan Sutherland
Music: Edwin Astley
Sound: Fred Turtle, Cecil Mason
Cast: Patricia Dainton (Sally), Stephen Murray (Garrett), Patrick Barr
   (Frank), Dermot Walsh (MacDonnell), Clifford Evans (Inspector
   Hudgell), Leonard White (Thompson), Reg Green (Toby), Alexander
   Dor (Carter), Frank Atkinson (Porter)

The Man from Tangier (US title: *Thunder Over Tangier*), 1957, 66 min.

Production company: Butcher's Film Service
Studio: Nettlefold
Producer: W. G. Chalmers
Director: Lance Comfort
Screenplay: Paddy Manning O'Brine
Director of photography: Geoffrey Faithfull
Editor: Peter Mayhew
Art director: John Stoll
Music: Wilfred Burns
Continuity: Phyllis Townshend
Sound: W. H. Lindop
Cast: Robert Hutton (Chuck Collins), Lisa Gastoni (Michele), Martin
    Benson (Voss), Derek Sydney (Darracq), Jack Allen (Rex), Leonard
    Sachs (Heinrich), Robert Raglan (Inspector Meredith), Harold
    Berens (Dr Kenyon), Michael Balfour (Spade), Emerton Court
    (Armstrong), Richard Shaw (Johnny), Frank Forsyth (Sergeant
    Irons), Marianne Stone (Woman in hotel), Frank Sanguineau
    (Montez)

The Ugly Duckling 1959, 84 min.

Production company: Hammer
Studio: Hammer, Bray
Executive Producer: Michael Carreras
Associate Producer: Tommy Lyndon-Haynes
Director: Lance Comfort
Screenplay: Sid Colin, Jack Davies
Director of photography: Michael Reed
Editor: James Needs
Art director: Bernard Robinson
Music: Douglas Gamley
Costumes: Molly Arbuthnot
Continuity: Marjorie Lavelly
Sound: Jock May
Cast: Bernard Bresslaw (Henry Jekyll/Teddy Hyde), Reginald Beck-
    with (Reginald), Jon Pertwee (Victor Jekyll), Maudie Edwards (Henri-
    etta Jekyll), Jean Muir (Snout), Richard Wattis (Barclay), David
    Lodge (Peewee), Elwyn Brook-Jones (Dandy), Michael Ripper
    (Benny), Harold Goodwin (Benny), Norma Marla, Keith Smith,

Michael Ward, John Harvey, Jess Conrad, Mary Wilson, Geremy Philips, Vicky Marshall, Jill Carson, Cyril Chamberlain, Alan Coleshill, Jean Driant, Reginald Marsh, Nicholas Tanner, Shelagh Dey, Ian Wilson, Verne Morgan, Sheila Hammond, Ian Ainsley, Roger Avon, Richard Statman, Robert Desmond, Alexander Doré

Make Mine a Million (US title: *Look Before You Laugh*), 1959, 82 min.

Production company: Jack Hylton Film Productions
Studio: British Lion Studios, Shepperton
Producer: John Baxter
Director: Lance Comfort
Screenplay: Peter Blackmore, with additional scenes by Talbot Rothwell and Arthur Askey, from a story by Jack Francis
Director of photography: Arthur Grant
Editor: Peter Pitt
Art director: Denis Wreford
Costumes: Dulcie Midwinter
Music: Stanley Black
Continuity: Yvonne Richards
Sound: Red Law, Buster Ambling
Cast: Arthur Askey (Arthur Ashton), Sidney James (Sid Gibson), Dermot Walsh (Martin Russell), Olga Lindo (Mrs Burgess), Kenneth Connor (Anxious Husband), Clive Morton (National TV Chairman), Martin Benson (Commercial TV Chairman), Sally Barnes (Sally), Lionel Murton (Commercial TV Director), Bernard Cribbins (Jack), Leigh Madison (Diana), George Margo (Assistant), Bruce Seton (Superintendent James), David Nettheim (Professor), Tom Gill. Guest Stars: Tommy Trinder, Dickie Henderson, Evelyn Laye, Dennis Lotis, Anthea Askey, Raymond Glendenning, Patricia Bredin, Leonard Weir, Sabrina, Peter Noble, Gillian Lynne, Television Toppers

The Breaking Point (US title: *The Great Armoured Car Swindle*), 1961, 59 min.

Production company: Butcher's Film Service
Studio: Walton
Producer: Peter Lambert
Director: Lance Comfort
Screenplay: Peter Lambert, from the novel by Laurence Meynell

Director of photography: Basil Emmott
Editor: Peter Pitt
Art director: John Earl
Costumes: Jackie Cummins
Music: Albert Elms
Continuity: Ann Besserman
Sound: Michael Hart
Cast: Peter Reynolds (Eric Winlatter), Dermot Walsh (Robert), Joanna
    Dunham (Cherry), Lisa Gastoni (Eva), Brian Cobby (Peter de
    Savory), Jack Allen (Ernest Winlatter), Geoffrey Denton (Debt
    Collector), Arnold Diamond (Telling), Richard Golding (Mintos),
    John Heller (Mei)

Rag Doll (US title: *Young, Willing and Eager*), 1961, 67 min.

Production company: Blakeley's Films
Studio: Walton-on-Thames
Producer: Tom Blakeley
Director: Lance Comfort
Screenplay: Brock Williams, Derry Quinn
Director of photography: Basil Emmott
Editor: Peter Pitt
Art director: John Earl
Costumes: Dulcie Midwinter
Music: Martin Slavin
Lyrics: Abbe Gail
Continuity: Marjorie Lavelly
Sound: William Buckley
Cast: Christina Gregg (Carol), Jess Conrad (Shane), Hermione Baddeley
    (Princess), Kenneth Griffith (Mort Wilson), Patrick Magee (Flynn),
    Patrick Jordan (Wills), Michael Wynne (Bellamy), Frank Forsyth
    (Superintendent), Marie Devereux (Ann), Eve Eden (Daphne)

Pit of Darkness 1961, 76 min.

Production company: Butcher's Film Service
Studio: Twickenham
Producer, Director, Screenplay (from Hugh McCutcheon's novel, *To
    Dusty Death*): Lance Comfort
Director of photography: Basil Emmott
Editor: John Trumper

Art director: John Earl
Costumes: Jean Fairlie
Music: Martin Slavin
Continuity: Phyllis Townshend
Sound: George Adams
Cast: William Franklyn (Richard Logan), Moira Redmond (Julie),
  Bruno Barnabe (Maxie), Leonard Sachs (Conrad), Nigel Green
  (Jonathan), Bruce Beeby (Mayhew), Humphrey Lestocq (Bill),
  Nanette Newman (Mary), Anthony Booth (Ted Mellis), Michael
  Balfour (Fisher), Jacqueline Jones (Mavis), John Stuart (Lord
  Barnsford), Ronnie Clark (Singer)

The Break 1962, 76 min.

Production company: Blakeley's Films
Studio: Pinewood
Producer: Tom Blakeley
Production Manager: John Comfort
Director: Lance Comfort
Assistant Director: Roy Baird
Screenplay: Pip and Jane Baker
Director of photography: Basil Emmott
Editor: Peter Pitt
Art director: George Provis
Costumes: Jean Fairlie
Music: Brian Fahey
Continuity: Jane Buck
Sound: Buster Ambler
Cast: William Lucas (Jacko Thomas),Tony Britton (Greg Parker),
  Christina Gregg (Sue Thomas), Eddie Byrne (Judd Tredgear),
  Gene Anderson (Jean Tredgear), Robert Urquhart (Pearson),
  Sonia Dresdel (Sarah), Edwin Richfield (Moses), Patrick Jordan
  (Driver), John Junkin (Harry), Marshall Jones (Jim)

The Painted Smile 1962, 60 min.

Production company: Blakeley's Films
Studio: Twickenham
Producer: Tom Blakeley
Director: Lance Comfort
Screenplay: Pip and Jane Baker, from an idea by Brock Williams

Director of photography: Basil Emmott
Editor: John Trumper
Art director: George Provis
Music: Martin Slavin
Continuity: Phyllis Townshend
Sound: Norman Bolland
Costumes: Maude Churchill
Cast: Liz Fraser (Jo), Kenneth Griffith (Kleinie), Tony Wickert (Tom), Peter Reynolds (Mark), Nanette Newman (Mary), Ray Smith (Glynn), David Hemmings (Roy), Craig Reynolds (Night-club singer), Harold Berens (Mikhala), Grazina Frame (Lucy), Lionel Ngakane (Barman), Gerald Sim (Plainclothes Policeman), Richard McNeff (Police Inspector), Rosemary Chambers (Gloria), Mia Karam (Dawn), Ann Wrigg (Manageress)

Band of Thieves 1962, 69 min.

Production company: Filmvale
Producer: Lance Comfort
Director: Peter Bezencenet
Screenplay: Lyn Fairhurst
Director of photography: Alex Thomson
Music: Norrie Paramor, Acker Bill
Sound: Robert T. McPhee, Gordon McCallum
Cast: Acker Bill (Himself), Colin Smith (Flash), Jonathan Mortimer (Fingers), Ron McKay (Scouse), Roy James (Dippy), Stan Greig (Haggis), Ernie Price (The Mole), Geoffrey Sumner (The Governor), Jimmy Thompson (The Honourable Derek), Jennifer Jayne (Ann), Maudie Edwards (The Duchess), Arthur Mullard (Getaway), Charmian Innes (Mrs Van Der Ness), Michael Peake (Chief Warder). Guest artistes: Norrie Paramor, Peter Haigh, Carol Deene

Tomorrow at Ten 1962, 80 min.

Production company: Blakeley's Films
Studio: MGM/Borehamwood
Producer: Tom Blakeley
Production Manager: John Comfort
Director: Lance Comfort
Screenplay: Peter Miller, James Kelly

Director of photography: Basil Emmott
Editor: John Trumper
Art director: Jack Shampan
Music: Bernie Fenton
Costumes: Rob Rayner
Continuity: Phyllis Townshend
Sound: Fred Turtle
Cast: John Gregson (Parnell), Robert Shaw (Marlow), Alec Clunes
    (Chester), Alan Wheatley (Bewley), Kenneth Cope (Sergeant Grey),
    Ernest Clark (Dr Towers), Piers Bishop (Jonathan), Helen Cherry
    (Robbie), William Hartnell (Freddy Maddox), Renee Houston (Mrs
    Maddox), Betty McDowall (Mrs Parnell), Harry Fowler (Smiley),
    Noel Howlett (Specialist), Ray Smith (Briggs), John Dunbar (Henry),
    Bernadette Woodman (1st Nurse), Marguerite McCourt (2nd Nurse),
    Edward Rees (Desk Sergeant), Anthony Ashdown (Constable
    Jackson), Neville Taylor (Bongo Player), Richard Armour, Kenneth
    Gilbert, Norman Coburn, Norman Hartley, Stephen Mayling,
    Peter Mason (Desk Men), Christopher Ellis (Chris Parnell)

Touch of Death 1962, 58 min.

Production company: Helion Films
Studio: Twickenham
Producer: Lewis Linzee
Production Manager: John Comfort
Director: Lance Comfort
Screenplay: Lyn Fairhurst, from a story by Aubrey Cash and Wilfred
    Joseph
Director of photography: Basil Emmott
Editor: John Trumper
Art director: John Earl
Music: Johnny Douglas
Costume: Muriel Dickson
Continuity: Doreen Soan
Sound: Stephen Dalby
Cast: William Lucas (Pete Mellor), David Sumner (Len), Ray Barrett
    (Maxwell), Jackie (Jan Waters), Frank Coda (Sergeant Byrne),
    Geoffrey Denton (Baxter), Mary Jones (Mrs Baxter), Lane Meddick
    (Morgan), Ann Martin (Mrs Morgan), Roberta Tovey (Pam), Chris-
    topher Brett (Mike), Clifford Earl (Mr Grey), Alethea Charlton (Mrs
    Grey), Reg Lever (Fred), Thomas Kiflin (Nick), Robin Sumner

(Davy), David Rosen (Chris), Eleanor McCready (Woman in shop), Frank Forsyth (Local Inspector), Victor Charrington (Loch-Keeper), Michael Martin, Keith Campbell, John Martin, Roy Evans, Glynn Dale, Barry Steele, Kenneth Gilbert, Clive Marshall, Frank Mayer

The Switch 1963, 69 min.

Production company: Philip Ridgeway Productions
Studio: Pinewood
Producers: Philip Ridgeway, Lance Comfort
Director: Peter Maxwell
Screenplay: Philip Ridgeway, Colin Fraser, from a story by Ridgeway
Director of photography: Stephen Dade
Editor: Tom Simpson
Art director: Duncan Sutherland
Music: Eric Spear
Continuity: Gladys Goldsmith
Sound: Peter Davies, Colin LeMesurier
Cast: Anthony Steel (Bill Craddock), Dermot Walsh (Inspector Tomlinson), Zena Marshall (Caroline Markham), Conrad Phillips (John Curry), Susan Shaw (Search Officer), Dawn Beret (Janice Lampton), Jerry Desmond (Chief of Customs), Arnold Diamond (Jean Lecraze), Raymond Smith (Mandreos), Tom Bowman (Polovski), Arthur Ludgrove (Harry Lewis), Gordon Boyd (Jack Kingston)

Live It Up (US title: *Sing and Swing*), 1963, 74 min.

Production company: Three Kings Films
Studio: Pinewood
Producer: Lance Comfort
Production manager: Roy Baird
Director: Lance Comfort
Screenplay: Lyn Fairhurst, based on an idea by Harold Shampan
Director of photography: Basil Emmott
Editor: John Trumper
Art director: Jack Shampan
Costumes: Eve Faloon
Music: Joe Meek, Norrie Paramor, Kenny Ball
Continuity: Phyllis Townshend
Sound: R. T. McPhee, C. LeMesurier

Cast: David Hemmings (David Martin), Jennifer Moss (Jill), John Pike (Phil), Heinz Burt (Ron), Steven Marriott (Ricky), Joan Newell (Margaret Martin), Ed Devereaux (Herbert Martin), Veronica Hurst (Kay), Penny Lambirth (Barbara), Peter Glaze (Mike Moss), David Bauer (Mark Watson), Anthony Ashdown (Bob), Douglas Ives (Bingo), Paul Hansard (Film Director), Geoffrey L'Cise (Assistant), Peter Haigh (Announcer), Trevor Maskell (Aldo), John Mitchell (Andrews), Anthony Shephard (Commissionaire), David Clarke (Recording Man), Pat Gilbert (Housekeeper), Guest artistes: Nancy Spain, Peter Noble, Kenny Ball, Patsy Ann Noble, Gene Vincent, Kim Roberts, Outlaws, Sounds Incorporated, Andy Cavell and the Saints

Blind Corner (US title: *Man in the Dark*), 1963, 80 min.

Production company: Mancunian/Blakeley's Films
Studio: Pinewood
Producer: Tom Blakeley
Production manager: John Comfort
Director: Lance Comfort
Screenplay: James Kelly, Peter Miller, from a story by Vivian Kemble
Director of photography: Basil Emmott
Editor: John Trumper
Art director: John Earl
Costumes: Eve Faloon
Music: Brian Fahey
Continuity: Lorely Farley
Sound: Robert McPhee
Cast: William Sylvester (Paul Gregory), Barbara Shelley (Anne Gregory), Mark Eden (Mike Williams), Elizabeth Shepherd (Joan Marshall), Alex Davion (Ricky Seldon), Ronnie Carroll (Ronnie), Barry Aldis (compre), Edward Evans (Chauffeur), Frank Forsyth (Plainclothes Policeman)

Devils of Darkness 1964, 90 min.

Production company: Planet Film Productions
Studio: Pinewood
Producer: Tom Blakeley
Production Manager: John Comfort
Director: Lance Comfort

Assistant Director: Roy Baird
Screenplay: Lyn Fairhurst
Director of photography: Reg Wyer
Editor: John Trumper
Art director: John Earl
Costumes: Muriel Dickson
Music: Bernie Fenton
Continuity: Muirne Mathieson
Sound: Robert T. McPhee, Gordon K. McCallum
Cast: William Sylvester (Paul Baxter), Hubert Noel (Sinistre), Rona
    Anderson (Anne Forrest), Tracy Reed (Karen), Carole Gray (Tania),
    Diana Decker (Madeline Braun), Eddie Byrne (Dr Kelsey), Peter
    Illing (Inspector Malin), Gerald Heinz (Bouvier), Avril Angers
    (Midge), Marianne Stone (The Duchess), Victor Brooks (Inspector
    Hardwick), Brian Oulton (The Colonel), Marie Burke (Old Gypsy
    Woman), Olwen Brookes (Landlady), Rod McLennan (Dave),
    Geoffrey Kenion (Keith Forrest), Burnell Tucker (Derek), Julie
    Mendes (Speciality Dancer)

Be My Guest 1965, 82 min.

Production company: Three Kings
Studio: Twickenham
Producer, Director: Lance Comfort
Screenplay: Lyn Fairhurst
Director of photography: Basil Emmott
Editor: Sydney Stone
Art director: John Earl
Costumes: Evelyn Gibbs
Music: Malcolm Lockyer
Continuity: Leonora Hail
Sound: William Buckley, Stephen Dalby
Cast: David Hemmings (David Martin), Stephen Marriott (Ricky),
    John Pike (Phil), Andrea Monet (Erica Page), Ivor Salter (Herbert
    Martin), Diana King (Margaret Martin), Avril Angers (Mrs Pucil),
    Joyce Blair (Wanda), David Healy (Milton Bass), Tony Wager
    (Artie Clough), David Lander (Routledge), Robin Stewart
    (Matthews), Monica Evans (Dyllis), Pamela Ann Davies (Zena),
    Douglas Ives (Steward). Guest artistes: Jerry Lee Lewis, The
    Nashville Teens, The Zephyrs, Kenny and the Wranglers, The
    Niteshades

The Ugly Ones 1968, 97 min.

This title is listed in one Internet source as having been co-directed by Gene (Eugenio) Martin and Lance Comfort. Its release date is given as 1968, two years after Comfort's death, and it is sometimes referred to as *The Bounty Killer* (the title of the book on which it is based and not to be confused with the 1965 American western directed by Spencer G. Bennet), as *The Price of a Man*, and as *El precio de un hombre*. The release dates are sometimes listed as 1966. The stars of this spaghetti western are Tomas Milian and Richard Stapley. I have been unable to confirm whether Comfort in fact worked on this project.

Television credits

The following credits are not complete but are intended to give a sense of the scope of Comfort's work in television. They are listed under the titles of the series in which the films (usually less than half an hour in length) were screened.

Douglas Fairbanks Jr Presents

1954

The Apples Director, Producer: Lance Comfort. Scriptwriter: Stanley Mann. Leading players: Ron Randell, Eunice Gayson.

Atlantic Night Director: Derek Twist. Producer: Lance Comfort. Scriptwriter: Arthur Bryant. Leading players: André Morell, Michael Goodwin.

Johnny Blue Director, Producer: Lance Comfort. Scriptwriter: Jerome Gruskin. Leading players: Sam Levene, Lee Patterson.

1955

The Heirloom Director: John Gilling. Producer: Lance Comfort. Scriptwriter: John Kneubuhl. Leading players: Sybil Thorndike, Judy Campbell.

Heritage Director, Producer: Lance Comfort. Scriptwriter: Joseph Schell. Leading players: Robert Beatty, Betty McDowall.

1956

Enchanted Doll Director: Harold Huth. Producer: Lance Comfort. Scriptwriter: Derry Quinn. Leading players: Freda Jackson, Douglas Fairbanks Jr.

Second Wind Director: Leslie Arliss. Producer: Lance Comfort. Scriptwriter: Jerome Gruskin. Leading players: Nora Swinburne, Michael Shepley.

The Awakening Director: Michael McCarthy. Producer: Lance Comfort. Scriptwriter: Lawrence B. Marcus, based on 'The Cloak' by Nikolai Gogol. Leading players: Buster Keaton, James Hayter.

The Hideaway Director: Arthur Crabtree. Producer: Lance Comfort. Scriptwriter: Stanley Mann. Leading players: Dorothy Alison, Mandy Miller.

Another Day Director: Arthur Crabtree. Producer: Lance Comfort. Scriptwriter: Jerome Gruskin. Leading players: Ron Randell, Clifford Evans.

The Mix-up Director: Tony Young. Producer: Lance Comfort. Leading players: Patrick Holt, Eunice Gayson, Jean Anderson.

The Refugee Director, Scriptwriter: Michael McCarthy. Producer: Lance Comfort. Leading players: Denis O'Dea, Ingeborg Wells.

A Lesson in Love Director: Leslie Arliss. Producer: Lance Comfort. Leading players: Dulcie Gray, Robert Coote.

The Wedding Veil Director: Charles Saunders. Producer: Lance Comfort. Leading players: Lana Morris, Nanette Newman.

The Man Who Heard Everything Director: Allan Davis. Producer: Lance Comfort. Scriptwriter: Lawrence B. Marcus. Leading players: Michael Gough, Brenda Bruce.

Provincial Lady Director, Producer: Lance Comfort. Scriptwriter: Miles Malleson, from the play by Ivan Turgeniev. Leading players: Margaretta Scott, Douglas Fairbanks Jr.

Mr Sampson Director: Lawrence Huntington. Producer: Lance Comfort. Scriptwriter: John Sherman. Leading players: Sybil Thorndike, Joyce Carey.

A Line in the Snow Director: Michael McCarthy. Producer: Lance Comfort. Scriptwriter: Gabrielle Upton. Leading players: Robert Beatty, Patrick Holt.

Flight One-Zero-One Director: Lance Comfort. Producer, Scriptwriter: Derek Twist. Leading players: Patrick Barr, George Coulouris.

The Thoroughbred Director: Harold Huth. Producer: Lance Comfort. Leading players: Eunice Gayson, Cyril Cusack.

Tony Director: Lawrence Huntington. Producer: Lance Comfort. Scriptwriter: Guy Morgan. Leading players: Muriel Pavlow, Fay Compton, Beatrice Varley.

Leave to Die Director: Derek Twist. Producer: Lance Comfort. Scriptwriter: A. R. Rawlinson. Leading players: Yvonne Mitchell, Ram Gopal.

Rain Forest Director: Lawrence Huntington. Producer: Lance Comfort. Scriptwriter: J. B. Williams. Leading players: Clifford Evans, James Hayter.

Guilt Director: Lance Comfort. Producer: Douglas Fairbanks Jr. Scriptwriter: James Parish. Leading players: Joan Miller, John Stuart.

Ship's Doctor Director: Derek Twist. Producer: Lance Comfort. Scriptwriter: Val Valentine. Leading players: Miles Malleson, Victor Maddern.

The Long White Line Director: John Gilling. Producer: Lance Comfort. Scriptwriter: John Larkin. Leading players: Nora Swinburne, Joyce Heron.

Myra and the Money Man Director: Michael McCarthy. Producer: Lance Comfort. Scriptwriter: Leigh Vance. Leading players: Margot Stevenson, Guy Middleton.

Pattern for Glory Director: Derek Twist. Producer: Lance Comfort. Scriptwriter: Abby Mann. Leading players: Anne Crawford, Ron Randell.

The Relative Truth Director: Leslie Arliss. Producer: Lance Comfort. Scriptwriter: Paul Vincent Carroll. Leading players: Patrick Holt, Liam Redmond.

The Rehearsal Director, Producer: Lance Comfort. Scriptwriter: John Q. Copeland. Leading players: Marius Goring, Lucie Mannheim.

The Lovely Place Director: Leslie Arliss. Producer: Lance Comfort. Scriptwriter: Gabrielle Upton. Leading players: Diana Dors, Ron Randell.

Gramma Bren Director: Lawrence Huntington. Producer: Lance Comfort. Scriptwriter: Mildred Cram. Leading players: Louise Hampton, Lou Jacobi.

The 90th Day Director: Terence Fisher. Producer: Lance Comfort. Scriptwriter: Malvin Wald, Jack Jacobs. Leading players: Donald Stewart, Alan Gifford.

Room 506 Director: Arthur Crabtree. Producer: Lance Comfort. Scriptwriter: James Patrick O'Neill. Leading players: Mary Jerrold, Eddie Byrne.

A Borderline Case Director: Roy Rich. Producer: Lance Comfort. Leading players: Greta Gynt, Robin Bailey, Bernard Lee.

Big Nick Director, Producer: Lance Comfort. Leading players: Rossano Brazzi, Valentina Cortese.

Dimitrios Director: Dennis Vance. Producer: Lance Comfort. Leading players: Dermot Walsh, Karel Stepanek, Ellen Pollock.

Pardon My Ghost Director: Leslie Arliss. Producer: Lance Comfort. Scriptwriter: Guy Morgan. Leading players: MacDonald Parke, Douglas Fairbanks Jr.

1957

Little Big Shot Director, Producer: Lance Comfort. Scriptwriter: William Wiener, Herbert Abbott Spiro. Leading players: Diana Wynyard, Diana Decker.

Gabrielle Director: Bernard Knowles. Producer: Lance Comfort. Leading players: André Morell, Ingeborg Wells.

Double Identity Director: Francis Searle. Producer: Lance Comfort. Scriptwriter: Charles Hatton. Leading players: Elsie Albiin, Lloyd Lamble.

The Trap Director: Arthur Crabtree. Producer: Lance Comfort. Scriptwriter: Gabrielle Upton. Leading players: Mary Parker, Sandra Dorne, Phil Brown.

The Face of the Law Director, Producer: Lance Comfort. Scriptwriter: Selwyn Jepson, Lance Sieveking. Leading players: Ron Randell, Patric Doonan.

The Happy McBains Director: Derek Twist. Producer: Lance Comfort. Leading players: Michael Denison, Dulcie Gray.

Dream Stuff Director: Charles Saunders. Producer: Lance Comfort. Scriptwriter: Gabrielle Upton. Leading players: Betty McDowall, Lee Patterson.

Four Farewells in Venice Director: Michael McCarthy. Producer: Lance Comfort. Scriptwriter: Charles Frank. Leading players: Douglas Fairbanks Jr, John Stuart.

Stand By Director: Derek Twist. Producer: Lance Comfort. Scriptwriter: Doreen Montgomery. Leading players: Clifford Evans, Sarah Lawson.

Forever is a Long Time Director: Lawrence Huntington. Producer: Lance Comfort. Scriptwriter: Tedwell Chapman, Gabrielle Upton. Leading players: Richard O'Sullivan, Terence Alexander.

Someone Outside Director: Lance Comfort. Producer: Douglas Fairbanks Jr. Scriptwriter: Martin Worth. Leading players: Lois Maxwell, Maurice Kaufmann.

Border Incident Director: Derek Twist. Producer: Lance Comfort. Leading players: William Sylvester, Paul Carpenter.

Pitfall Director: Roy Rich Producer: Lance Comfort. Leading players: Douglas Fairbanks Jr, Betta St John.

Honeymoon Deferred Director: Dennis Vance. Producer: Lance Comfort. Leading players: Betta St John, Robert Arden.

Crime A La Carte Director: Dennis Vance. Producer: Lance Comfort.

Scriptwriter: Stanley Mann. Leading players: James Hayter, Martin Benson.

Only Son Director: Michael McCarthy. Producer: Lance Comfort. Leading players: Cyril Cusack, Eithne Dunne.

The Immigrant Director, Scriptwriter: Michael McCarthy. Producer: Lance Comfort. Leading players: André Morell, Gene Anderson.

The Milkman Director: Arthur Crabtree. Producer: Lance Comfort. Scriptwriter: Lawrence B. Marcus. Leading players: Leslie Dwyer, Mary MacKenzie.

The Hero Director: Harold Huth. Producer: Lance Comfort. Scriptwriter: Abby Mann, Ben Arbeid. Leading players: Frank Latimore, Constance Smith.

Together Director, Producer: Lance Comfort. Scriptwriter: Paul David. Leading players: Lee Patterson, Luciana Paluzzi.

The Auction Director: Bernard Knowles. Producer: Lance Comfort. Scriptwriter: Stanley Mann. Leading players: Adrienne Corri, Douglas Fairbanks Jr, William Hartnell.

The Treasure of Urbano Director: Harold Huth. Producer: Lance Comfort. Scriptwriter: Paul Tabori. Leading players: Douglas Fairbanks Jr, Marina Berti.

The Fast Buck Director: Dennis Vance. Producer: Lance Comfort. Scriptwriter: Berkeley Mather. Leading players: John McCallum, Lois Maxwell.

Another Day Director: Arthur Crabtree. Producer: Lance Comfort. Scriptwriter: Jerome Gruskin. Leading players: Ron Randell, Clifford Evans.

The Sound of Your Voice Director: Leslie Arliss. Producer: Lance Comfort. Leading players: Ian Hunter, Eleanor Summerfield.

While the Circus Passes Director: Lawrence Huntington. Producer: Lance Comfort. Scriptwriter: John Haggarty. Leading players: Eva Maria Meinecke, Oliver Hassenkamp.

Crown Theatre

1956

Blue Murder Director: Roy Rich. Producer: Lance Comfort. Scriptwriter: Emery Bonett. Leading players: Douglas Fairbanks Jr, Joyce Carey.

Street of Angels Director: Arthur Crabtree. Producer: Lance Comfort. Scriptwriter: Paul Ericson, Guy Morgan. Leading players: Eileen Moore, Douglas Fairbanks Jr, Martin Benson.

King High Director: Terence Fisher. Producer: Lance Comfort.

Scriptwriter: Andrew Solt, Glen Bohannan. Leading players: Patricia Medina, Douglas Fairbanks Jr, Peter Illing.

International Settlement Director: Lawrence Huntington. Producer: Lance Comfort. Scriptwriter: A. R. Rawlinson. Leading players: Karel Stepanek, Mary Parker, Douglas Fairbanks Jr.

Deadline Vienna Director: Harold Huth. Producer: Lance Comfort. Scriptwriter: Kent Donne. Leading players: Delphi Lawrence, Douglas Fairbanks Jr.

One-Way Ticket Director: Lawrence Huntington. Producer: Lance Comfort. Scriptwriter: Paul Bauman. Leading players: Douglas Fairbanks Jr, Eunice Gayson.

The Last Knife Director, Scriptwriter: Michael McCarthy. Producer: Lance Comfort. Leading players: Sheila Shand Gibbs, Lilly Kann.

Counterfeit Director: Roy Rich. Producer: Lance Comfort. Scriptwriter: Abby Mann, Howard Apter. Leading players: Robert Beatty, Douglas Fairbanks Jr.

Success Train Director: Dennis Vance. Producer: Lance Comfort. Scriptwriter: Abby Mann, Jack Wilson. Leading players: Douglas Fairbanks Jr, Colette Dereal.

The Patriarch Director: Michael McCarthy. Producer: Lance Comfort. Scriptwriter: Derry Quinn. Leading players: Finlay Currie, Renee Asherson.

Assignment Foreign Legion

1956

The Sword of Truth Director: Lance Comfort. Producer: Anthony C. Bartley. Scriptwriter: Paul Monash. Leading players: Merle Oberon, Allan Cuthbertson.

The Anaya Director: Lance Comfort. Leading players: Eddie Byrne, Christopher Lee.

The Outcast Director: Lance Comfort. Leading players: Michael Gough, Rosalie Crutchley.

Dollar a Year Man Director: Lance Comfort. Producer: Anthony C. Bartley. Scriptwriter: A. R. Rawlinson. Leading players: Merle Oberon, Anton Diffring.

The Man Who Found Freedom Director: Lance Comfort. Producer: Anthony C. Bartley. Leading players: Merle Oberon, Lee Patterson.

The Stripes of Sgt Schweiger Director: Lance Comfort. Producer: Anthony C. Bartley. Scriptwriter: Paul Monash. Leading players: Merle Oberon, Anton Diffring.

1957

Testimonial to a Soldier Director: Lance Comfort. Scriptwriter: Paul
Monash. Leading players: Martin Benson, Nigel Stock.

The Volunteer Director: Lance Comfort. Leading players: André
Morell, Leo McKern.

The Gay Cavalier

1957

Lance Comfort directed the following episodes of this Civil War swash-
buckler for George King Productions, to be broadcast by ITV. The
regular cast included: Christian Marquand, Larry Burns, Ivan Craig.

Dragon's Heart Scriptwriter: Brock Williams. Leading players: Joyce
Linden, Willoughby Goddard.

The Lady's Dilemma Scriptwriter: Jack Andrews. Leading players: Jean
Anderson, Christopher Lee.

The Masked Lady Scriptwriter: Charlotte Hastings, Gordon Wellesley.
Leading players: Colette Wilde, Henry Oscar.

Angel Unawares Scriptwriter: Charlotte Hastings. Leading players:
Simone Silva, Charles Farrell.

Flight of the Nightingales Scriptwriter: Brock Williams. Leading
players: Ivan Craig, Charlotte Mitchell.

The Lost is Found Scriptwriter: Anthony Verney. Leading players:
Hazel Court, Anthony Dexter.

The Little Cavalier Scriptwriter: Anthony Verney. Leading players:
Simone Silva, Charles Farrell.

Return of the Nightingale Scriptwriter: Brock Williams. Leading
players: Robin Bailey, Sara Gregory.

Forsaking All Others Scriptwriter: Charlotte Hastings, Gordon
Wellesly. Leading players: Paul Hansard, Christine Labiez.

A Throne at Stake Scriptwriter: Jack Andrews. Leading players: Joyce
Linden, Sydney Bromley.

Martin Kane, Private Investigator

1957–58

Lance Comfort was one of three regular directors (the others were
Cliff Owen and C. Pennington-Richards) on this series involving a New
York private eye (William Gargan) who cooperates with a Scotland
Yard detective (Brian Reece).

Ivanhoe

1958–59

Lance Comfort directed the following episodes of this series based on Sir Walter Scott's romance for Sydney Box Productions, to be broadcast by ITV. The regular cast included Roger Moore, Robert Brown, John Pike, and Andrew Keir.

Freeing the Serfs Co-director: David MacDonald. Scriptwriter: Joel Carpenter. Leading Player: Alex Scott.

Slave Traders Scriptwriter: Saul Levitt. Leading Player: Patrick Holt.

Black Boar Scriptwriter: Richard Fielder. Leading players: Betty McDowall, Edwin Richfield.

Whipping Boy Scriptwriter: Larry Forrester. Leading players: Terence Longden, Leslie Perrins.

The Witness Scriptwriter: Geoffrey Orme. Leading players: Martin Wyldeck, Patrick Holt.

Ragen's Forge Scriptwriter: Sheldon Stark, Larry Forrester. Leading players: Ann Sears, Martin Wyldeck.

Search for Gold Scriptwriter: Saul Levitt. Leading players: Derick De Marney, Noel Johnson.

Look at Life

1964

Sound of a City Producer: George Grafton Green. Scriptwriter: Lance Comfort. Commentator: Tim Turner.

Select bibliography

Part of the reason for the present book is that there has been so little written about the films of Lance Comfort, except for brief reviews of individual films in newspapers, fan magazines and trade papers. For references to these, see the notes at the end of each chapter. Other than these reviews and production reports, many of which can be found in the BFI's microfiche collection on individual films and in the 'Lance Comfort Collection', held by the BFI, the following have been consulted for what material, limited in most cases, they have to offer on the subject of Comfort. A few others are included for their relevance to related matters.

Ambler, E., *Here Lies: An Autobiography*, Glasgow, Fontana Collins, 1986 [1985].

Aspinall, S. and Murphy, R. (eds), *Gainsborough Melodrama*, London, British Film Institute, 1983.

Bourdieu, P., *The Field of Cultural Production: Essays on Art and Literature*, edited and introduced by Randal Johnson, Cambridge, Polity Press, 1993.

Brooks, P., *The Melodramatic Imagination: Balzac, Henry James, Melodrama and the Mode of Excess*, London and New Haven, Yale University Press, 1976.

Durgnat, R., 'Some lines of enquiry into post-war British crimes', in R. Murphy (ed.), *The British Cinema Book*, London, BFI Publishing, 1997.

Gledhill, C. (ed.), *Home is Where the Heart Is: Studies in Melodrama and the Woman's Film*, London, BFI Publishing, 1987.

Harper, S. *Picturing the Past: The Rise and Fall of the British Costume Film*, London, BFI Publishing, 1994.

Heilman, R. B., *The Iceman, the Arsonist and the Troubled Agent:*

Tragedy and Melodrama on the Modern Stage, London, George Allen & Unwin, 1973.

Landy, M., *British Genres: Cinema and Society, 1930–1960*, Princeton, Princeton University Press, 1991.

Landy, M., 'Melodrama and femininity in World War Two British cinema', in R. Murphy (ed.), *The British Cinema Book*, London, BFI Publishing, 1997.

MacDonald, K., *Emeric Pressburger: The Life and Death of a Screenwriter*, London, Faber & Faber, 1994.

Mason, J., *Before I Forget*, London, Hamish Hamilton, 1981.

McFarlane, B., *An Autobiography of British Cinema*, London, Methuen, 1996.

McFarlane, B., 'Lance Comfort: melodrama and an honourable career', *Journal of Popular British Cinema*, 1 (1998).

McFarlane, B., 'Lance Comfort, Lawrence Huntington, and the British program feature film', in W. W. Dixon (ed.), *Re-Viewing British Cinema, 1900–1992*, Albany, NY, State University of New York Press, 1994.

McFarlane, B. 'Pulp fictions: the British B film and the field of cultural production', *Film Criticism*, XXI:1 (Fall 1996).

Murphy, R., *Realism and Tinsel: Cinema and Society in Britain 1939–1948*, London and New York, Routledge, 1989.

Pitt, P., 'The men who called Action!', *The Veteran*, 75 (Autumn 1995).

Pitt, P., 'A reminiscence of Elstree', *Film and Television Technician*, February 1989.

The main journals consulted were *Kinematograph Weekly*; *Today's Cinema*; *Daily Film Renter*; *Monthly Film Bulletin*; *Picturegoer*; *Picture Show*; *Variety*; *Motion Picture Herald* and *Films and Filming*.

The following works which provided the basis for various of Comfort's films were available (though not necessarily still in print) and consulted. Other source material proved terminally elusive.

Ambler, E. *Epitaph for a Spy*, London, M. Dent, 1938.

Caspary, V., *Bedelia*, London, White Lion Publishers, 1972 [1945].

Catto, M., *They Walk Alone*, London, The Richards Press, 1948.

Cronin, A. J., *Hatter's Castle*, London, Gollancz, 1931.

Pertwee, R. and M., *The Paragon*, London, English Theatre Guild, 1948.

Priestley, J. B., *When We Are Married*, London, Samuel French, 1938.

Storm, L., *Great Day*, London, English Theatre Guild, 1945.

Young, F. B., *Portrait of Clare*, London, William Heinemann, 1927.

Index

Note: Though there are many scattered references to aspects of Pierre Bourdieu's theory of cultural production, the Index lists only those occasions when major terms are defined. The main reference to each of Comfort's films is given in bold. Page numbers in italics refer to an illustration on that page.